Eating Together

4/14

Eating Together

Food, Friendship, and Inequality

ALICE P. JULIER

University of Illinois Press

URBANA, CHICAGO, AND SPRINGFIELD

© 2013 by the Board of Trustees
of the University of Illinois
All rights reserved
Manufactured in the United States of America
1 2 3 4 5 C P 5 4 3 2 1
♾ This book is printed on acid-free paper.

Library of Congress Cataloging-in-Publication Data
Julier, Alice P.
Eating together: food, friendship, and inequality / Alice P. Julier.
pages cm.
Includes bibliographical references and index.
ISBN 978-0-252-03763-4 (cloth : alk. paper)
ISBN 978-0-252-07918-4 (pbk. : alk. paper)
ISBN 978-0-252-09488-0 (ebook)
1. Food habits. 2. Dinners and dining. 3. Table etiquette.
4. Eating (Philosophy) 5. Social networks.
I. Title.
GT2850.J85   2013
394.1'2—dc23   2012050854

25.00

Contents

Acknowledgments

Being about food, friendship, and community, this book has emerged from the generosities of others who fed me, gave me spaces to write, reasons to take a break, and always things to think about. It is likely that those who are unnamed were instrumental, and I apologize if I am remiss in remembering. Most importantly, this book would not exist were it not for the people who agreed to talk to me, let me into their homes, and allowed me to participate in their lives.

Gratitude for starting it out goes to the people at the University of Massachusetts, Amherst. Naomi Gerstel, Jack Hewitt, Robert Zussman, and Ellen Pader offered support and ideas, despite some consternation at my shift to the then-suspect area of food. The feminist writing groups in all their permutations, from meals at home to coffee in restaurants, offered solace and solidarity, and I miss them, especially the late Valerie Moore. Particular thanks to Patricia Hanrahan and Amy Wilkins, who commiserated, and Art Redman, who made me laugh, even if I wasn't cool enough. Thanks to Dan Cooley for cheerleading from the science side of the campus and Miliann Kang for those coffee shop summers. Jane Riley, from among many, will always be the student who could.

Thanks to many people at Smith College, where most of this work was germinated. I still reap the benefits of the conversations about Bourdieu with Rick Fantasia and the kindnesses of Marc Steinberg and Nancy Whittier. I am a better teacher and scholar for having known Colleen Boyle, Sarah Freedman, Rachel Noto, Jake Lipman, Christi Smith, Kristen Lanzano, and Julia Fischer-Mackey, among many other incredibly insightful women. At Smith and beyond, Jayne Mercier is everything and more, even though we can't really escape being restaurant workers. Smithies beyond Northampton who help me think critically about food include Simran Sethi, Emily Bailey, and Kerstin McGaughey.

The Women's Studies Program at the University of Pittsburgh provided me with an academic home when I most needed one. Jean Ferguson Carr offered support, amazing feedback, space to write, and a model of what's important. There were also those graduate students, such as Greg de Saint Maurice and Carolyn Zook. Thanks also go to friends, students, and colleagues at Chatham University. Eden Hall, our sustainable space and farm, is where the future of Food Studies is just beginning to take shape. Although this work mostly precedes my time with them, every day I am astounded by what I have learned from the graduate students in my program and grateful for the chance to support and train new activists in the struggle for community and sustenance.

Many years ago Peter Conrad welcomed me into his home and fed me, and he has always pushed me to be a good Brandeis sociologist. As deus ex machina he introduced me to Marjorie DeVault and nurtured my zigzagging approach. Marj's work, which sparked this whole endeavor, her writing on feminist methods, and her general example as a scholar have helped me enormously, and I appreciate her gentle but sharp insights into the inequalities embedded in our everyday world. Both of them inspire me.

Ages ago Jeffrey Sobal sought me out, even though I was pregnant and grumpy, at a hot ASA meeting in Washington D.C. and invited me to attend a small food-related conference. Thanks to Jeff for guiding me to the Association for the Study of Food and Society—but more so, for support, intellectual rigor, and a willingness to answer even the stupidest question with solid empirical data.

The Association for the Study of Food and Society and its sister organization, the Agriculture, Food, and Human Values Society, form my perfect intellectual and social home. It is my fortune to have colleagues and dear friends with whom I have the great pleasure of sharing at least one or two collective meals in a new city every year. Thanks to everyone for feeding body and soul, but especially: Jenny Berg, Amy Bentley, Krishnendu Ray, Jonathan Deutsch, Annie Hauck-Lawson, Lucy Long, Jan Poppendiek, Ken Albala, Rick Wilk, Beth Forrest, Laura Lindenfeld, Carol Counihan, Rafia Zafar, Jeff Miller, Liora Gvion, Danny Block, Gil and Ardy Gilespie, Doris Witt, Cara de Silva, and Christy Shields-Argeles. For more insights, I thank Laura Shapiro, Cory Bernat, Barbara Haber, Jan Whitaker, and David Sutton. Among the mensches, Alex McIntosh, Warren Belasco, and Jeff Sobal have provided a rare thing: a model of how men who are senior scholars can be feminist mentors. Anne Murcott offered that and more. The graduate students in the Gastronomy Program at Boston University all inspire me, especially Ilona, Kristina, Kerstin, Paige, and Syd.

I thank Warren Belasco, most notably for being tall, for eating falafel with me in Northampton, and for always showing that food is fun and serious all at once.

I am amazed at the people who kindly and continually take responsibility for my intellectual and emotional good health, and I hope I can offer back a tiny bit of the same to Psyche Williams-Forson, Charlotte Biltekoff, Elaine Power, Fabio Parasecoli, Lisa Heldke, Abby Wilkerson, and, forever my noisy muse, Netta Davis.

So many people have fed me I can't name them all: almost everyone in Pelham and Amherst, especially Sarah Bramen, Debbie Rice, Tom Hidas, and their families; Sue Dexter, who taught Zoe to eat peas and pork chops; Carol Bigelow, Barbara and Lindsey, Dan and Sue, Marcia and Lynn, and especially Claudia and Matt. My niece Emily will always be an honorary Valley person. I miss Sherrie and everyone at the late great Food Bank Farm of Western Massachusetts. And of course, many bagels were shared with Ruth and Alan, Joel and Ana, and Rich and Lise.

My thanks and love to my family, siblings and spouses, nieces and nephews, in-laws and out-laws, especially my parents—for whom food matters deeply—and my sisters, who keep tradition alive and plan the winter holiday menus in July. No less of a debt goes to my partner's family, who all indulge my love of food, each with their own special twist, from borscht and schmaltz to ginger and chocolate.

I am profoundly and deeply fortunate to have Arlene Voski Avakian and her partner Martha Ayres in my life and to have known their daughter Leah Ryan, whose too-short life inspires me to keep working and to find value in words of all sorts. I learn the meaning of sustenance from them.

Thanks to Scarlett, who always makes sure I am paying attention and spend time outside. Above all, I am grateful for Zoe and Esme and Zack for love, patience, and laughter, a thousand good meals, and the best conversations in the world.

Eating Together

1. Feeding Friends and Others

> Like my mother, I like to know what everybody ate. My friends are
> constantly driven crazy by me because I want to know what they
> had for dinner. I want to know what they had and how they cooked
> it. I'm not very curious about what people had out. I'm interested
> in what people have in, because I'm very interested in people's
> domestic lives. I used to think I was fretting away my time, but the
> fact is, what is more interesting than how people live? I personally
> can't think of anything. Maybe war or death or something, but not
> to me. I like to know how they serve food, what they do with it,
> how it looks.
>
> —Laurie Colwin, *More Home Cooking*

> Drinks are for strangers, acquaintances, workmen, and family.
> Meals are for family, close friends, honored guests. The grand
> operator of the system is the line between intimacy and distance.
>
> —Mary Douglas, *Deciphering a Meal*

"Putting Yourself Out"

When my partner and I began living on our own, our house was a place
where friends visited often, especially during evenings or weekend days.
I believed that people felt welcome because good food that they liked was
readily available. Somewhat consciously I thought that if there was some appropriate meal handy, then our home would be a comfortable base, a place
where my circle of friends centered. Creating meals became a way to draw
people to where I lived, to interact socially, bringing together friends from
across the various social groups we knew, from work colleagues to college
friends to basketball acquaintances. Since I enjoyed doing this, I never questioned my actions until a friend began trying to mitigate what he called my
"unnecessary work." He often encouraged us as a group to go out to eat or
get take-out food. Finally one day he offered to get prepared food because
he didn't want me to "put yourself out so much."

For a long time after he said this, I reflected on what my actions meant:
what was I attempting to ensure in my household? What assumptions guided

my activities? This seemingly small incident of everyday life became the springboard from which I began to think sociologically about what people do when they invite others into their homes to share food. In particular, I recognized that my so-called larger sociological interests—unequal access to resources faced by marginalized groups such as women, people of color, and poor or working-class communities—were not separate from my everyday concerns. Meals provide a landscape from which to explore all manners of cultural and economic dilemmas. Decisions about whom we eat with, in what manner, and what kinds of food are inextricably tied to social boundaries. The personal, after all, is political.[1]

In the fifteen years since I began thinking critically about food and social life, the academic landscape has changed dramatically, such that this book does not need to begin with disclaimers or long explanations of why it's so important for social scientists to study food.[2] The relationship between the material and symbolic dimensions of our lives still begs for serious analysis, but where once I could point to only a handful of important texts, the wealth of scholarship that supports this pursuit is now so enormous that Warren Belasco claims we have entered a "Golden Age of Food Studies."

Even so, I offer this as a partial and preliminary map of the landscape of social meals. Additionally, voluntary relationships—friendships, for lack of a better, all-encompassing word—are also an elusive topic, one whose analysis sits at the margins of mainstream sociology. Because these topics are not overtly political and public, it bears asserting that our understandings of inequality in America might benefit from looking at the domestic, where the seemingly private, mundane components of daily life unfold. While asserting the mainstreaming of food studies, Belasco also suggests that such work is inherently subversive, requiring scholars to cross boundaries and "ask inconvenient questions" (Belasco, 2008, 6). Like Laurie Colwin and Mary Douglas, I am profoundly interested in asking about people's domestic lives, particularly in the part that food plays in constructing social relationships. In a slightly different manner than my friend suggested, I am "putting myself out" to write this book about eating in with friends and others.

Food and the Social Order

In *Deciphering a Meal*, Mary Douglas writes:

> Sometimes at home, hoping to simplify the cooking, I ask, "Would you like to have just soup for supper tonight. I mean a good thick soup—instead of supper. It's late and you must be hungry. It won't take a minute to serve." Then an argument starts: "Let's have soup now, and supper when you are ready."

"No, no, to serve two meals would be more work. But if you like, why not start with the soup and fill up with pudding" "Good heavens! What sort of meal is that? A beginning and an end and no middle." "Oh, all right, then, have the soup, as it's there, and I'll do a Welsh rarebit as well." When they have eaten soup, Welsh rarebit, pudding, and cheese: "What a lot of plates. Why do you make such elaborate suppers?" They proceed to argue that by taking thought I could satisfy the full requirements of a meal with a single, copious dish. Several rounds of this conversation have given me a practical interest in the categories and meanings of meals. I need to know what defines the categories of a meal at home. (Douglas, 1972, 61–62)

What counts as a meal? Does it need to be cooked in the home? Include rice? Can it be cold? How much can come from cardboard boxes? What about popcorn eaten together while watching television? In *The Migrant's Table*, the Bengali Americans interviewed by Krishnendu Ray (2004) talked about miscommunications and misperceptions of meals (such as gigantic servings, plain pasta and salad, and hors d'oeuvres instead of a main course) when being invited over to the homes of white Americans (80–81). More critics are joining public health pundits to find fault within the food industry and convenience foods, portion sizes, and endless snacking when exploring American eating habits. Even though our understandings of what counts as a meal have some consistent cultural characteristics, it is also contested terrain. Within that landscape, I want to demonstrate how people construct meaningful everyday practices.

To begin, I explore some of the moral discourses and texts that shape our understandings of food and social life in the United States. The majority of this narrative is organized around stories told by a small sample of people who held dinner parties, potlucks, brunches, buffets, and other uncategorizable social meals. The meals and relationships they describe are tied up in particular understandings of difference and inequality, understandings that emerge from the historical and contemporary configuration of gender, race, and class. While other dimensions of experience might be salient, I find these to be the most powerful in shaping everyday life in the United States. Put simply, people with greater access to resources that accrue from gender, race, and class privilege have access to more variety and more nutritionally rich food and can focus on the meal as a social accomplishment rather than a necessity. At the same time, social networks of reciprocity provide people with different skills and relationships that are often specifically useful for their communities, since shared meals, like other aspects of cultural capital, are situated in historical and geographic contexts.

Despite a growing interest in everyday life as the site where inequality is made manifest, we know very little about what people actually do in their daily domestic lives, particularly the parts that are not primarily defined by familial obligations. Mary Douglas, who spent a large part of her illustrious career taking food seriously, outlined an unfulfilled agenda, stating,

> Many of the important questions about food habits are moral and social. How many people come to your table? How regularly? Why those names and not others? There is a range of social intercourse, which is based on food, on reciprocity, on frequency of exchange and other patterns. We ought to know more about patterns of social involvement so as to understand rejection, since it appears undeniable that starvation and undernourishment are the result of social rejection more than of physical deficiency of food supplies. (Douglas, 1984, 13)

The material and social aspects of providing food are central to social life, but because it is routine, such activities often appear mundane. Yet, connecting food activities or "commensality" to larger social arrangements that stratify people demonstrates how choices about food and sociability are guided and constructed within a range of opportunities and constraints. Anthropologist Audrey Richards (1932) rightly claimed that food more than sex determines the nature of our social groupings and the form of our activities.[3] Like it or not, the basic questions of human survival and of human culture are questions about food—how we acquire it, how we prepare it, and who is responsible for its distribution. Some would suggest that agrarian culture cemented the rise of private ownership and entrenched inequality. The capacity to preserve and store food has both freed and constrained human social development. As Amartya Sen (1981) demonstrates in his global exploration of famine, hunger is usually not about lack of food, it's about lack of entitlement and rights. Worldwide, women and poor people of color predominate in the production and provision of food—as agricultural workers, domestic servants, as farmers, producers, cooks, and servers in both domestic and commercial settings. To study food, particularly the procuring and preparing of food, is to study the nature of inequality in our culture. In its extreme outcomes, commensality exists alongside the possibility that people starve if not included in shared meals. In less dire, but equally determinant situations, exclusion from shared meals means isolation from important and useful social and cultural resources, or "capital" (Bourdieu, 1984). As historian and culinary curator Barbara Haber (2005) has said, if you want to understand the workings of a society, "follow the food" (65).

Deciphering Meals, Decoding Patterns of Social Life

Currently across the United States, people are eating out in restaurants more frequently. They also eat socially "on the go," ordering pizza while watching their children play sports or grabbing prepared foods (from sushi to soup to sports bars) on their way to or from work. Even so, domestic kitchens have not disappeared and the rhetoric of domestic mealtime and its social benefits remains constant. Activists concerned with everything from the "agro-industrial food complex," the "obesity epidemic," environmental change, and global food aid all invoke the significance of the shared table and the social organization of eating together.

Here, I examine only one particular type of sociable activity, the shared meal—and more narrowly, the shared meal that occurs in households and includes non-kin. Even so, the analysis is based on the understanding that such activities occur as part of a much larger pattern of sociable events with food based on temporal cycles, such as weekly meals, annual celebrations, special events, and changes across the life course. Mary Douglas (1984) argued, "a radical approach to food's place in civilization would require the whole range of food's social uses to be considered" (6). The study of shared meals needs to be situated among a larger body that examines rituals, holidays, ethnic and regional variations, global migrations, historical permutations, and prognostications about the future.[4]

According to Douglas and Nicod (1974), the meal is different from other food-related activities (such as eating a snack) because it is distinguished by having some kind of formal structure, including the types, order, and presentation of foods as well as the order and mode of consumption. These formats vary across cultures and historical timeframes, but they all adhere to some social rules (Murcott, 1982; Sobal, 2000; Meiselman, 2000; Wood, 1995). The meal is particularly interesting because it is both physical and social, both a "metaphor for communication" and "a physical event" (Douglas, 1984). Simmel suggests that eating together is a profound intersection of the social and the individual since "what the individual eats, no one else can eat under any circumstances" (Symons, 1994, 346). Symons explains, "we might sit down together at a meal, but we must understand what we share. We must accept that we never really share food" (344). Paradoxically, this individual material act of consumption may also be the very basis of sociality since the necessity to eat is something all humans share. This type of sociability is so important that political campaigns, union drives, and religious organizations rely on community suppers to create solidarity.

In contemporary American society, I found that what counts as a meal is a highly contested and ideologically charged question that is also filtered through people's biographies and social locations. Who people spend time with in a domestic setting and under what circumstances tells us about social boundaries. Consider the family meal as a site where fears of social disintegration get centered. Arguments about the kind of food that is created or served in people's homes often frames a debate between a powerful food industry and its vocal critics. In this chapter, I examine more aspects of these historical and contemporary discourses that fuel these questions and affect the choices people have in determining with whom and how to eat.

Staging and participating in such a food event requires that participants share some understandings of what activity they are engaged in. In Georg Simmel's terms, the meal is a *social form*, a way of classifying different kinds of social interaction. As Levine (1971) describes them, social forms "are the synthesizing principles which select elements from the raw stuff of experience and shape them into determinate unities. . . . And they are not fixed, and immutable but emerge, develop, and perhaps disappear over time" (xv). If everyday practices seem idiosyncratic and individualized, perhaps a focus on the social form allows us to see the common patterns of interaction and behavior that help organize the complexity of individual experiences. Consider the forms that seem most prevalent in American society: potlucks, dinner parties, brunches, and barbecues all express something about the relationships being enacted. Each involves different degrees of formality, different roles and social expectations for participants, and different divisions of labor in the actual production of the food, the event, and social interactions. People choose to participate in these events as a way of constructing close relationships that are not necessarily rooted in the obligations associated with kinship. These forms are not the only ones available to contemporary Americans—in fact, one segment of my analysis is dedicated to events that defy existing labels—but these particular events have both historical and cultural resonance for many people, such that their choice of social form reflects important insights into their social experience. But how do people choose which among these forms will constitute the stage for the production of these relationships? Which people eat out? Watch old movies and eat popcorn? Invite fourteen people for brunch? As I elaborate through people's stories, learning the role expectations and "rules" of various sociable occasions is not always a straightforward process.

Given the lack of sociological studies on this topic, I framed my inquiry with an eye toward larger questions that cannot be easily answered: How does the negotiation of appropriate forms occur among people who wish to arrange sociable moments? What discourses, cultural discussions, and ideologies do they draw upon in creating these events? To what extent are they constrained by structural conditions? What changes do we see across the life course? And how does the presence of food, in the ordered form and expectations of a meal, affect the choices, the interactions, and the meanings given? How is the cultural geography of space in households—the size of a kitchen, the privacy of bedrooms and bathrooms—implicated in the structuring of the event and the kinds of relationships that develop? Starting with a small-scale qualitative study, a starting point to suggest answers to these questions, I went on to map some of the language, concepts, and concerns that deepen our understanding of relatively underexplored topics.

Engendering Meals

By describing cooking as "putting yourself out," my friend perhaps unintentionally highlighted the gendered way I was easily recruited into this work, driven by a belief in the importance of shared intimacy over food (DeVault, 1990). Not surprisingly, at the time of his comment, I was immersed in the feminist literature on close relationships, family, and most importantly domestic labor, with scholars such as Dorothy Smith eloquently questioning the sociological understanding of "work" as something outside the realm of emotion, caring, or even pleasure. This relationship between work and care is intricately played out in the act of cooking and feeding others, and as such, is a critical component of gender as a lived experience and a set of social structures.

These issues are articulated by Marjorie DeVault's *Feeding the Family*, which germinated my own interest in this topic. Using interviews with a variety of families, DeVault expertly dissects the hidden aspects of feeding work, such as cleaning, provisioning, keeping track of preferences, and cooking, which contribute to its role in creating and maintaining gendered expectations. DeVault argued that women were often unaware of the extent of the work they did on a daily basis to produce meals for their family members. This work was often disguised as "caring" and "love," rendering it invisible and naturalizing domestic food labor as a central form of "doing gender" and creating family life as well as enacting social differences of class (1991, 13). Invisible labor includes everything—from the physical work of provisioning, planning, and cooking, but also the emotion work of coordinating family members, fostering interactions over meals, and creating a sense of the family as a group characterized by affection.[5] Whether the shared meal is for a family or non-kin, it depends on creating a balance of uniqueness and connectedness for all participants. Such "kin keeping" is entwined with gender expectations (Rosenthal, 1985). For example, Michaela DiLeonardo (1987) points to the "female world of cards and holidays" as evidence of women's work maintaining social ties. These kin scripts, which delineate lines of obligation and support across networks, often include more than blood relations, and are often critical both for the maintenance of power in wealthier groups and for the basic survival of economically marginal communities (Ostrander, 1984; Stack, 1974). What this work recognizes is that women are recruited into this type of labor through ideologies that posit women's caregiving as innate and consistent across differences of race and class and culture. As Lisa Adkins (2005) suggests, "Because it is theoretically untenable to associate women with affective labour, it doesn't mean that we disregard that women do most of it. Perhaps the distinction that matters here is . . . between being and doing. While women may not be naturally caring, they end up doing the work" (197).

While doing gender is centrally implicated in this process, it is also a way in which systems of class and race are perpetuated. For example, Randall Collins and others demonstrate that it is "largely women who perform the Weberian task of transforming class into status group membership" (1992, 219), including navigating the marketplace and maintaining awareness of food and nutrition discourses. Such work also involves making sense of taste cultures for the household and for its social networks, a task compounded by the fact that the landscape of what counts as good and appropriate food is constantly shifting, often highly politicized, and definitely ideologically charged. Dana, a working-class African American woman I interviewed summed this up in an interesting example:

> Well, you know, my kids always ate what I made, no complaints. And we made do, that's for sure. I wasn't baking or anything much any more, because of work, you see, but there was always something around. But you know, then the one of them started going to, you know, and bringing friends after school and I was glad . . . because she just wasn't so social before that, but she said something about the food, the food at her friend's, like a pantry full of snacks, you know, I'll never forget her saying, "she's got a cabinet full of snacks, all the ones you see on TV." And we just wouldn't . . . couldn't do that, but I tried for a while, you know, to buy a few of the things she asked for, just so she wouldn't feel funny when those kids came over and you gotta have a snack. Maybe popcorn, but even that, you gotta buy the right kind or it doesn't count.

Some of the most highly charged terrain rests between the industrially produced and "homemade" foods, a set of distinctions that are, themselves, often problematic. In considering my own experiences, I realized that for me, events such as the one my friend tried to mitigate had to involve food: not just any food, but food that had come from my imagination and my hands. For me, cooking was pleasurable, even as it was often implicated in complicated class codes: at different times in the last twenty years, it has been an accomplishment, a necessity, an expectation, a gift, and an imposition. Most of the early feminist literature on cooking tended to see it only as a source of oppression rather than pleasure and skill.[6] One exception was the work of African American feminists, who often centralized reclamation of the domestic realm. Whereas black women had domestic service for others imposed upon them, caring for their own families was framed as an act of resistance. For racial-ethnic women in the United States, their food labors were sometimes a means of exercising some control over family and kin.[7] At the same time, McIntosh and Zey (1989) point out that statements about women's gatekeeping confuse "responsibility for" with "control over." For women of color, participation in food production crossed public and private divides and exists in a complicated nexus of both empowerment and oppression.[8] As Avakian and Haber claimed, "cooking is something that was and continues to be imposed upon women, but is also an activity that can be a creative part of our daily lives" (2005, 6). As our understandings become more richly textured, I hope to illuminate spaces where multiple and often contradictory feelings about food are expressed and experienced.

The vast majority of what we know about food and the domestic realm focuses on what Dorothy Smith calls SNAF, the Standard North American Family, which is more an ideological code than a lived reality for many people (1993). The stories of DeVault's interviewees rang true to what people told me, although I was keenly aware that her research focused only on the experiences of heterosexual families with young children. My own world reflected a more varied and permeable construction of households, which I wanted to explore. My graduate school colleague, Chris Carrington (1995) produced an oft-cited corrective in his study of domestic labor in gay and lesbian households, demonstrating that, despite different gender ideologies, many kinds of households had one main "food" person. Building on his work, I was particularly interested in whether feeding work was always tied to particular ways of doing gender for women and men. To that end, I ensured that my interviews included men, single people, families without children, and blended households.

Once uncovered, many people still weren't comfortable seeing feeding work as invisible or emotional labor. This was particularly true when we move beyond the realm of family and kin-keeping activities. Arlene Kaplan Daniels (1987) argues that "resistance to conceptualizing interpersonal activities as work comes from the expectation that emotional interpersonal gestures are natural expressions that come spontaneously" (410). Yet cooking and feeding others is almost never a completely spontaneous act, reliant as it is on knowledge, supplies, and other existing resources. Even people who described a practice of feeding friends who "just drop by at dinner time," were working from a storehouse of prior knowledge. Lavinia, a Lithuanian-American woman in her eighties, revealed this when she talked about her own cooking practices in relation to her daughters:

> Well, Cassandra and the other girls, you know, they'll just call me up and say, "Can you make this for Julia's birthday party" or "Would you mind bringing a

tray of the pasta when you come?" They all have families of their own but, it's different—they haven't learned to cook these things. I learned all new foods when I got married, because my husband was Italian and I wanted to cook what he liked, but these girls, well, it's different. Jean, my eldest, who lives in Washington, she just calls a catering company, because that's what they do there, but you know, she still asks me to bring something, her favorites, so I do. And sometimes it's the day before, but I do it. The other ladies—we're all widows—where I live, they don't cook much so I bring food when we are going to be together. I know what to make and, you know, even if it's not what they're used to, they eat it. A hot meal, not so bad.

Friends, Family, and In-Between: Beyond Social Capital

Finally, in thinking through feeding others and eating together as social activities, I also began to question what kinds of relationships I was unquestioningly trying to ensure by my actions. I must have had an image or ideal type that encapsulated the social relationships I wanted: at the time, I was not long out of college, without children, still within social circles established from school, but fairly diverse in terms of the class and racial ethnic groups. In the fifteen years I have been considering this question, those networks have changed considerably. When I spoke to some of my original interviewees again after a few years or kept in touch for much longer, this was often true for them, as changes in their relationships and the composition of their households brought shifts to their commensal lives.

When my friend made his comment, I was not clear what I expected or wanted: the language available to me to describe these experiences still seems inadequate. "Family" was not a label shared by all members of my group of friends. "Community" seems too broad, and "entertaining" too distant. Although, as my friend pointed out, other social arrangements could have been possible, my need for a consistent pattern of social interaction with a particular group of people centered on providing food in my own household. I believe my inability to describe this, even armed with the analytical tools of sociology and anthropology, reflects a puzzle in the larger disciplines. What, after all, could one say about this enormous swath of social life that seemed to stand outside of social scientific scrutiny, to vary tremendously in people's everyday vocabularies, and yet to matter enormously in their sense of themselves as members of the social world? At the same time, in the late 1990s, there was very little to describe this and the literature on friendship, despite repeated calls for reclaiming and expanding, has not expanded to include domestic meals (Rawlins 1992, 2009).

In the ensuing decade, the concept of social capital has captured the theoretical and empirical discussions about social networks in political science and public policy, fueled by the work of Pierre Bourdieu in one direction and Robert Putnam in another. Social capital, with its emphasis on the generative nature of social contacts from work, family, education, and geographic environment, seems like a useful, process-oriented umbrella under which we can explore the kinds of relationships people engender. However, studies of social capital have often focused on measuring networks and framing its functionality around exchange and use value. So, for example, women's social networks are seen as generative in the sense that they provide potential resources for families when or if crises emerge. Some feminist theorists have called for an outright rejection of the concept, since even revisions operate on a romanticized presumption that women are "naturally" the central creators of social networks and social goods (Franklin and Thompson, 2005; Adkins, 2005). Some analysts suggest it would be useful to challenge the idea of a public/private divide and recognize shifts in informal and formal interactions. Given this critique and the specifics of my interviews, I believe this exploration of social meals is an ideal opportunity to reconsider social capital, particularly as people described their experiences through a surprising juxtaposition of formal models and affective expectations. Because inequality is a lens through which these experiences are filtered—in this case, in the form of the differential access to social and cultural knowledge that supports people outside work and family—I retain some of Bourdieu's construction of social capital, particularly as a factor in reinforcing social boundaries. The varieties of exchanges as well as the intangibility of some of the effects of commensal sociability, combined with the material experience of eating together, raise questions about whether it's even possible to name social relationships based on effects and layers of reciprocity. Indeed, even after doing this research and thinking about these issues for almost two decades, I remain curious about mapping the boundary crossings, the encounter with Simmel's stranger, and the paucity of intellectual vocabulary for understanding a variety of social relationships beyond work and family.

Studying Commensal Relationships

I pursued those questions through qualitative approaches, from interviewing people to observing events, to codifying popular texts—exploring historical shifts in etiquette and dining together—and finally, to unpacking larger cultural discourses about food, which are increasingly important in the contemporary global debates about food. In thinking through and about meals, I drew upon the insights of Institutional Ethnography, a method of inquiry pioneered by Dorothy Smith, which uses a triangulation of approaches to explore knowledge as a social accomplishment specific to various sites and people. The main goal of the research strategy is to allow particular subjects to speak about how they understand their situation, but it is incumbent upon the researcher to move from the standpoint of the subjects under investigation to a conceptual problematic that accounts for how people are related to their everyday worlds through institutions and relations of ruling. In this case, I began with what people told me about their commensal lives, looked at texts where such experiences were codified, and then returned to talking to people, often some of the same ones, five or more years after our original interviews.

Although the stories constitute the heart of this exploration, I also analyze books and other materials related to hospitality, suggesting that the context in which people conduct their social lives are shaped by the available discourses about commensal activities. Although hospitality is now dominated by commercial contexts and industries that profit from service such as restaurants and hotels, the original meaning, of making guests comfortable in a domestic setting, was a starting point for my investigation.[9]

In a world shaped by words, people routinely conduct their work through taken-for-granted texts such as books, forms, and reports. Institutional Ethnography helps map out relations of ruling, the shaping of texts and ideas that organize people's lives. While most practitioners of Institutional Ethnography examine the world of paid labor, in this study, the method helps explain a different kind of interactional and physical work—the work of producing meals and relationships. In this case, it was generally difficult to find actual texts (even consistent online sources) that people used to construct their understandings of sociable meals—in fact, I began with those that were overtly mentioned, such as entertaining and etiquette books, but I also considered unnamed texts that were of the same genre, comparative books directed at African Americans, and eventually other moral directives about food that are part of the larger discursive context in which Americans make decisions about what to eat.

Rather than seeing these texts as actual sources of information, they represent an example of crystallized social relations. The intent is not to try and understand these people's specific experiences in a way that claims to get directly at meanings and intentions for individuals, but rather to see how their experiences are bound up with various social structures and institutions that mediate people's lives outside work and family. The stories and descriptions provided by the people I interviewed allow me to identify some of the translocal relations, discourses, and institutional work processes that shape everyday work.

Originally, I conducted a large number of formal or standardized interviews but then continued talking to people (both some of the original interviewees and new contacts) over the next five to ten years as a means of building understanding of the coordination of activity in multiple sites. Each conversation, whether formal or not, provided an opportunity to learn about a particular piece of the extended relational chain, to check the developing picture of the coordinative process, and to become aware of additional questions. Text and discourse analysis helped examine how forms and practices of knowledge get created and acted upon—how they end up organizing work processes and how individuals must then fit themselves into these unnamed but prefigured arrangements. In the end, the relationship between these levels remains speculative, but I believe this multifaceted approach provides some framework from which we can begin to think about how relationships, food, and domesticity fit together to create and maintain social boundaries.

Shared Meals and Stories

Popular culture abounds with images of sociable events with food, from films and advertisements narrating "good times" to an array of books and magazines about entertaining and cooking. Many of the social events that characterize contemporary American society center on people sharing food with family or friends in their homes. Our categories for these events evoke historically and culturally specific images, denoting social arrangements of greater or less formality—potlucks, dinner parties, brunches, barbecues. The reasons attached to social gatherings vary—some are associated with holidays or festive occasions such as birthdays and graduations, some are connected to other events such as watching sports together on TV or playing cards—and yet each invokes a particular structure and form, such that the design and presentation of the meal expresses ideas about the social relationships being enacted. When people invite friends, neighbors, or family members to partake of a meal within their household, they are engaging in forms of sociability, delineating lines of intimacy and distance.

Although ultimately I focus heavily on the social, the food is as important as the relationships, considering what is served, how, and to whom, and of course, why. The stories I collected, through interviews, observations, and informal conversations, focus on specific "food events," including the shared meal and the sociable moments surrounding it, as well as the performances of self that are created through these everyday interactions.

More specifically, from the late 1990s to the present, I interviewed and observed a small sample of people in contemporary American society, mapping the contours of their experiences with food and socializing. My goal was to explore uncharted territory, gathering a variety of descriptions and multiple versions of experience rather than attempting to find a "typical" set of stories (DeVault, 1991, 21). Originally, I interviewed and observed forty-seven people, which involved thirty-five households containing over a hundred people. Some of the people knew and socialized with each other, creating approximately six groups or "networks" of friends and acquaintances who socialized together. This offered some comparative understandings of how different people view the same relationships and events. I also found it important to talk to group members who were not cooks and had to negotiate different avenues of reciprocity other than cooking for friends. I also spoke to both members of a couple when possible, which allowed for some comparison about the division of labor and the construction of meaning between partners.

Most of the original interviews took place in the New England region. I met people through word of mouth, by putting up fliers in churches, synagogues, chain stores, local businesses, and supermarkets. Some people contacted me directly after a local food writer wrote a newspaper column about my research. People in Michigan, Chicago, New York, and Pennsylvania also recruited acquaintances for me to interview. Among these, I chose people whose social networks did not fall on extreme ends of the spectrum, neither social isolates nor individuals with extremely large social networks. I also tried to avoid talking only to people who claimed to be "serious cooks" or liked to "entertain," because those labels are often class-coded. In questioning the very categories we have to describe commensality, I sought certain kinds of respondents rather than trying to construct a representative sample. I spoke to men who cook, people with a variety of family structures, gays and lesbians, and single people, and people who did not cook but attended a lot of events at other people's homes. Most people identified themselves as middle class, although their self-reported household incomes ranged from what would be barely managing to being part of the upper brackets in the United States. Over time, I became particularly interested in the differences between the experiences of the African Americans and euro-whites who did not self-identify ethnically and focused much of my thinking on these comparisons.

Over the course of five years, I also conducted participant observations. Originally, the observations focused on six sets of people, some of whom I subsequently interviewed. As I continued to do interviews, I participated in events whenever possible. In order to observe, I often had to be a legitimate member of the circle of people invited to the event. No one offered to invite me to observe parties unless they felt I had some previous contact or relationship that sanctioned my presence. In contrast, I was often encouraged to interview and observe people at home during their daily routines with family. There was a clear sense that I was acceptable among family and not guests. At first these seemed counterintuitive because family is often perceived as the private realm, providing sanctuary from the outside world. On the other hand, it's possible that people were more comfortable presuming what would be acceptable to their *family members* than what would be acceptable to their *friends*.

In structured interviews, I asked questions about whom they spent time with outside of the workplace and who they invited to their homes for food and companionship, constructing a thorough but loose social network list. The stories and analyses are centered on their non-kin relationships, that is, with friends, colleagues, neighbors, and acquaintances. The stories they told defined both the events that make up the patterning of their social experiences and the relationships constructed through that work. I use these narratives to analyze the nature of commensality, with a specific focus on various forms of socializing that people make use of in their everyday lives. I was particularly interested in how they defined hospitality, how their social lives were similar or different from what they experienced in childhood, and the forms of event that people hosted. The events ranged from formal dinner parties to potlucks, from highly structured buffets to the evening meal where friends "just drop by." Given what people told me about hospitality, I also analyzed etiquette and entertaining books that describe the ideal forms of these events. Although I begin with the texts, it should be clear that the interviews came first, establishing the language and concepts that followed.

Food and Moral Panics

The context for these stories is the social, economic, and political climate of the United States in the late twentieth and early twenty-first century. While people may have only touched upon moral and social issues in their interviews, these particular discourses shape the universe in which they make choices about what to eat, what kind of meals to serve, and with whom they want to spend time socializing. Like sexuality, attitudes and behaviors surrounding food and eating are shaped by available cultural meanings as well as economic and social configurations. Both involve material and physical processes that must be translated, explained, and analyzed through a social lens in order to be comprehensible as a source of collective and individual identification. As Bourdieu suggests, if food is a field, then it is both an object and a subject caught in webs of signification. People's choices are embedded in moral and social discourses. While there are numerous ways to consider the moral organization of food in America, in this section I explore only the outlines of some significant discourses. What we eat and who provides it offer some broad contexts that shape domestic food practices.

What We Eat

At one point, I interviewed Margaret, a white woman in her midfifties who works as a school secretary, while she cooked dinner for her family and a friend. She summed up the most direct way that the moral discourses about food get translated directly onto the plate:

> Well, we used to have a lot of people over from church or we'd do potlucks at the social hall, but you know it's getting harder—it's not that I don't like to cook, I really do, you can see that. But now you have to ask, is anybody a vegetarian, . . . is anybody allergic to something, or is there anything you don't eat. It's not—well, like Stephanie's eating dinner with us tonight, she does a lot, and I know she won't eat mushrooms, but she doesn't ask, she just picks them out. Maybe once, there was something [she couldn't eat.] But, I mean, for the potlucks, I'm not just making the same thing over and over again—there are some of these church people that do, for the potlucks I mean—and that's fine because people expect it, you know the bean salad or something, but I like to try stuff and I'm always worried it's not going to be okay and now you gotta ask—or sometimes, I mean, they'll tell you and that's okay. I mean, if it's an allergy, you have to know, but some of these people they'll just come right out and say, well, I don't eat fish or I don't like broccoli and I'm thinking, is it going to kill you?

It's not surprising that people's anxieties about the well being of their social world, culture, and individual selves often coalesce around food. Alan Warde (1997) surmises, "the structural anxieties of our age are made manifest in discourses about food" (56). Anthropologists and material historians have long understood that social order—indeed, the very choice or necessity for people to live in groups—is built on a need to generate a sustainable food supply. That said, we also know that what counts as edible and sustaining varies greatly among groups across history and geography—and that disgust, taboo, and rejection are as much social as physical constraints on the cultural production and consumption of food. Social groups are defined by what they will or will not eat, creating ethnic and national boundaries based on cuisine and consumption. All major religions circumscribe the universe by what is or is not edible to practitioners. As social life and institutions change, food—its availability, its safety, its symbolism—is often a conduit for people's attempts to ground their collective beliefs and identities.

As with many moral issues, public debates about food ebb and flow. Currently, food is increasingly the center of transnational controversies, only some of which are related to control, trade, and policies. Although numerous issues pushed these topics into the public light, Lien and Nerlich (2005) suggest that the BSE scare ("mad cow disease") along with battles over genetically modified foodstuffs made the politics of food more global in the 1990s (5). For most of our earlier recorded history, collective concerns about food centered on its availability, such that cycles of abundance and shortage parallel changes in civilizations. The safety of food—what's good to eat and what's not—becomes part of the collective responsibility, whether transferred through culture, religion, or the state. Some of the other issues that coalesce as moral panics around food begin with agriculture and include crop and livestock diseases, the influence of science genetic engineering, environmental concerns centered on pesticides and the critique of monoculture agroindustrial farming, trade, and agriculture in relation to global development, and cultural preservation through geographically designated foodstuffs.

The stability of food supplies has been one of the most dramatic changes wrought by industrialization and urbanization. Indeed, as John Goody (1997) points out, whatever bad things one can say about commercial and industrial food, it has drastically improved the nutrition and health of many populations of people across the globe (albeit often concentrated in wealthier areas). Although food safety has always been a concern for human communities, modernization and industrialization shift the focus from more "natural" issues such as crop loss, disease, and distribution limits to concerns about the impact of what Goody calls "industrial decadence." In particular, the development of what some call the industrial food complex—a series of industries, political lobbying groups, marketing and advertising organizations, and regulatory agencies—has generated concerns about the quality and availability of food. Today many moral panics about food center on the successes and excesses of agro-industrial production. The good and bad are summed up by the contradictions between the amazing variety and quantity of foods available and the concern that this food is overabundant, environmentally dangerous, and nutritionally suspect. "Safety" becomes a more complex issue as the global food industry has evolved into a monolithic entity that produces most of the world's food (much of it highly processed), more foods than the population can support.[10] It protects its interests through government regulations and subsidies, financial support of favorable research, and billions of dollars of advertising promoting industrial foods, particularly processed foods, to children (Nestle, 2002). Food safety and security—the ability of populations to have access to good quality, nutritionally adequate, and culturally appropriate food—remains a concern, often presented as a failure of government or as part and parcel of the profit motive of the industrial food complex. While food safety and availabilities are more stable than in other times, famines and widespread hunger continue to exist and are often a result of global political conflicts, inequalities, and most centrally, a lack of entitlements—a failure of distribution—rather than as a result of a lack of available foodstuffs. The debate over food is profound and divisive, particularly since the reliance on a global industrial food supply can be presented as either a triumph of modernity and technology creating choices and opportunities for more people or a moral failure of governments and individuals who allow corporations to run rampant and people to acquiesce to convenience (Belasco, 2008; Lien and Nerlich, 2005; Atkins and Bowler, 2000). However, in a highly industrialized world shaped by ideologies of personal responsibility, the outrage over inequities of distribution and consumption often focus less on the food supply itself than on those who consume it and how they should navigate these problems. For example, Maxine Baca Zinn (1998) argues "research on women of color demonstrates that protecting one's family from the demands of the market is strongly related to the distribution of power and privilege in society" (16). Similarly, debates about growing obesity levels across the globe can be seen as a touchstone for anxieties about shifts in economic, social, and cultural conditions (Julier, 2007; Campos et al., 2005; Saguy, 2006; Guthman, 2012).

For most people, their lives intersect with these debates from a vantage point as consumers, since the vast majority of foods are grown and produced outside the individual household and brought in as purchases. Although variety and choice are the hallmarks of a westernized country like the United States, such choices are not equally distributed across the population. Although the "smart shopper" is supposed to be classless (DeVault, 1991), even market researchers concede that knowledge about the marketplace is stratified. In particular in the United States, what counts as good food—and as safe and accessible food—is shaped by class-based discourses about quality. In an unprecedented shift away from some small-scale production at home (in the form of local agricultural products and home gardens), reliance on the global agricultural-food conglomerates is now necessary for people with fewer resources. Indeed, even supermarkets are distributed unequally. Convenience stores and fast-food chains dominate the landscape, but more palpably in low-income areas where fresh foods are scarcer, creating what some have called "food deserts."[11] Ironically, local products, farm-produced items, and foods from geographically specific peasant cuisines are now more expensive than the convenience foods that are so ubiquitous in westernized countries. Once easily available, these items are embedded morally in questions about health and variety, part of household projects related to identity and self-expression. Eating "the other" has become both a mark of status and a mark of the ordinary, where sushi is available in supermarkets and locally produced meat is a culinary luxury. "Food adventuring" becomes, as Lisa Heldke (2003) describes, one version of this as culinary colonialism, where contact with experiences of the exotic other makes a bland cultural background more interesting.

In the last ten years, public debates about food safety, organics, natural foods, meat consumption, and processed foods have increased dramatically so that people (as consumers) are bombarded with often contradictory messages presented as guidelines from various sources like mass media, social contacts, and social institutions. For example, Alan Warde (1997) suggests that when we examine the various kinds of advice people receive about what to eat, we find a series of long-standing structural oppositions that are often mobilized to express appreciation of food and to make choices. Warde calls these deep-seated contradictions "antinomies of taste," which capture larger structural anxieties and parameters of uncertainty in contemporary western cultures. They include extravagance and economy, novelty and tradition, health and indulgence, care, and convenience. What we eat is filtered through a political economy of food and a set of cultural discourses that stratify people and, as Margaret so aptly points out in her interview, adds one more layer of complication in opening up the domestic realm to non-kin for a meal.

Who Provides Food

A second, related moral panic about food centers on who provides meals. The debates about food in this case often center on the decline of the family meal. Laments about the loss of cooking are commonplace alongside the fear of the loss of the family meal. Even commentators who wish to be careful cannot avoid pointing to women's increased role in the paid labor force as the reason why people watch television cooking shows but no one cooks at home any more. Critics of fast food are quick to point to busy lifestyles and a desire for convenience over care as the culprit. For example, Michael Pollan, whose exploration of the food system has become one of the most talked-about critiques, begins drawing conclusions about our food system by lamenting a loss of cooking and a rise in food television shows instead. Questioning the popularity of the latter, he writes,

But here's what I don't get: How is it that we are so eager to watch other people browning beef cubes on screen but so much less eager to brown them ourselves? For the rise of Julia Child as a figure of cultural consequence—along . . . whoever is crowned the next Food Network star—has, paradoxically, coincided with the rise of fast food, home-meal replacements and the decline and fall of everyday home cooking. . . . That decline has several causes: women working outside the home; food companies persuading Americans to let them do the cooking; and advances in technology that made it easier for them to do so. Cooking is no longer obligatory, and for many people, women especially, that has been a blessing. But perhaps a mixed blessing, to judge by the culture's continuing, if not deepening, fascination with the subject. It has been easier for us to give up cooking than it has been to give up talking about it—and watching.

Pollan's point—that cooking is no longer obligatory—is a gendered one, despite his shift to a more gender-neutral "us" at the end of his complaint.[12] It's generally assumed that the entrance of women into the work force is responsible for the collapse of home cooking. However, women with jobs outside the home spend less time cooking—but so do women without jobs. Women with jobs have more money to pay corporations to do their cooking, yet all American men and women now allow corporations to cook for them when they can. Those corporations have been trying to persuade Americans to let them do the cooking since long before large numbers of women entered the work force (Shapiro, 2005). In this case, there is no empirical correlation between food television consumption and a decrease in home cooking—indeed, it's not clear that these activities draw from the same subpopulations.

The moral discourse about cooking is also an opportunity to complain about changes in the race- and class-based structure in the United States. In contemporary society, laments about fast-paced social and economic changes in family life are often expressed through anxiety about families who do not sit down to "home-cooked" meals together. By imposing products and selling cultural meanings, commercial food changes the experience and function of family. In his original treatise on McDonaldization, George Ritzer (2000) indicts convenience in the home kitchen, where the microwave, frozen foods, and supermarket "value-added" products such as ready-to-go burritos or rotisserie chickens bring the commercial attitudes as well as products into the private home. Buying and using mass-produced food alters not only the amount but also the nature of labor within the household. For Ritzer and others, by extension, it changes the meaning as well: "Those qualities of the family meal, the ones that impart feelings of security and well-being might be lost forever when food is 'zapped' or 'nuked' instead of cooked." Lamenting kids who make their own meals with microwaves, Ritzer equates not having to cook with not having to care. Furthermore, people who cannot create "proper meals" for their families are to blame for all manner of social problems.[13]

This discourse, while tapping into deep-seated anxieties about shifting gender expectations, also helps render the world of commercial food labor invisible and unnecessary. The people who do the vast majority of low-paying but vital food production—from fast-food employees to ketchup-processing plant workers, from supermarket sales clerks to agricultural workers—tend to be women, people of color, immigrants, and working-class individuals. The marketing end of the industrial food system does its best to point attention away from the actual people who make meals, but critics are also equally culpable in missing the fact that whether it's in the household or in the processing plant and fast-food restaurant, the person doing the work is undervalued, given the absolute central nature of their work to societal continuity.

In terms of everyday life and the people whose social events I examined, these discourses enter into their experiences tangentially, through a valorization of home-cooked food and a certain amount of guilt and anxiety over foods prepared in the commercial marketplace. Correspondingly, regardless of social class, the cook is usually a gendered being, who cannot completely escape the expectations of women at hearth and home.

Starting here, I considered how these attitudes and actions related to food—our ideas, habits, and patterns—shape the possible social choices and environments for close social relationships. In particular, how do people find the like-minded others in this environment? How do they "break bread" with those whose bread is unrecognizable in their symbolic and material universe? To start, in Chapter 2, I offer an analysis of texts—etiquette and entertaining books—that establish the groundwork from which people are supposed to make these decisions. How people define hospitality—and how that definition has evolved—creates the space from which all their sociable events must emerge.

2. From Formality to Comfort

The Discourse of Meals and Manners

The Lovell-Mingots had sent out cards for what was known as "a formal dinner" (that is, three extra footmen, two dishes for each course, and a Roman punch in the middle), and had headed their invitations with the words "To meet the Countess Olenska," in accordance with the hospitable American fashion which treats strangers as if they were royalties, or at least their ambassadors.

—Edith Wharton, *The Age of Innocence*

No meal was ever planned or balanced or served. Nor was there any gathering at the table. Pilate might bake hot bread and each one of them would eat it with butter whenever she felt like it. Or there might be grapes, left over from the winemaking, or peaches for days on end. If one of them bought a gallon of milk, they drank it until it was gone. If another got a half-bushel of tomatoes or a dozen ears of corn, they ate them until they were gone, too. They ate what they had or came across or had a craving for.

—Toni Morrison, *Song of Solomon*

The two approaches to meals described above seem like the extreme ends of a continuum from formal and structured to informal and haphazard, from upper-class urban white culture to working-class rural black culture. Although the ensuing narratives about these two meals reveals a more complex distribution of affect, reciprocity, and taste, what unites them is that both rely on an acquired storehouse of knowledge about food, meals, and interactions.

When people share meals, they rely on social knowledge about what to do and how to do it. Their events work from "cultural templates," to use Warde and Martens' term, even as their actual activities deviate or shift the form in its specific manifestation (2001). Exploring these cultural templates that people draw upon, I asked people in a variety of ways about how they learned to cook, where they developed their ideas about parties, and what these events might have looked like in their families of origin. In my interviews, some people talked specifically about magazines and cookbooks, friends and family members who gave them ideas, training, and information about food and cooking. But the larger question about how such an event should be shaped was not clearly articulated. Lacking another word to describe it, in interviews I asked people how they would define "hospitality"—how was their definition similar or different from that of other people or from the kind of sociable activities that went on in their families of origin. This chapter explores how people's definitions of hospitality—and consequently their social meals—reflect cultural discourses about sociability. After considering what people said, I turn to textual sources from which such ideas develop. Concerns about how people construct their social lives emerge in debates about propriety, etiquette, formality, intimacy, comfort, style, and display. As Bourdieu (1984, 1987) demonstrates, such debates are never trivial, but rather illustrate how struggles for control over symbol and meaning are the real sites of conflict in contemporary society.

Defining Hospitality: Balancing Comfort and Civility

When I asked people to define hospitality, almost everyone said "making guests comfortable." This is significant not only because it was evoked so consistently, but also because "comfort" is not central to the kind of formal hospitality that dominates nineteenth- and early-twentieth-century American culture. Historically, informal sociability certainly coexisted with more formal models, but the latter had a cultural ascendancy due to its class and race associations. Ideologies of upward mobility tied to discourses of assimilation and class conduct posit the more formal mode of hospitality as the one to which people aspired. According to Murray (1904), hospitality involves constructing rights and membership for nongroup members. In the case of domestic hospitality, this takes the form of bringing people into the "private" household and providing for their needs, which, in contemporary times, is often limited to a meal and drinks. However, as Olesen (1993) and Gusfield (1994) point out, what rights and expectations guests have are dependent on historical and cultural conditions.

The people I interviewed evoke a sense of familial boundaries rather than the formal welcoming of strangers and non-intimates. For example, one woman, Cindy, made an explicit contrast between two approaches to hospitality. She preferred "putting people completely at ease and making them feel like they are at home. And indulging and pampering them. . . . I'm sure there's that really stuffy attitude where it would be a real success if it was really fancy and formal and everybody was afraid about dropping something on the rug."

Another interviewee Nora, echoed these sentiments when she described "learning to relax and allow grace in the moment. . . . I don't want to be like my mother-in-law following them around with a DustBuster so they don't get crumbs on the couch." However, there were differences both in the ways people evoked comfort for guests and in the degree of formality in their sociable activities. Given this, it's worth unpacking people's use of that term and then its reflection in larger discourses of sociability. The emphasis on discourses allows us to consider a larger universe of ideas that create categories and expectations, but may be only vaguely connected to direct experience.

Comfort seems, foremost, to be about access to someone else's home. One woman who works in commercial hospitality said, "It's all about comfort; where you can find comfort, the couch, the nice chair to sit in . . . and I can smell the food cooking."[1] Of course, there are differences in what people mean by comfort: How much of the home do guests have access to? How is the household altered because of their presence? Do they get served or serve themselves in the manner of intimate family members? Do they participate in the production of food and the cleaning up, or are they only responsible for good conversation and a bottle of wine?

Because the interviews focused on commensal events, "feeding guests well" was an important part of the way people defined comfort. As Mary Douglas remarked, relationships are constructed by the kinds of meals one shares. Helen said, "I like the kind of ambiance, no not ambiance, comfort. It's the relationship that develops around food . . . we're talking about a way you have people enter your life." Comfort becomes the staging for greater intimacy among people. Alcohol, good food, and comfortable furniture allow people to be more relaxed around one another, a way of physically attending to guest's needs.

Many of the African Americans I interviewed were first- or second-generation migrants to the north: this social and geographic shift was referenced in their conversations about inviting people in. Both Daniel and Perry's descriptions of "southern hospitality" centered on offering people something to eat or drink, notably home-made food, even if they just "dropped by" unexpectedly. Perry complained that one adjustment he had living in New England was "when people says let's get together, it usually means eating in a restaurant rather than having them cook for you. I miss that about the South. . . . [F]or me, part of meeting people is inviting them into your home and sharing food with them. . . . I think food—extending food to someone is a way of making them welcome."[2] This understanding of hospitality is shaped by the history of the African American experience in the United States, notably the ways in which sociability and community sharing were integral to group survival.

For example, while people of both races often distinguished comfort defined as "providing food" from "waiting on guests," in the end they seemed to have different reasons as to why. Pam, an African American professional, began by saying "I don't think of what I do [as] hospitality," pointing out a difference between herself and hosts, "who say come right in, seat yourself, can I get you a drink, whereas in my house, people know where the refrigerator is." Listening carefully, to agree but clarify, her friend Kendra asserted, "That's still hospitality . . . because whatever she did from the beginning made that person feel comfortable to do that." In Pam and Kendra's formulation, real comfort comes from access to the home, a (possible) familiarity with the inside of kitchen cabinets and refrigerators that family members experience. To Pam, the comfort and care she extends to guests comes from providing food, not service.

Although no one asserted this explicitly, some of the distinction between hospitality as comfort and hospitality as service may be a result of commercial control over so many contexts we associate with hospitality. Murray (1990) points out that the only references to hospitality in contemporary texts are connected to the hotel and restaurant industry. More and more, Americans are dependent on the growing service sector to meet at least some of their daily needs. "Service," is a form of caring work and, increasingly in everyday experience, becomes something more people pay for. In fact, race and class distinctions are often manifest by the extent and character of individual and household reliance on the paid service work of others. In her now-classic work, *The Managed Heart*, Arlie Hochschild (1983) uses examples from service work in the airline industry to illustrate the commercialization of emotional labor. She describes, "the management of feeling to create a publicly observable facial and bodily display; emotional labor is sold for a wage and therefore has exchange value. [It] produces the proper state of mind in others—in this case, the sense of being cared for in a convivial and safe place" (7).

In a comparable experience, Harry Murray (1990) found that similar attitudes began to shape the Catholic Worker shelters and soup kitchens, such that he saw Max Weber's rationalization of society extending into hospitality. Hospitality is supposedly accessible to everyone, but codifying and commodifying voluntary service to others "destroys the openness towards the stranger that is a requisite of hospitality in the traditional sense . . . [and it] undermines the practice of hospitality, since it gives the trainee predefined categories into which to fit one's clients" (4). In particular, service work in contemporary American society is not seen as individualized and valuable labor, but rather performed by anonymous and interchangeable workers at the low end of the wage scale. Not surprisingly, such work is often done by women and people of color. When the people I interviewed centered their definitions on different aspects of hospitality, they were implicitly invoking a contrast between the practices in their homes and the impersonality of the commercial marketplace.[3] More recently, in informal interviews, people were much more explicit about rejecting eating out at certain kinds of restaurants, centering their social lives around eating in and insisting on food they defined in contrast to the industrial food system's productions.

In defining domestic hospitality, a focus on food is not surprising, given the way food has taken on increased cultural value in the last twenty years. Associations between caring and food are long-standing, particularly in terms of gendered labor on behalf of families. Interestingly, in Alan Warde's analysis of changes in the food columns from British women's magazines, he describes a shift in rhetoric about "care": from the 1960s to the 1990s, he finds less emphasis on caring in general and notes that most of the references to care in the 1990s are about caring for *guests* rather than *family members*. In con-temporary western society, time is often experienced as a scarce commodity, so that cooking for someone (rather than relying on prepared or convenience foods) is a highly valued form of caring that need not be accompanied by other attempts to attend people's needs. He suggests that "cooking becomes more a technical matter, the food stands for itself, the result of effective performance, a demonstration of culinary expertise and knowledge about food" (Warde, 1997, 137). People cook for each other both as a performance of self and as a way of pleasing others. Paula explicitly asserted the personal rewards of her cooking as the main reason for the gathering:

> I feel like a hostess is someone who says, "this is my home, welcome, I'm here to serve you." . . . I feel like I'm not here to serve you, you can go get what you want. Some water? Help yourself. But what I guess I want to show you what I can do [as a cook] and want you to enjoy it and tell me that I'm great—it's more of an ego thing and not a serving thing. I want to do something for you that I think you might like.

Such uses of food as display are, of course, class-based. People with more economic means were more likely to describe the food as the main "gift" in their hospitality. However, across class lines a number of others echoed Daniel, who said, "I like to watch their faces when they eat my food." Harry, who does both everyday family meals and a variety of sociable cooking, as-serted that food, not formality, was central to hospitality: "I think of food as nurturing. My mom was a nurturer . . . giving to people and sharing [the experience] with her. That's what I like to think I do." Although he cooks a variety of cuisines and constructs dinners with six courses, Harry says that "elaborate is not a good word, because to me, elaborate would be centerpieces and candelabra and I'm really stark about that kind of stuff." Interestingly, among the people I interviewed, Harry had the economic and cultural capital to create elaborate dinners with ease. Instead, these descriptions focus on the meal as the central gift to guests, a way of meeting their physical and aesthetic needs.

Although comfort and formality are historically opposed, they emerge simultaneously in many people's descriptions. Even people whose sociability centered on formal meals evoked an ethos of care based in comfort. Amy, who held formal dinners regularly, said "hospitality is making people feel comfortable. And I want people to have a great time in my house, which they do! I mean, the word 'hostess' sounds so formal, like very proper . . . but hostess with the mostest I think I want to be. It makes me feel good when people come here and they say, 'oh, your house is so warm and comforting. And there's just this cozy feeling here, we love coming here.' And they love the food."

While Amy wanted people to be comfortable, she also described setting the table with fresh flowers, crystal glasses, silver, and good china, and making sure her children used proper manners. The desire for comfort is not completely at odds with the formal structuring of a sociable event, but there are shifts and readjustments in how people enact these two modes. As Amy envisions it, formality rests in the setting, the presentation of the meal, and the sensuality of the food: "To come through to my kitchen or as people go to the living room, they've got to go through the dining room. And I feel that the table makes a statement, that if you've got a table that's very festive looking and very inviting, people's mouths are going to start to water. And the smell of the kitchen . . . everything blends together."

However, for many people blending comfort and hospitality is not always straightforward. With formal hospitality, the rules and role expectations are clear. To many of my interviewees, hospitality as "comfort" implies degrees of intimacy that usually need to be negotiated. Many participants described a practice of "asking what we can bring," as a way of finding out the form of the event and the expectations on them as guests. People desire cultural and social guideposts for less formal social events. There were numerous discussions of the effort involved in constructing a menu that suited the tastes and needs of one's guests. Knowledge of food preferences can be a function of intimacy, of shared tastes and social capital, or of routine interaction. Socializing together on an ongoing basis allows people to develop shared definitions of the situation.

Although ideas of comfort appeared in people's descriptions, there were no clear-cut rules for behavior explicitly invoked. Given the lack of directives, how do people come to a shared sensibility about social occasions? People whose sociability centered on comfort often described problems in getting some guests to understand their definition of the situation. Cindy and Mary described a friend who comes to their house for dinners and "jumps up from the table and . . . absolutely insists on doing the dishes . . . and the next thing you know she's got them all done. It just drives me nuts. I just don't want her in there. . . . Recently they were here and dinner's on the table . . . and she's got to wash the one or two dishes before she sits down. . . . It's always an argument." When sociability is guided by an ideology of "comfort," people are able to construct a greater range of roles and selves than those afforded by a more formal ethos. However, this can also lead to greater uncertainty about appropriate behavior, food, and expectations about levels of intimacy, and an ongoing negotiation of shared definitions of the situation. People's practices suggest that more formal norms still circumscribe social interactions in the domestic setting. In a short story, Lorrie Moore (1995) asks, "is the dinner party a pantomime of the family or a paradigm of society?" Although the ethos of comfort suggests that sociable moments often mirror the intimacy of family life, that intimacy is circumscribed by persistent ideas about social boundaries. For example, almost no stories were about events with outright rancor between guests. Houses were cleaned or modified in some degree to accommodate guests for almost all occasions except the spontaneous and extremely informal. Daniel said hospitality and comfort mean "my house is your house for right now . . . of course, there are doors that you close that you don't want opened." There were still certain expectations for guests, too: Interviewees describe guests offering to help or bringing flowers, dessert, or wine; people dressed more formally for some occasions: and conversations modified to suit the group. Even potlucks, the most informal format where everyone shares the labor, operated on some shared assumptions about appropriate behavior. Participants must arrive within a reasonable time frame, contribute food that fits with the general expectations of the group, and participate in sociable and mobile conversations without drawing too much attention to one individual.[4]

These discussions of hospitality point to a complex and often conflicting set of concerns about the nature of formality in contemporary sociable gatherings. On the one hand, among the people I talked to, comfort is a central feature of commensality. On the other hand, many descriptions demonstrated that ideas about formality and structure still held considerable sway over people's activities. According to John Kasson (1990), the cultural tensions between civilized behavior and comfort are not a new phenomenon but rather reflective of other social, political, and economic issues such as democracy, urbanization, and commodity culture in America. I explore how these contrasting concerns get expressed and acted upon today.

Discourses of Distinction:
Etiquette and Entertaining in Texts

> Manners, especially the manner of relationship to legitimate culture, are the stake in a permanent struggle. There can be no neutral statement in these matters.
> —Pierre Bourdieu, *Distinction*

Although their food ideas came from a wide range of sources, when people did reference textual sources for their ideas about hospitality, two particular names came up frequently: Emily Post and Martha Stewart. Both women made their names part of popular discourse by publicly prescribing and providing guidelines for sociable activities with food. Because I interviewed many African Americans, I also considered the historical and contemporary manifestations of the hospitality discourse through texts that were specifically written for people of color.

Emily Post's *Etiquette* was widely disseminated in the 1920–1940s. From the same era, Edward S. Green's *National Capital Code of Etiquette* (1920) is full of photos of exemplary African Americans from Washington D.C.'s "Negro Four Hundred" whom Green held up as exemplars in his guide for the mainly middle-class African Americans in other parts of the country. Charlotte Hawkins Brown's *The Correct Thing To Do—To Say—To Wear* was published in 1940 as an extension of her lifelong work as an educator and founder of the Palmer Institute. Palmer began as a vocational and agricultural college founded on Booker T. Washington's principles for racial uplift but gradually, due to funding issues, evolved into a finishing school for the children of black elites. In both incarnations, Hawkins Brown insisted that social graces were an integral part of the curriculum.

To capture the shift from formality to comfort, I also analyzed more contemporary evocations of hospitality, with Stewart's first few books, including *Entertaining* and Smith's books, *Entertaining and Cooking for Friends* and *Rituals and Celebrations*. Given the emphasis on dinner party manners, I compared additional material from two etiquette books for African Americans: *Basic Black: Home Training for Modern Times* (1996) written by Karen Grisby Bates and Karen Hudson, and Harriet Cole's *How to Be* (1999).

Although it's impossible to talk about these books in terms of direct influence on the people I studied, we can see these books as iconic texts, reference points that contain a concise version of the templates most people consciously or unconsciously draw upon in their own sociable events. Editions of Post's book have appeared regularly since 1922. Today there's the Emily Post Institute, countless publications, and a Web site. Hawkins Brown was one of the most well known among a number of educators at African American schools, women's clubs, and training associations.

Stewart's media output began with the 1982 *Entertaining* and evolved into a multimillion-dollar empire of books, goods, and programs. B. Smith, a former model and restaurateur, has been called "the black Martha Stewart," perhaps unfairly constraining her particular contributions to advice about style and cuisine. Both author's books sell well to white and black audiences.

Other than Green, a former diplomat, all the writers are women, as is common in twentieth-century American advice literature. Although there are certainly men who serve as experts of the same sort, these writers inherit a tradition of "advice writing as an emerging vocation for middle class women in the late 19th century" (Kasson, 1990, 49). In many ways, these women are establishing a performance of gender as well as prescribing sociable behavior. Examining the similarities and differences between the two time periods also illustrates some continuing and shifting themes in the discourse of commensality. Most notably, while status and aesthetic display are apparent in both, contemporary ideologies of "choice," "materialism," and "individualism" have meant a reconfiguration of rules of sociability and food. For the African American writers, a notion of home and community center an emphasis on behavior that transcends public and private. In terms of food and style there is a greater emphasis on food traditions rooted in a specific history rather than appropriating style from many cultures.

Emily Post and Charlotte Hawkins Brown

Although advice books on manners have a long and interesting history, as a genre they are also linked to the social, economic, and technological changes of the late nineteenth century. Both Kasson (1990) and Williams (1987) argue that the need for instruction on manners came from the Victorian era and the bourgeois desire to distinguish members of their class in an increasingly complex urban society. Certainly the need to cultivate appropriate behavior for social settings is part of the "civilizing of bodies and selves" explored historically by Elias and Foucault. By formalizing rules for interaction and social behavior, people internalize restrictions as morally appropriate rather than oppressive. These prescriptions for behavior are in greatest demand for "public" situations, that is, where one interacts with individuals who are not intimate members of one's household. Domestic sociability, inviting non-kin into the private realm of the household, is a key site for the enactment of such prescriptions, for it is the crucial intersection of public and private behavior. Eating with others, in particular, was a central test of "bodily management and emotional control" (Kasson, 1990, 182). As such, etiquette and advice books emphasize dinner parties and informal entertainments involving food and drink in the home. In order to be fully accepted in upper-middle-class society, one must survive "trial by fork." To put it another way, etiquette is a system of accountability for "doing class," determining the boundaries of sociable relationships.

Although there are numerous etiquette books that focus on proper deportment at dinner parties, one of the most-often-cited and reissued versions belongs to Emily Post. Visser (1991) calls her "the doyenne of a new breed of experts" (75). Her articulation of formal etiquette remains a reference point for many Americans. In debates about propriety, the refrain, "Look it up in Emily Post," has become a colloquialism. The book is organized like a dictionary in size and format, with a fat index and table of contents designed to make it easier to locate the exact rules one needs. Illustrations are line drawings that show specific behaviors (elbows off the table) and samples (invitations and letters) or black and white photographs of table settings (when does the spoon go across the top of the place setting). One indication of their place in the cultural landscape is that *Etiquette* and its subsequent editions are often found in the reference section of most libraries and bookstores.

In America in the 1920s and 1930s, the rich didn't require Emily Post.[5] But the newer classes did, especially as a way of identifying with the wealthy and distinguishing themselves from new immigrants. According to Kasson (1990), etiquette writers "must be viewed within the larger concern of how to establish order and authority in a restless, highly mobile, rapidly urbanizing, and industrializing democracy. Seeking to avoid overt conflict, they turned issues of class and social grievance back upon the individual. They redefined issues of social conflict as questions of social propriety and 'good taste'"(62). Emily Post's rules are important because they speak to people who are uncertain about the specifics of such interactions. If the ideology of upward mobility is central to American culture, advice books can be seen as crucial tools in people's efforts to advance or sustain themselves in that endeavor. Susan Williams (1987) surmises,

> Middle class Americans worked hard to elevate themselves socially and to maintain and symbolize that position by emulating the cosmopolitan lifestyles of the elites, adopting social practices and codes of behavior that would at the same

time distinguish them from the laboring classes. Yet middle class Americans also felt it necessary to set themselves apart from the negative characteristics of elites, the tendencies towards indolence and luxury that they perceived great wealth to have wrought. They viewed the constant exercise of self-control and personal and social propriety essential to the preservation of their distinct culture, especially in the face of rapidly increasing population pressure from large numbers of southern and eastern European immigrants. These newcomers brought with them traditions and customs that were perceived by many as a threat to the hegemony of middle-class values. (21)

"Gentility" was increasingly seen as socially desirable and simultaneously "a purchasable commodity" (Kasson, 1990, 43). In general, as industrial capitalism advanced in the United States, Kasson argues that people shifted their expectations to the consumer market, such that mobility was linked to the abundant consumer choices (258). The American experience of social mobility is predicated on the notion that one could acquire the skills to function in different class setting. Manners, particularly those necessary for social interaction, were key. For example, Hawkins Brown emphasizes the correct thing to say through twenty-two chapters, including a short list of "helpful hints" for social interaction at the very end. Above all, she claimed, "Manners first, the rest will follow."

In a similar vein, Green's *National Capital Code of Etiquette* was an attempt to offer the same skills to mobility-aspiring African Americans outside the elite social center of Washington. The successes of the upper strata of American blacks were seen as a model for all, especially as more and more African Americans migrated north to urban centers. A few themes appear in Green's book and in the advice columns published in black weeklies and magazines of the time frame: one is the importance of restraint in all manners, from emotion to expression to dress; another is the necessity for consistency in those manners across public and private domains. Genteel behavior, as defined through Victorian mores and bourgeois respectability, was presented as a means for African Americans to distinguish themselves as a group worthy of full entitlement, citizenship, and rights.[6]

As migration moved many African Americans into new urban environments and workplaces, the discourse of racial uplift was wielded through advice on manners—black elites suggested in these newspaper columns that many Jim Crow laws were a result of the "lack of good manners" among the black masses. Promoting values of restraint through dress, demeanor, and deportment was a means of controlling public opinion. At the Palmer Institute, Hawkins Brown had the explicit goal of trying to create graduates who would, through their cultured behavior, "establish good will and understanding between the races." Hawkins Brown, a follower of Booker T. Washington, hoped to create an educated pool of desirable workers, providing African Americans with opportunities and showing white America why blacks were so important as full citizens and workers. However, as federal funding dried up during the Depression, the Palmer Institute shifted to becoming a finishing school for elite blacks wealthy enough to pay for their children's tuition. Training in social graces mirrored that of segregated elite white preparatory schools, with a focus on morality, civility, discipline, and industry. These books emerged as one avenue to help people navigate urban life, shifting class statuses, and the racial-ethnic tensions associated with migration and immigration.

Public and Private: Race, Class, and Restraint

The first four chapters of *Etiquette* focus on sociability as a form of interaction. Post begins with "the art of conversation," asserting the significant of language and public appearance: "Nothing reveals our background, training, self-discipline, and education as quickly as the words we choose and how we pronounce them. Well-educated people, for example, invariable use certain expressions and appear to avoid others instinctively. . . . Usually, to speak as the educated people in one's hometown speak is sufficient for all social and domestic purposes" (22). Bernstein (1977) and Heath (1982) have argued that linguistic capital is often a necessary component to educational success, upward mobility, and class-based social interaction. Among the French, Bourdieu (1984) suggests that the petit bourgeois are most concerned with language and grammar, leaning toward "hyper-correction, a vigilance which over-shoots the mark for fear of falling short and pounces on linguistic incorrectness in oneself and others" (331). It is significant that Post begins her tome with an array of guidelines for very public interactions: greetings, public speaking, traveling, correspondence, restaurants, outdoor events, and meetings. Sociability, as Simmel attests, is achieved through interaction. Post's job was to delineate proper modes. She codified appropriate modes of conversation, listing good topics, things to avoid, and types of bad conversationalists, such as people who talk too much, who only talk about problems, or are "overly humorous."

Among the upper class, the rules of sociable interaction are a part of early socialization. Such social competence is a matter of habitus, of early sociable learning through family and immediate environment. According to Wacquant (2001), "the most fundamental and distinctive competencies that we have are embodied knowledges and skills that operate beneath the level of discourse and consciousness, in an incarnate sense, arising out of the mutual interpenetration of being and world." To Bourdieu, even though

the habitus is an active, ongoing aspect of experience, its durability is, in part, a product of its early establishment in the individual's experience. Thus, although not impossible, it is extremely difficult for adults to comfortably embody a new set of interactional rules. Post attempts a "how to" of cultural capital, foreshadowing the contemporary situation where there are myriad advice manuals instructing how to order wine, sculpt muscles, or "win friends and influence people." Self-help and self-improvement focus on shaping the personality and the body, as commodities. Kasson (1990) suggests that today, "as etiquette has penetrated deeper into emotional life, these [books] are the true successors [of advice manuals] in the 20th century" (259). Norbert Elias pointed out that a distinguishing feature in contemporary society is the degree to which such rules for behavior have been thoroughly internalized by people: compared with these earlier societies, in ours an all-embracing feeling of shame is cultivated. Social differences are certainly still fairly great, but in the course of the process of democratization, the power differentials have lessened. Correspondingly, we have had to develop a relatively high degree of self-restraint in dealing with all people, including social subordinates (1978, 239). Books like *Etiquette* contribute to this process by providing people with a laundry list of all possible public occasions in which one might have to account for a performance of self.

After covering sociable interactions, Post turns her attention to formal entertaining, focusing on "official dinners, luncheons, formal afternoon entertaining, and balls and dances." She delineates these from informal entertaining in the next chapter, which includes cocktail parties, informal dining, buffet dinners, informal luncheons, dances, picnics, barbecues, showers, house parties, and overnight guests. The lines between formal and informal are clear-cut, although she makes it clear that both require structured behavior and settings.

As dinner parties spread to the white middle classes at the turn of the century, after the Depression, and again in the post–World War II era, even women without household servants were expected to have the social skills to cook and act as a hostess. Taste still mattered. Emily Post provides categories of behavior and detailed rules that leave no room for mistakes. To function successfully, one need only carefully memorize and enact these guidelines. The book rests on the fundamental idea that social respectability can be purchased and learned, particularly through sociable interactions with food. Individuals learn to do class, gender, and race by following these models. At the same time, Hawkins Brown, Green, and others concerned with racial uplift were able to use the basic knowledge put forth in books like Post's, adding and adapting it to speak to the particular needs of African Americans. Hawkins Brown herself attended Cambridge Latin High School and her patrons and donors were women from the established white New England elite. Both Post and Hawkins Brown stress that true good will and gentility had to underlie the codes of conduct they laid out. For African Americans, however, the actions of the individual stood as emblematic of the collective, a fear that those assimilated and nonethnic or racial whites reading the book would not share.

Although etiquette is an emulation of upper-class standards, its embodiment is not necessarily confined to the upper classes. One way we can see this is in how the texts distinguish public and private—for Post, there is a clear distinction, such that the private home becomes public when hosting an event. For Hawkins Brown and Green, the distinction between home and outside is blurred. Because good graces had to be on display at all times, there has to be a much greater sensibility about restraint. Both authors assert that manners must be on display at home. The notion of "home training" was the province of black female boarding schools before it traveled into the vernacular (as in "she has no home training"). For example, Anna Julia Cooper mentions it in her speech, "I Speak for the Colored Women of the South" (1990). Among the people I spoke to, African American women were most likely to mention "upbringing" in the same manner.

Home training was established as the grounds for public behavior, too. Green asserts, "To eat gracefully is an art that few of us ever acquire—to commit as few blunders as possible and to avoid unpardonable actions should be our chief ambition. There is but one safe way to accomplish the desired result and that is to be just as careful when dining at home with one's family as at dinner or banquet."

On one hand, we can read this as an example of the extreme measures to which African Americans had to go in order to combat negative stereotypes. On the other hand, we can also read it as an early assertion of the importance of family and community as deserving moral regard. This also translates into family expectations. Hawkins Brown writes, "Never permit Mother or the woman at the head of the house to take more steps than necessary to give you service. In families where there are no maids, children may easily take turns waiting on the table" (44). Given the disproportionate number of African American women in domestic service, Hawkins Brown's command can be read as a commentary on black women's home lives. This is supported by Hawkins Brown's other published work, which was a work of fiction, a novella attempting to rescue the Mammy figure from cultural disregard, suggesting that even through her subjugation, she was a cultural icon worthy of great respect from both whites and blacks.

In many ways, African Americans were able to turn their segregation in domestic service into a body of knowledge. Scholars of African American culinary history point to the ways in which African American women's cooking was appropriated by white southerners and yet became a training ground and set of skills that followed African Americans beyond domestic service (see Rafia Zafar, in Bowers, 2009).[7] This was exemplified by Celia, a middle-class African American woman, who described the source of her ideas about formal sociability. Although she said, "I don't have an inbred kind of tradition thing that says 'oh, invite some people over,'" she talked about why she believes in formal manners in social settings:

> Some of it comes from my grandma, who had so much influence on us. . . . She was a live-in servant in a house. You know, these places had, I don't want to call them rules, but there were ways to do things and here she was, you know, half white, half colored girl in this white man's house and she was a servant. So there were places for her to be and ways for her to act. My grandmother (was) proper, you know, courteous, polite and having all that stuff really served my mother well with her thirteen children. Christmas at my grandma's house, people didn't get up until everybody was done.

For Celia and her family, knowledge of formal behavior came from passed-down experience—in particular, experience that was filtered through deference expected in service work but translated into expectations for one's own domestic household. For etiquette writer Harriet Cole, the lessons learned were incorporated into formal meals at home: "Both my parents had been taught by mothers who were domestic workers in service of wealthy, well-traveled white folks for much of their lives, so they had learned the 'proper' art of fine dining and intended for us to incorporate these basic behaviors into our lives. . . . Today I am grateful. What I learned as a child I now practice effortlessly" (1999, 312). Although the very premise of *Etiquette* is that one can, in fact, learn to do all this, Post makes it clear that class differences and experiences do matter. Post is probably not referencing the kind of experiences that Harriet Cole's or Celia's grandmothers had as household servants.[8]

"No Odd Food": Balanced Tables and Respectable Menus

In Post's articulation of formal entertaining, the event, the food, the setting, and the roles required of participants are all highly structured. *Etiquette* is detailed down to prescribing particular greetings that aspiring hosts can use to make guests feel welcome.[9]

Post delineates these rules with certainty. She writes,

> The requisites for a perfect formal dinner, whether for two hundred people or for eight, are as follows:

Guests who are congenial (by far the most important requirement)

Servants who are competent and suited to your needs

A *lovely table setting*—furnishings in perfect condition and suitable; immaculate linen, brilliantly polished silver, shining glassware

Food that is perfectly prepared, a well chosen menu

A *cordial and hospitable host*

A *charming hostess*—a requirement that includes tact, sympathy, poise, and perfect manners

She goes on to say, "Although these requisites are much the same for all dinners, the necessity for perfection increases in proportion to the formality and the importance of the occasion" (163). The emphasis and order in which she lists the rules for formal entertaining are not arbitrary. First and foremost, she constructs the interactional setting where all participants have clearly delineated roles of guest, host, or servant. Formality served to make the sociable possible, since it limits people's confusion or uncertainty about what is expected of them. The fact that the hosting roles are gendered is central, in that both are charged with interactional labor, but the woman has a more clearly articulated job of emotional management. The production of formal sociability is a production of gender. Post makes clear that sociable occasions should have a "balanced number" of men and women, arranged for managed mixed-gender interactions.[10] As Visser asserts, "Post makes it very clear that it is the woman and she alone who bears the brunt of any horror that might occur at a dinner party" (1991, 90). Indeed, the husband is mentioned only in passing, unless he has a high-status rank where he must participate in establishing the guest list. However, once having done that, it is the wife's responsibility to organize the rest of the occasion. Both Post and Visser also assume that formal dining is exclusively the province of married heterosexuals. For example, Post makes no provisions for men who might entertain on their own. "The Single Woman Entertains" and advice for "Widows, Divorcees, and Bachelor Girls" appear in the chapter on informal entertaining. The majority of the advice for single women concerns who the appropriate male is to help you bartend, host, or carve (214, 224).

Most importantly, formal dinner parties depend on the availability of servants. Even in the 1969 edition Post asserts, "By its most essential definition, it is not possible to give a formal dinner without the help of servants" (164).[11] Although the book is about making upper-class activities accessible to those not socialized into such skills, Post ends up making it clear that formality in sociability is not attainable for those without resources to hire help—and "good help." In her description of a formal dinner that didn't heed her dictums, the servants are to blame for the major mishaps. Historically, in the United States, servants were most often women of color.[12] Given this racial dualism, dinner parties must be seen as a way of maintaining class boundaries and constituting racial difference.

Of course, most members of the middle class were, increasingly, unable to hire servants as regular household help. By 1928, *Etiquette* included a new section entitled "On the Servantless House," which reflected this change. In Post's 1969 edition, she adjusts her rules further, stating,

> The fact that few households except such official establishments as embassies have staffs that include butlers, footmen, or kitchen maids need not keep you from entertaining formally at home. The hostess who wishes her dinner to be formal can hire temporary help. All cities and many smaller communities have catering services that provide not only servants but excellent meals, either prepared by a cook sent to your home or partially cooked in their kitchens and finished in yours. If the servants are efficient and well trained, a small (that is, for no more than twelve) formal dinner may be beautifully handled by a cook, a butler, and a footman. (173)

At the same time, even informal occasions can warrant paid help. When hosting a cocktail party or any other informal gathering for more than eighteen guests, she contends that bartenders and waiters are necessary (213). Green even notes that sometimes it's necessary to hire help, which was economically possible for the Washington elite from which he drew his inspiration.

In Post's world, formality is also associated with a historically class-based set of goods. Again, in her writing, there are continual reminders that everyone can benefit from good manners, that taste is not restricted to the upper class—and yet, specific tastes are more attainable for some than others. One's sociable performance must be in line with one's economic and cultural resources. In the 1922 edition, Post writes,

> It is scarcely necessary to point out that the bigger and more ambitious the house, the more perfect its appointments must be. If your house has a great Georgian dining-room, the table should be set with Georgian or an earlier period English silver. Furthermore, in a "great" dining-room, all the silver should be real! "Real" meaning nothing so trifling as "sterling," but genuine and important "period" pieces made by Eighteenth Century silversmiths, such as de Lamerie or Crespell or Buck or Robertson, or perhaps one of their predecessors. Or if, like Mrs. Oldname, you live in an old Colonial house, you are perhaps also lucky enough to have inherited some genuine American pieces made by Daniel Rogers or Paul Revere!

Effort means knowledge of appropriate styles for appropriate class-based settings. Post evokes a Victorian-era sensibility about a formal table with symmetrical settings, albeit somewhat modified with each changing edition. In general, she eschews "fancy napkin folding" and encourages a certain level of practicality with the number of utensils and glasses provided at any given occasion.

However, one key point is that a formal meal is always a meal seated, which is, in itself, a very modern construct. Surveying sociable meals across history, Visser (1991) asserts that "the idea, which we take for granted, that everyone usually sits round a table to eat is in fact very specific to our own culture" (149). There is a distinct difference between being seated at a table and having the mobility to move around and choose who to talk to, what to eat, and how much one is under constant scrutiny. Being seated means greater control and greater formality as well as more circumstances for display and ostentation. Post contrasts the sit-down meal with informal entertaining. Informal meals have a different protocol about reciprocity. Cocktail parties "along with open houses, barbecues, and picnics . . . provide a relatively simple answer to the rule that all invitations must be repaid" (209). In other words, one does not need household help or a caterer; it's less expensive, easier to do, and numerically "you can entertain many more people at once in a small house." At the same time she makes it clear that invitations to such events are not the same level of honor and reciprocity as a dinner party. For example, she warns against big cocktail parties that are not really the equivalent to many invitations to small dinner parties. However, the main difference between a formal and an informal occasion is the expectations put upon guests. Post writes, "No matter how elaborate the meal, if the guests have to help themselves from a buffet, or if the hostess has to rise to clear the table, the dinner immediately becomes informal" (164). Service is at the heart of formal hospitality.

The dining room, a fairly recent edition to most middle-class homes in the early twentieth century, was the focal place of sociable meals. Having people in a dining room rather than a kitchen or living area meant that they were separated from the physicality of the meal preparation. According to Visser (1991), "cooking smells were thought to be suggestive both of food in its purely nutritive function and of the intimate background workings of the household; the smell of food was therefore considered to be an imposition upon the guests" (83). This, of course, is easier to achieve when one has servants to bring the food all the way from one room to another. No matter what, the sensual aspects of eating are to be controlled. In contrast with many of the people I interviewed, Post asserts, "The one thing every hostess tries to avoid is the risk of the smell of cooking." In Post's formulation, the food is secondary to the rest of the sociable environment.

After ten pages establishing all the behavioral standards and rules for guest lists, seating arrangements, atmosphere, and settings, Post devotes approximately one page to the actual food at formal gatherings and two pages to wine and drinks. In fact, the menu specifications for informal meals are more elaborated, since there is less need to "balance" the menu so tightly. *Etiquette* contains six or seven possible menus for a buffet, and only one for the formal meal. Even so, there are no actual recipes, which means that people hosting a party must either already know how to cook these dishes, have access to appropriate recipes and cookbooks, or have hired help who can prepare food according to their specifications. Although menu construction is important to Post's concept of formal and informal meals, cooking instruction is outside the boundaries of her advice. Both Green and Hawkins Brown offer the same kind of limited menu, with more emphasis on knowing how to behave than what to serve. They each provide two or three buffet menus and the briefest allusions to dinner party menus. Hawkins Brown states, "food should be good, but inexpensive." Even so, there are no actual recipes.

The type of formal meal that Post elaborates is extremely restricted in terms of components and patterning, resembling what Mary Douglas (1972) has analyzed as "A plus 2B," where *A* is a main protein and *2B* represents 2 side dishes, usually a green vegetable and a starch. The meal is a pattern based on "a system of repeated analogies," such as stressed and unstressed elements. This "proper meal" has a long history in Britain and the United States, where many people feel they have not eaten unless it involves these components. For example, Anne Murcott (1982) uncovers this system in South Wales, where a "proper meal" consists of "meat and two veg" or a starch, a center, and trimmings. This meal format or structure renders the meal recognizable and familiar in particular cultural contexts. The proper meal is conflated with middle- and upper-middle-class white American-ness. For example, Bentley (1998), Avakian (1997), and Ray (2004) document the ways that immigrants "become American" by deliberately de-emphasizing aspects of their ethnic foodways, at least partially assimilating to certain food habits.[13] Biltekoff (2005) and Shapiro (1986) suggest that home economists, social reformers, and cooking schools designed to teach servants to cook all deliberately promoted Americanization through food habits. The ordered meal was central to that process.

The meals cooked by African American women in their employment as domestic cooks also adhered to this general pattern, albeit with a greater emphasis on sides and relishes. It appears that cookbooks from this era by and for African Americans also adhered to some of these constraints. For example, Ann Bower examines the cookbooks published by the National Council of Negro Women (NCNW)—the 1958 fundraiser, *The Historical Cookbook of the American Negro* includes a smattering of African American history, listing great achievements by notable men and women and indeed, "many of the recipes in the book draw upon distinctly African American foodways and use food derived from African heritage. However, the rhetoric of the book never dwells on that history. The impression created is that, to a large extent, the food that the NCNW contributors prepare and eat is part of mainstream cuisine" (159).

In Post, the menu for formal meals is so restricted as to not allow for much deviation from the basic six courses: "soup *or* fresh fruit cup *or* melon or shellfish (clams, oysters or shrimp); fish course (*or*, on rare occasions, a dish such as sweetbreads); the entrée or main course (usually roast meat or fowl); salad; dessert, coffee" (1969, 178). Hawkins Brown and Green offer comparable menus: they all focus on the idea of a "well-balanced" menu but these principles are not highly elaborated, other than to suggest that the hostess "combine flavors intelligently." The emphasis is on the color, spice, and richness of each item in contrast with the others. In 1922 Post writes, "One should always try to choose well-balanced dishes; an especially rich dish balanced by a simple one. Timbale with a very rich sauce of cream and pâté de foie gras might perhaps be followed by French chops, broiled chicken or some other light, plain meat. An entrée of about four broiled mushrooms on a small round of toast should be followed by boned capon or saddle of mutton or spring lamb. It is equally bad to give your guests very peculiar food unless as an extra dish."

Given her menu selections, by "very peculiar food" Post must mean ethnic or regional dishes that are not blandly reconstituted for "white bread Protestant" palates. The only deviation was Green's willingness to assert a more ostentatious menu with Lobster Newburg as a main course. One does wonder how many middle-class African Americans were moved to emulate the Washington 400's tastes.

Other than the reference to "chops," Post avoids French haute cuisine, which had, according to Levenstein (1988), "reoccupied its place at the pinnacle of status" by 1961 when the Kennedys hired a French chef for the White House (140). Haute cuisine is problematic to Post's formulation because it is ostentatious and too revealing of differences and preferences among guests and hosts. Formal entertaining is about a circumscribed set of circumstances in which people experience sociability. If, as Simmel suggests, the menu is distracting or not accommodating to all tastes, the communal elements dissolve into too much individualism. Formal occasions, after all, are not intimate. Knowledge of people's individual preferences suggests too much intimacy, unless, of course, one is the guest of honor. Otherwise, the use of a supposedly neutral bland menu avoids these problems. In *Perfection Salad*, Laura Shapiro (1986) demonstrates that literally and metaphorically) "white food" encouraged by social reformers and home economists from early American cooking schools was an assertion of middle-class morality, racial virtue, and health, about drawing boundaries between the assimilated and the immigrant. It is necessary to include the African American migration and urbanization as part of that same process. Tracy Poe demonstrates how middle-class African American reformers in Chicago sought to restrain the southern food tastes of southern migrants as part of a larger campaign to reform manners, public behavior, and cultural differences (1999). The *Chicago Defender*, an African American newspaper, had a regular column where "the housekeeper" urged African American women to prepare foods that were fashionable in the white women's magazines of the day, emphasizing European dishes, eschewing vegetables, and avoiding spicy condiments. However, the two hallmarks of migrant cuisine were its southern-ness and the emphasis on mealtime commensality. Poe argues that local merchants began catering to the migrants' culinary needs, which allowed them to assert their culinary and domestic traditions despite reformer's pressures to assimilate!

Interestingly, for Post, meals are gendered as well. She complains: "too many women order trimmings rather than food" (1969, 164). Gender-segregated events required gendered menus. A tea or ladies' luncheon can consist of "clear soup, escargot, squab, potato croquette, string beans, green salad and sherbet," but "don't feed hungry men bouillon, daubs of hors d'oeuvres, samples of fruit salad, and meringues" (234). Both informal and formal meals, which were required to be mix-gendered, must account for men's tastes as the primary concern.

The A plus 2B format is essentially a white western model of meals. If format and balance do not, in and of themselves, provide clues to the type of class and race-based food preferences being constructed, one need only examine the role of "ethnic" foods in Post's descriptions. She writes,

> Some people love highly flavored Spanish or Indian dishes, but they are not appropriate for a formal dinner. At an informal dinner, an Indian curry or Spanish enchilada for one dish is delicious for those who like it, and if you have another substantial dish such as a plain roast which practically everyone is able to eat, those who don't like Indian food can make their dinner of the other course.
>
> It is the same way with the Italian dishes. One hating garlic and onions would be very wretched if onions were put in each and every course, and liberally. With Indian curry, a fatally bad selection would be a very peppery soup, such as croute au pot filled with pepper, and fish with green peppers, and then the curry, and then something casserole filled again with peppers and onions and other throat-searing ingredients, finishing with an endive salad. Yet more than one hostess has done exactly this.

Informal occasions allow more latitude for "ethnic" foods because people have some choices at a buffet or cocktail party that they do not at a formal dinner. However, even the menus for informal meals reflect a white middle-class sensibility about food, remaining in the format of stressed and unstressed elements. "Elaborate," is two main courses, but they "must be complimented by the same vegetables and condiments or you will have more preparation than you can easily handle" (234). The buffet menus include a few "ethnic" labels—Hungarian goulash, Italian spaghetti, and curried lamb—but these are anglicized foods, paired with items like "glazed carrots," "scalloped potatoes," and "green peas and onions." Luncheon menus are also based on a white Anglo-Saxon format, always a meat, starch, vegetable, condiment, bread, and dessert. Even more than the manners expected, the type of food prescribed for sociable entertaining establishes it as a white upper-middle-class ideal against which others should model themselves. Notice that so-called "southern food" does not exist in Post's imagination. Although the menus provided by Hawkins Brown and Green are generally of the same order, Green offers "chow chow" and "india relish" as condiments to his brunch and dinner menus. In one of the first published cookbooks by an African American woman, *What Mrs. Fisher Knows about Old Southern Cooking* (1881), there is a recipe for chow chow: cabbage, salt, cukes, brown sugar, cayenne, vinegar, turmeric, and onions. "You can add more pepper if you like it hot." Creole Chow Chow had tomatoes. But in this case, all the etiquette writers, black or white, offer a distancing from foods deemed too regional or racial-ethnic.

Advice about hospitality in the early twentieth century centered on control of interactions and setting. However, this approach is not sufficient for contemporary social life, since we are, in fact, more inclined toward informal sociable relationships outside the workplace. For Post, Green, and Hawkins Brown, etiquette acts as a restraint on comfort, but a restraint that allows sociability to emerge by constructing an "imaginary middle" where no outlying behavior disrupts the sociable possibilities. However, contemporary sociability has changed. For example, Levenstein claims that shifts in food tastes are related to immigration and racial-ethnic nationalist ideas, increased transnational travel since World War II, the whole foods movement, and the advent of cooking programs, generating a broader public interest in a wide range of food tastes and styles. During this same time frame, "soul food" solidified in northern cities like Detroit and Chicago as a distinctive African American cuisine, making it less palatable for black households to emulate the white middle class.

In his overarching food history of the time, Levenstein (1988) suggests that since the 1960s cooking has reemerged as a status symbol, where variety and food knowledge operate as cultural markers. He states, "unlike previous eras of food snobbery, high status could now be derived from preparing the right foods, not just consuming them. A Palm Beach reporter noted that in 1977, 'there is nothing more chic right now than a small gourmet party prepared by the hostess instead of her staff'" (222). As Beardsworth and Keil (1997) surmise, "We have moved from the situation where food is not a topic of conversation because we eat food appropriate to status and respectability to a context where food is always a topic of conversation as we seek to select that which displays taste, respectability, knowledge, and a 'search for marginal differentiation'"(103).

Food, therefore is crucial to contemporary sociability. Warde (1997) argues that since World War II, "of the long term trends, the steadily enhanced availability of a wider variety of products, particularly of foreign provenance but also resulting from manufacturing innovations, is probably the most momentous" (166). As food choices broaden, so do options for sociability. However, in examining both people's practices and discourses of sociability, the notion of "choice" needs to be problematized to account for its connection to the increasing commodification of daily life.

The Rise of Style: Martha Stewart and B. Smith

Many of the people I interviewed used Martha Stewart as a cultural reference point, in the same way they used Emily Post when we talked about hospitality and good manners. However, none of the people I interviewed mentioned her without some reservations, as if claiming an affinity toward Stewart's ideas was problematic. This does reflect cultural tensions about Stewart—even with a multimillion-dollar empire that spans class categories of consumption, she is often parodied and criticized for promoting an unattainable and gender-regressive set of ideas about domesticity. Among my respondents, Stewart was often invoked as a disclaimer such as "I'm no Martha Stewart but . . ." or, "well, I wouldn't want it to be Martha Stewart-y." For example, when I asked Cindy for her definition of hospitality, she said, "well, I hate to think that it's only what Martha Stewart thinks it is." Another woman, Margaret, evoked Stewart positively, but with hesitation when she talked about the differences between her way of doing things and her relatives, saying, "It's cold, you know, there's no care put into it . . . it doesn't have to be fancy, expensive. It doesn't have to be shrimp. . . . I usually bring something [to my mother-in-law's house] and my sister-in-laws tease me to no end 'cause when I bring it, it's garnished, it's on a pretty tray and they call me the parsley queen. . . . But it makes a difference how you present it. . and that sounds kinda Martha Stewart and kinda silly, but it makes a difference . . . it's more attractive and more edible, I think, and conveys a certain love and care."

Socializing with food has become the textual province of "lifestyle" publications, most notably embodied by Martha Stewart and her domestic empire. Her 1982 book, *Entertaining*, provides a model for the evolution of social norms and expectations for having people over to one's house for dinner. Like the earliest editions of *Etiquette*, *Entertaining* set the parameters for all of Stewart's other statements about domestic hospitality. Stewart's success allowed others like Smith to move from restaurant work to the growing lifestyle publication industry.

Entertaining was, at the time of its publication, unique. It looks and reads like an oversized glossy magazine and is clearly meant to be used very differently from Emily Post. Starting with a personal narrative, Stewart invokes Edith Wharton and Tolstoy as part of her own imaginings of an upper-class literary discourse about dinner parties.

After naming these formal and historical models, Stewart claims, "Entertaining always seemed natural to me" (2). Like Post, Stewart models a contradiction between innately embodying the necessary qualities for proper sociability and being assertive enough to acquire them. Smith is a bit more sanguine about the process, gently asserting that her life in fashion gave her the skills to be comfortable in a variety of settings. In Stewart's case, her "naturalness" can be read as a desire to invoke the reader's trust in her expertise. It might be easy for her, but others can learn it too. Unlike Emily Post's book, which is almost entirely devoid of personal reflection, Stewart and Smith narrate their own relationship to food and entertaining. In this way, they contribute to a shift in social norms by giving visual examples from personal life of how domestic entertaining works. The insistent "I" in Stewart's writing personalizes it, makes it seem authoritative yet friendly, very different from the "one should" of Emily Post. While Post's examples rely on imaginary situations and guests with invented tags like "Mrs. Noteworthy" and "Doris Debutante" and "Mrs. Notable."[14] Stewart and Smith, in contrast, describe real family members, famous socialites, places, and events (Roy Lichtenstein, the Museum of Folk Art in Manhattan, book publishing parties, and beach trips to Nantucket). Stewart insistently establishes herself as authentically "down to earth" with photos of her Polish immigrant family's butcher-block table. However, the photos of Martha on her big Connecticut estate among her lilies, beehives, and heirloom chickens speak more to images of landed gentry and sophisticated social circles than "down-home folk." It's probably no coincidence that Smith, a former model, had sensibilities shaped by experience in the world of advertising and fashion but continues to evoke her family roots as guiding her entertaining choices. Both Stewart and Smith represent a shift from manners to style, from *how to behave* to *how to appear.*

Much has been made of the ways Stewart carefully constructed her biographical self—and how this is part of her success, since she is not only selling products, but herself. In exploring this, the introduction and format of *Entertaining* are instructive, because it is her first foray and sets the tone for all others like it. After describing her evolution from a working-class Polish girl to stockbroker to caterer, she situates her experience in a larger cultural and social framework:

> I am not alone in my feeling that home is not only the most natural but the most evocative place to entertain. Everyone now seems to be choosing a home setting over expensive restaurants; caterers are thriving because they accommodate and facilitate entertaining at home. . . . Whatever its shape and specifics, home is a very welcome place. . . . I hope to show that there are many ways of entertaining and that each ultimately depends not on pomp or show or elaborate technique, but on thought, effort, and caring—much like friendship itself. (9)

To Stewart, the household as private arena is an appropriate place for sociability—and that status in and of itself is not necessary—or, ultimately enough—to make for appropriate social situations. In this sense, she follows a tradition established by Post and other etiquette writers, democratizing the cultural capital of the elite classes by codifying it for outsiders. Cynthia Duquette Smith (2000) argues that the rhetoric of Stewart's publications encourages readers to create particular kinds of selves "who are domesticated and exercise self-discipline, valorize the home and understand it as a therapy center, and are accustomed to self-expression through consumer purchases." Stewart writes, "In the last several decades, home entertaining in America has evolved dramatically from a matter of rules and regimens into a very personal freewheeling affair. There are no longer rigorous prescriptions . . . for the growing body of experience in America—social as well as culinary—has fostered a new openness and respect for diversity. . . . There is no such cause for anxiety today, for there is no longer one proper behavior, or one taste (to be offended), but many to celebrate" (12).

For Stewart, there is an underlying assumption that people have internalized generally appropriate behavior for public sociability and that, by being gracious, one has accomplished all that is necessary. Stewart does spend about two pages talking about "making guests comfortable." She has a tendency as a writer to try and cover both sides of each issue. Although most of the book asserts style as key, she spends a few pages on how to choose appropriate guests, but the narrative she provides is not one that people can emulate, like the rules in Post. She starts with a vignette from D. H. Lawrence and moves into some of her own reminiscences. Both stories of sociability are predicated on a "kind of extraordinary spontaneity" that's "unpredictable." Like Post, Stewart and Smith see the hostess's work of choosing the guests who will make a "convivial occasion" as the key. They are more explicit about the emotion work behind the caring ethos, though, illustrating how a hostess invites people in, picks good music, and introduces people to each other. Speaking of one hostess, Stewart emphasizes how "she . . . made everyone comfortable enough to be his own natural, impulsive, expressive, social self." Unlike Post, such work is about more informal interactions. Kasson (1990) suggests that contemporary advice about sociability centers on the construction of personality over character.

Creating these sociable environments sometimes requires a shift in how people conceptualize the private space of their homes and the role of guests in participating in that construction. In a controlled and individualized way, Stewart gets people involved in creating the atmosphere: "I get them a drink and, depending on their interests, I might ask them to lend a hand with the salad or the coffee grinding. . . . As other guests arrive, the kitchen expands, and when it is full, we adjourn to the parlor" (14). In this way, Stewart also articulates another shift in hospitality, where the smells and work of cooking are moved to front-stage visibility, indeed, becoming part of sociability. Stewart implicitly references Post when she writes about kitchens, "Now what was once hidden is flaunted" (102). Since Post's time, popular culture provides numerous examples of food writers, television chefs, and new culinary ideas that, in fact, make food and cooking more visible. Margaret Visser writes, "Being asked to eat in the kitchen was for a long time, in houses and apartments large enough to possess dining rooms, the ultimate gesture of intimacy, extended in principle only to close family. It has become entirely normal these days to hold dinner parties in the kitchen . . . turning [it] into a large and splendid room, gleaming with technology but also comfortable, attractive, and hospitable" (1991, 83).

Similarly, Stewart undoes the back-stage–front-stage propriety of dining rooms by situating food in hallways, inviting guests to "help," and cooking individual omelets to order. The kitchen, "a warm easy place," becomes public space, albeit one that must be transformed into a site of display. Joanne, one interviewee who cooked elaborate dinner parties said, "People want to be in your kitchen when you cook . . . what I'm realizing now is they want to be where you make food and hang out where you make food because they have such a comfort feeling watching it, knowing someone else is making food for them and . . . just being there while it's all happening."

If, as Stewart asserts, sociable events with food are "productions not unlike theatrical productions," then an analysis of such events needs to explore this shift in where and how they occur. In later chapters, I explore how a number of my interviewees contend with cooking in front of guests and socializing in the kitchen. Interestingly, Smith does not mention deliberately involving guests. Echoing the comments of some of my African American interviewees, Smith focuses on "making people feel important," which is more about honoring them as guests of honor or providing special foods they like. One rather important difference, however, is that Smith very plainly talks about the pleasures of hosting parties at someone else's home, since her own apartment is often too small or inappropriate for the kind of event she wishes to construct. This is a different form of "guest involvement," sharing the home and the honor or responsibility of hosting that normally goes with it.

Food, Style, and Personality

A main focus in the output of Stewart and Smith is style. Rather than learn a detailed set of behaviors, what people really need to be successful at sociability is knowledge of the visible signs, the symbolic aspects of display that illustrate "good taste." Given this, it's not surprising that the food, which is barely specified in Post (since, after all, caterers and servants do the vast majority of this work), becomes central to Stewart's guidelines. A section on "making food look beautiful" precedes all the recipes and settings. In the introduction, Stewart situates the ethos of caring in shifting ideas about food:

> In the decade I have been a professional caterer, there has been a culinary revolution. It has taught us to appreciate the aesthetics of food—the fresh, the simple, the homemade—and shown us the possibilities of many different tastes and styles. It has made food an adventure to be shared. It has also fostered a new style of entertaining that is informal, relaxed, and expressive, based not on intimidating prescriptions and pretensions, but on personality and personal effort. (12)

However, Amy Bentley (2001) argues that Martha Stewart's food "has transformed food culture, no less by upping the ante in haute cuisine by taking an idealized meal to another level of complexity" (6). In some ways Stewart's food is different from Post's only in its complexity, not in its invocation of a more sophisticated or luxurious model of food. The items themselves are not of a different order, but rather the patterning of the meal is more complex. Douglas (1984) writes,

> Many people assume intuitively that complexity mainly depends on the variety of materials available. . . . But complexity depends on pattern order as well as on variety, and the way it involves socioeconomic factors is indirect. If the rich household used six sauces every day, its food system would be no more complex than the poor household using one sauce. Throwing in extra items is not in itself as complex as extra interlocking of a few items with others to produce patterns of "if . . . then" entailments, which also lock into the outside world. (22)

It's instructive how Stewart herself links a shift in social rules about "entertaining" to shifts in food rules. In one way, her statements link entertaining to a nostalgic past, asserting friendship and community connectedness as American values. At the same time, she calls for a reconfiguration of etiquette—undoing Emily Post as a set of rules—in the name of some other American ideologies, most notably those of "individualism," "choice," and "equality." She says, " Entertaining is . . . an opportunity to be individualistic, to express your own ideas about what constitutes a good party" (1982, 12). Interestingly, she reasserts these ideas in a new preface to the 1998 reissue of *Entertaining*: "How we entertain, where and when, are questions that will always be centered on our personal tastes and style." And yet, what follows in the remaining three hundred pages of text is a series of rules, albeit rules that function as guidelines in specific contexts.

Comparatively, in her etiquette book, Harriet Cole (1999) situates the desire to entertain and socialize with others in a different attitude about freedom that is less about the individual and personal taste. She states, "Being black in America means that you are descended from survivors, from people who dared to discover unique and creative ways to enjoy whatever liberties were afforded to them." She goes on to situate those freedoms in African traditions of collective responsibility: respect for self, family, community, environment, and religion (21). Thus, while Cole's book is titled *How to Be*, which sounds like the quintessential self-improvement statement, her objective in creating a manners manual is grounded in reasserting collective traditions while navigating the dominant culture. This is quite different than the freewheeling appropriation that Stewart embraces.

Contemporary sociability also requires rules of appearance and the palatability of food; otherwise, Stewart's recipes and ideas would not be relevant or popular. Alan Warde (1997) argues that cultural texts about food, "[p]urvey style. Standards of appearance, of presentation of food on the plate, are particularly important. So too, is the transmission to the reader of the sense that he or she can read various culinary styles. In a world of styles, there is an obligation to become acquainted with the rudiments of many, even those one would never seek to engage with, because being acquainted with their variety is essential to deciphering those expressed and discussed by other" (186). Since women are most frequently responsible for the food work and the status production in households, they are also usually the ones who have the additional obligation to keep abreast of variety. Thus, style becomes code for gender-, class-, and race-based constructions of self. Rather than constructing an obvious divide between formal and informal meals, both books are divided into chapters based on the format of the event, from "cocktails and hors d'oeuvres" to omelet parties, buffets, dinner parties, holidays, and dessert parties. To a certain extent, some of the guidelines are, indeed, reflective of Post's. Within each chapter, the format of the event is elaborated based on menus for smaller to larger numbers of guests. Many of the larger parties are, in fact, predicated on hiring servers, "assistants," or caterers. For Stewart, even a small dinner party requires "one person in the kitchen to rinse plates, stack dishes, and make coffee" (1982, 28). Smith demonstrates some parties where she and her husband manage alone and others where they hire help.

Again, Stewart invokes a number of contradictions: she insists that this book "is not intended only for the culinary elite . . . but especially for all those people who regard cooking . . . as drudgery or duty—and entertaining an even greater worry" (9). At the same time, critics repeatedly point to the luxury of time, goods, and skills that an individual would have to possess in order to re-create one of her events. People comment that no "real person" could possibly emulate Martha unless they too had a team of gardeners, cooks, and household help. There is a continuous tension between her asser-tion that she democratizes taste and her reassertion of a hierarchy of "good things" particularly when those good things are not realistically accessible.[15] Indeed, Bentley finds that the food in MS publications is so technically con-structed through photography that "a real dish of food placed in front of a patron—or family—is destined to disappoint" (2001, 14).

To a certain extent, Smith's entertaining advice comes from the same vi-sual and moral universe that celebrates variety. On the other hand, Smith's advice is more lightly presented—she embraces spontaneity and mistakes, acknowledges that what she lacks in space in her own apartment she makes up for it by using friends' houses for bigger parties, and incorporates social causes into the reasoning for an event or party. Smith's culinary choices pull from a wide range of styles, mainly from the international settings where she traveled and lived, but at least one item in each menu is rooted in her southern family heritage, including her mother's chittlins recipe and peach cobbler. She promotes her Afro-Caribbean roots in the Kwanzaa Christmas buffet.

Like most etiquette writers, Harriet Cole does not provide recipes in *How to Be*; however, she does discuss the need for care of the body, especially since many of the foods that have come to be associated with black culi-nary traditions can be contributors to high blood pressure and diabetes. As Psyche Williams-Forson (2006) points out, "the connections among food, body, and politic are also closely associated with race issues" (13). Cole also provides an annotated cookbook bibliography, with categories including low-fat, vegetarian, Caribbean, southern, African, African American, and Jewish cooking. This is quite different from the kind of appropriation in the name of personal style that's going on in Stewart's books and magazines.

In *Etiquette*, Post evokes rules and the reader is expected to apply them. In their books, Smith and Stewart expect the reader to envision specific settings and unique menus specially constructed for possible occasions. These newer advice publications are visually organized around exquisite photographs of food, table settings, people, places, and events. Although we can only speculate about how much people use those models simply as reading material or a form of vicarious living versus actually trying to "emulate Martha," the point is that they provide cultural reference points. Ideally, the reader is supposed to emulate Martha, whereas Post was speaking to a generic set of circumstances. The narratives in *Entertaining* often focus on specific events that Stewart catered or hosted: for example, she describes two weddings that she helped organize, one of which involved relatives. In the early books like *Entertaining*, photos of context were part of what Stewart was promoting, as specific visions of "new" events. "Lifestyle" books, of which this is one of the models for many others, provide readers with a visual image of how other idealized lives are actually lead. In comparison, Post's narratives and pictures are static and lifeless. Stewart's images are populated, most notably with Stewart herself, who, after all, is the main product being promoted. Interestingly, no one is visibly racial or ethnic in the events that Stewart features.[16] In Smith's comparable photo-studded entertaining books, her guests are equally well named, positioned as celebrities or elites. The main difference is that Smith features family members as well and her guest list is racially mixed. She inserts a bit of her own social justice and philanthropic interests into almost every party.

For both Stewart and Smith, the books are organized around a short story, large glossy photos of events and specific serving ideas and food items along with recipes. Although Stewart does not adhere to the strict WASP dictums of Post's silver, china, and crystal, one still needs a particular kind of cultural capital to find or own green glassware, "yellow ceramic bowls," and "old tin scoops"—although Martha's new versions of these items are available at Kmart or through her catalog. In fact, some critics argue that Stewart is selling commodified and sometimes mass-produced versions of upper-middle-class sociability. This is true of the food and recipes as well.

Bentley suggests that this represents a shift in the "proper meal," which must go beyond the mainstream American ideal to something more elaborate.[17] For example, among Stewart's dinner party menus, one mirrors the structure of Post's, involving five dishes: sautéed wild mushrooms, loin of pork with prunes, fennel puree, celeriac and potato puree, and a dessert. However, almost all the others include many more dishes, particularly "side" notes, sauces, condiments, and additional desserts. Bentley makes a compelling argument that Martha Stewart's food has a twofold effect. The first is making food expectations more complex. The Anglo-American food pattern for meals as A plus 2B. Indeed,

Post's menus are structured accordingly. However, as Bentley demonstrates, A plus 2B is "too mundane, too bourgeois" for Martha Stewart. Instead, the ideal meal formula more resembles something like "BAC plus D over E"—a more complex and thus perhaps more sophisticated version of standard American fare. As important as the food itself, all are ensconced in silver, plateware, glassware, napkins, tablecloth, and centerpiece (*E*).

Alan Warde suggests that the need for cultural mediators and taste experts arises in contemporary culture in response to growing anxieties over food choice as many people's options are constantly expanding with global capitalism. He concludes, "There are no clues about the means by which particular items might convey a particular sense of style or identity" (1997, 161). Stewart is a perfect advisor for this situation. She contributes to the glorification of variety that is so central to commodity culture, insisting on the "right" bowl for just the right menu item and occasion, creating complicated meals that offer potential experiences (the Cape Cod beach party, the estate wedding, the Chinese New Year dinner), and finally, suggesting that there are, in fact, "perfect" ways to do things even amid the complex array of choices. Bentley argues that "embedded in the instructions is a tone of moral authority and a hyperawareness of aesthetics, as if Stewart feels the need to educate the upwardly aspiring in the proper mode of production and presentation" (9). When Smith enters into the same territory—indeed, her menus are only slightly less elaborate than Stewart's—her events are more tightly tied to family or personal history. The use of ethnic or racial food is a key example. In Stewart's companion volume *Menus for Entertaining*, her party ideas range from Thai to Tuscan, from southern BBQ to Thanksgiving on Turkey Hill (whose WASP aesthetic is not based in Martha's actual ethnic heritage). As Bentley points out, the ethnic is simply another party tool, not an actual invitation to understand or participate in different cultures. Indeed, it's been assimilated into whiteness: the best example of this is in her "Fried Green Tomato Brunch," a menu that culls freely from southern cuisine without acknowledging geography beyond the "Tennessee Iced Tea." For the "Southern Shrimp with Grits," Stewart writes about the chef—a friend (white and female) who collaborated with her on this menu, as "it reflects her ability to take old-fashioned recipes and make them brighter and better than the originals" (1994, 228). Compare this to Smith, who speaks specifically of her mother's recipes, her aunts teaching her to cook. If she modifies one of these recipes, she talks about the necessity for health reasons.

Note that Stewart's aesthetics are still based on a white middle-class model that appropriates what is useful from other cultural contexts and reconfigures them into the standard mold. In contrast, Smith offers an aesthetic grounded in the reality of global migration but firmly linked to particular traditions and places as speaking to African American communities.

In Emily Post's world, effort is about overseeing the construction of an event, but with a kind of bourgeois freedom from the gritty details (hence, no recipes and the constant invocation of paid help). In Martha Stewart's world, the effort of constructing the event is a kind of pleasurable artisanal control, where the cadre of helpers is rendered invisible.

It's not clear the extent to which these books' guidelines influence people's actual practices. However, there are some recurring issues that emerge from analyzing these texts. One is that formal entertaining is invariably associated with a white upper-class model of action, one that also depends on rigid roles between hosts and guests, men and women, servers and participants. The work of such activities is supposed to be invisible and easily reciprocated. A second concern is that even as consumer culture provides us with a myriad of "choices" about sociable activities with food, looking closely at Martha Stewart shows that the notion of choice needs to be carefully analyzed. The ideal of comfortable entertaining is still predicated on someone's labor, even as that labor is positioned as part of the "fun" of the event. Discourses of class, gender, and race still affect the social forms of shared meals: people are supposed to be able to recognize the appropriate styles and signs for their social equals.

Murray (1990) argues that the rationalization of society that Max Weber described has extended into hospitality, commercializing and commodifying it, particularly in the sense that one must have specialized training in order to provide hospitality. Smith and Stewart contribute to a construction of sociable behavior that rests on the presumption that people can choose from a variety of possible "selves" if given a guided tour through the possibilities.

However, real choices about the work involved are beyond the economic means of most people. While Smith and Stewart diverge on the appropriation of different culinary cultures in the pursuit of style and variety, they are both engaged in the same activity. Thus, although their pursuits are different across race, they remain part of the same class-based strategies for distinguishing self from others. As Crawford (1980) points out, reconstructing one's self and body through material practices requires a certain amount of time and leisure. Although the desire for comfort in hospitality can be considered part of a "democratization" of elite practices, an examination of people's practices and the texts from which they draw their ideas illustrates that underlying concerns about self control and boundaries of distinction based on taste cultures still shape these voluntary occasions. Ultimately, the kind of sociability people produce rests upon their ability to adapt these circumstances to fit the material and social constraints of their daily lives.

3. Dinner Parties in America

If you accept a dinner invitation, you have a moral obligation to
be amusing.
—The Duchess of Windsor

Is the dinner party a paradigm of society or a vicious pantomime
of the family?
—Lorrie Moore *Beautiful Grade*

In 1990, the writer Susan Orlean traveled the United States looking at what
people do on Saturday night. She found people who cruised in their cars,
played in cocktail lounge bands, polka-danced, ate in restaurants, and
watched television with friends. Orlean figured that hosting a dinner party
would be a quintessential Saturday night activity, so she sought out people
from wealthy New York social circles. This is what she found:

> There are many people in the world for whom giving a party would be an
> unnerving prospect, but Mrs. Thomas Kempner is not among them. [She] is
> not just a skillful hostess but an ardent and confident one who has a hostess's
> temperament and poise and instincts, as well as all those other things that go
> along with being good at giving nice parties, such as a big apartment on Park
> Avenue, an investment-banker husband, a butler, a masseuse, a cook, and a
> horse.... I once asked someone who attends a great number of New York so-
> ciety dinner parties how a person could go about achieving pre-eminence as a
> hostess, and she said "Unless they're very rich or quite attractive, they should
> stay where they are." (1990, 142–152)

The party for a European countess involved ambassadors, attaches, and
other members of New York society, a "phalanx of waiters, cooks, housekeepers and butlers," and what the hostess described as a "very American"
menu, including ham, crabmeat in aspic, corn muffins, and Apple Brown
Betty. Orlean's description of Mrs. Kempner makes it clear that such dinner
parties are the terrain of a narrow socioeconomic and cultural segment of
American society.[1] Despite a democratization of goods and greater variety

and access to different cuisines and foods, the majority of people simply do not have the wealth, the time, or the social necessity to construct elaborate and formal rituals as a way of maintaining relationships. But while the *New York Times* society page dinner party creates an ideal type, many people do construct their own version of a dinner party.

At least twenty-two of my original interviewees held what one might consider a dinner party. Many of them used the phrase "dinner party" to describe their social events. These were parties where one person (the hostess or host) was usually responsible for all the food and cooking, where guests were seated at a dinner table and served, and where there were some stated expectations about the formality of dress, manners, and table setting. A number of these people had incomes and education that placed them as members of the professional managerial class. In this chapter, I use stories from both formal and informal interviews to travel from those that dutifully adhere to the cultural template of dinner parties to those that deliberately alter some important aspects while still insisting that what is occurring can be considered a dinner party. The first stories are about "traditional" dinner parties where women in heterosexual marriages perform interactional and physical labor to ensure the social networks of their family. Then, I examine a dinner party that is potentially a burlesque of normative ideas about dinner parties and who holds them. Questioning whether the gender of the cook is the most salient factor in the performance of a dinner party, I analyze the narratives of men who cook on weekends. The chapter ends by raising questions about the boundaries of dinner parties, focusing on the experiences of a lesbian couple who incorporate real and fictive kin into dinner parties and other events.

How does one decide whether an event is a dinner party? I took the most obvious approach: if someone labeled an event, I accepted the designation. For example, many of the people I interviewed who had spouses or partners often had dinners where one other couple was invited over. However, it was rare for people to call such an event a "dinner party" even if the hosting couple did all the cooking and serving, so those events are not the focus of this chapter. In the general usage of my respondents, a dinner party was an event, one that involved more than two guests. Numbers matter in terms of sociability. Simmel suggests that the dyad has a "different reference to each of its two elements than have larger groups to their members" (123 in Wolff, 1950). The dyad has very specific features. He suggests, "this is shown not only by the fact that the addition of a third person completely changes them, but also and even more so, by the common observation that the further expansion to four or more by no means correspondingly modifies the group any further" (138).

In general, more participants mean more interaction and differentiation and careful orchestration. Emily Post suggests that without paid help or servants, eight is the maximum for a formal dinner party. In a section on "Entertaining" in *Joy of Cooking*, author Irma Rombauer (1975) advises that the ideal number for a dinner party is eight and, "Unless the guests are very close friends, the minimum must exceed two." She explains, "back in the living room afterward, first time acquaintances must be able to exercise options and establish small centers of mutual interest; and we suggest that this can only be engineered with any degree of success among groups of at least eight. Twelve is an even happier number" (15).[2]

Both Rombauer and Simmel agree that more participants increases the amount of interaction and differentiation. However, Rombauer implies that there is in fact more significant differentiation among various size groups. In general, the number of people attending and participating in a formal event has an impact on the experience. For the people I interviewed, a dinner party ranged from six to twenty people.

Another determinant was whether the hosting person or persons were responsible for the provision of almost all the food. I did not analyze catered meals since I wanted to explore the invisible labor of planning, preparing, cooking, and serving. Most people considered a dinner party an event where guests were not expected to contribute to the meal, other than perhaps a bottle of wine or some nonfood gift such as flowers. They contrasted these meals with a much more informal form, such as the potluck or providing "take-out food" spontaneously after some other social activity. Sociable moments are predicated on reciprocity, but such reciprocity in potlucks is immediate (we all contribute to the construction of the food and the event) whereas the dinner party contains a sense of extended obligation, the promise that the host and guest roles will eventually be reversed. Sometimes guests were not expected to reciprocate in kind. For the most part, people limited what their guests could contribute to the immediate event. In most cases, meals were served as courses, with everyone seated at a set table.

Almost everyone who used the label "dinner party" described events that did not include kin beyond the immediate household members (usually partners and sometimes children). For most people, a party that involved both extended family and friends was often defined differently and frequently took a more informal form than a dinner party. Discussing triads, Simmel posits that mediation becomes a central component of the family as a group of three or more. The family acts as an affective unit, already bounded by bonds of intimacy. Theoretically, including family in formal sociability would change the character of "free play" associated with the dinner as a social form.

Again, Simmel finds that expectations of intimacy in families are different than those achieved in sociable occasions. He contrasts marriage and friendship, stating, "This entering of the whole individual ego into the relationship may be more plausible in friendship than in love for the reason that friendship lacks the specific concentration upon one element which loves derives its sensuousness. . . . Friendship lacks this vehemence, but also the frequent unevenness of this abandon" (325 in Wolff, 1950).

The discourse of dinner parties described in Chapter 2 strongly suggests that dinner parties are, foremost, performances of class, race, and gender. Participants establish who they are in relation to each other and to the larger world by their inclusion in such events. Furthermore, they reinforce gender inequities by relying on a gendered division of labor. Providing domestic hospitality is a gendered activity. What follows is an example of a dinner party that, in many ways, conforms to the Emily Post traditional discourse of entertaining.

Women's Work: The Dinner Party and Commensality in Marriage

> The hostess must be like the duck—calm and unruffled on the surface and paddling like hell underneath.
> —Anonymous

> When my mother had to get dinner for eight she'd just make enough for sixteen and only serve half.
> —Gracie Allen

Sociologists Virginia Olesen and Joseph Gusfield each describe domestic hospitality as a shifting social form that corresponds to changes in gender and class-based social conditions. Historically, the dinner party is seen as a product of the invisible physical and interactional labor of women, most typically white upper-middle-class women as hosts and women of color as servers. Given various shifts in contemporary American society, particularly the changing occupational circumstances of women and people of color, such a performance is both out of the reach of most people and unsuited to their social experiences. As the types of households in the United States continue to shift away from the nuclear family, this also changes who creates the meals for the household. Most obviously, as more women of all classes participate in the paid labor force, they may be less able or willing to maintain social networks based on one person doing the work of "entertaining." The ideal image of a dinner party, of host and hostess, of appropriate guests, and of the management of their social interactions, has historically depended on the intersection of class and gender ideologies. These narratives demonstrate how shifts in the social world in terms of gender and class play themselves out in the social lives of people who attempt to hold dinner parties.

Marion is a white woman in her early sixties, married to a prominent lawyer and politician. She holds dinner parties that are fairly traditional in the sense that as a wife in an upper-middle-class household, she does the vast majority of the interactional and physical work to produce these social events. For most of their marriage John and Marion have lived in a large historic colonial house located in a small New England town just outside the city where John works. They grew up within thirty miles of their current home, in the same region where both attended prestigious private schools. Their friends include other couples their age who were "school pals" or college roommates, family friends, and old colleagues from John's professional life. Marion also seemed to know most of the longtime residents and neighbors in her small town and spoke about running into people in the post office frequently. At the time I interviewed Marion, she and John were in the process of retiring, with plans to sell the large house and move to a small seaside condominium. When they were younger and his career was not yet established, they held many dinner parties. I single out their story because Marion and John's social events approximated the Emily Post vision. They have the material wealth, inherited goods, social connections, and spatial requirements to hold such parties.[3] When I asked Marion about where she got her ideas about hospitality, she talked about being raised by two aunts who believed in proper etiquette and manners. Her own dinner parties seem like a "natural" connection to her family's traditions.

In explaining why they did so much entertaining when they were younger, Marion emphasized their house:

> Well, we have this big old house and it's about a hundred and sixty years old. . . . Our house is on a hill and the other people [previous owners] never had anybody. So when we first moved there years ago, you know, everybody wanted to get inside. And see. And over the years, we've done it all over. . . . Because it's a wonderful place to have people come, plus I love to have people come. We have an open house at Christmas and we used to have an Easter egg hunt on the lawn. And the dining room is probably even longer than this. So, we have this table, it's at least [twenty feet] long and it has, you know, the pedestal thing with leaves. . . . The dining room opens onto a big enclosed porch and you have a view of the mountain across the fields. Our barn is really falling down but it still looks pretty. When we do the Christmas thing [a neighbor] hitches up a sleigh and horses and people get to ride up the yard to the house. There are candles in every window. Inside we set the table beautifully and there's a Rose Medallion bowl with punch and lots of little foods for the children. It's very lovely, very Norman Rockwell.

In her description, owning such a "showpiece" historic house obliges them to share it publicly and use it as an appropriate space for socializing. The social geography of this historic New England town includes ideas about community relations, such that "everybody" wanted to see their historic house. For example, one of the neighboring towns requires village residents to restrict their holiday lights to white candles in the windows. John's vocation in politics, which gives him local prominence, adds to the public nature of domestic life. John and Marion live in a world where certain kinds of socializing are "expected."

Marion's reference to Norman Rockwell is not an accidental evocation of American life. Rockwell's 1943 series, "Four Freedoms" were intended to illustrate the American values that justified our involvement in World War II. The most famous, "Freedom from Want," is centered on ideas about domestic hospitality, depicting a grandfatherly patriarch standing behind his wife, who is setting an enormous turkey before a table surrounded by eager faces. Amy Bentley (1998) suggests that this image functioned as a visual metaphor for prescriptive notions about expectations of abundance, societal order and stability, and maintenance of the status quo; depictions of bountiful meals with women as servers and cooks connoted stability to many Americans mostly because the images reinforced the status quo of gender roles (60).

By referring to Rockwell, Marion suggests that the presentation of her home embodies those symbolic meanings. Their holiday open house in a quaint New England town is a cultural performance, one that invokes a nostalgic and idealized past, where neighbors and family were welcomed into one's home frequently, and women or women servants created community through food and caring work. According to Bentley (1998), "Freedom From Want is important not only for the abundance it portrays but also for the social and familial relations it conveys" (60).[4] Marion and John's social events evoke the same kind of symbolic universe.

Marion described pressed linens for the table and centerpieces from flowers in their gardens. She did most of the shopping and cooking, but it was often based on a menu that John had planned. For all the social events, "we really used to set the table, you know. If we have a dinner party, of course, we use the silver and stuff like that . . . things I inherited from my aunts. Some we got when we were married. And we used to have soup plates, you know, the plate you take away when the bowl is empty. We started off so fancy, I don't know why, because that's how we—most of us—our friends and such—were brought up."

Marion implies a stereotypical New England WASP upper-middle-class upbringing and social circles. As a result, she has knowledge of etiquette and the "proper" way to set a formal table. This formality in goods is mirrored in the formality expected among the guests. She and John were given or inherited the kinds of material goods that historically signify a particular class standing: silver, linens, and antique furniture. These special items, reserved for entertaining, along with the fresh flowers arranged on a formal table, are meant to mark the occasion as out of the ordinary.

Ordinarily, many of their parties were for groups of friends, people they'd known from college or from John's early days as a lawyer. She described a latter part of their marriage where parties were held specifically to help further John's career, with prominent businessmen or people connected to city politics as guests. "When John was a young associate, there were [clients] or ... whatever he did to bring in business, so we had all these parties and then we'd go out with them the next night. . . . Like for two weeks, so you had to have different things each night. When it was like that, some of them [the parties] were catered."

The people at these parties were not exclusively friends but mostly work associates, such that the dinners were about status and display but also obligation and formality. John and Marion engaged in friendliness and hospitality with these colleagues, but with boundaries and limits established through the formality of the party.

For Bourdieu, cultural capital has a number of forms, most notably as "long lasting dispositions of the mind and body," but also in the "objectified state, in the form of cultural goods" (1984). John and Marion convert both of these forms of cultural capital, the WASP dispositions and the inherited goods, to social capital. The dinner parties allow them to invest in social networks that maintain their social position and assist in John's career. By producing these sociable occasions, Marion enacts a performance of gender and class that contributes to her family's status. Sociologists have suggested that "the affluent white housewife, epitomizing the last vestiges of the cult of domesticity, had become a 'worker' for her husband's livelihood by producing hospitality significant for his success" (Olesen, 1993, 89; Pyke, 1996). Marion's matter-of-fact way of describing this work suggests that she saw it as an ordinary, uncomplicated part of marriage, an easily met obligation. For example, although she talked about her volunteer work, Marion did not mention (until I asked directly) that she had never worked for pay outside the home.

Even though she held many food events in her house, Marion describes herself as someone who "does not like to cook." Interestingly, Marion's stories rarely focus on the food and menu. In describing the events that were held during the ascent of John's career, she told me about a party that "went badly" when they invited people who drank too much: "You know, they're not really there to see each other, just to get sloshed." In these cases, the food was less significant, even less so than the decoration of their house.

As Mary Douglas (1972) explains, allowing people into one's home for food demarcates boundaries of inclusion and exclusion. Her famous structuralist analysis demonstrated that categories of people were matched by "appropriate" categories of socializing. Marion constructs her own version of Douglas's boundaries: there are clear distinctions between the main social groups in their lives: work-related acquaintances, neighbors, old friends, and new acquaintances from their AA support groups. Some of the requisite dinner parties were for people from John's work life, which, while pleasurable and social, involved more obligation than choice. The social capital necessary for upper-middle-class sociability and male careers was important enough for Marion to subordinate many of her own desires to do this work. Where she could, she established limits, making clear the levels of intimacy. She stated, "We are not really party people—I like having everybody there. Yes. But I'm also glad to see them go, because I'm not a night person. We never tell anyone it's time to leave, but we do sort of set a limit on how late we'll stay up."

The formal dinner party, with its specified rules and control over the format and sequence, creates both connectedness and distance. The line drawn here is different from the one drawn for close friends. Marion described neighbors generally as people they know but don't socialize with regularly—"I see them maybe in the post office once in a while"—who are invited for the holiday open houses, but not for sit-down dinners. Friends include John's Princeton roommates, people from Marion's childhood, and connections through private school and family. For friends, Marion sets a formal table and everyone dresses "nicely," but she cares about "making everyone comfortable" so they can all relax and reminisce. Here is how she described the food: "Well if we have that group (our old friends), there are usually about sixteen of us at this big table. So we usually have pilaf rice, this traditional thing, and put parsley on the chicken. People don't even notice, they're just so glad they don't have to cook. That's what I think. You know, we'll have rolls, we'll have salad, and then a dessert. But mostly we talk."

The meal itself is the standard A plus 2B, in keeping with the white upper-middle-class expectations. For old friends, the group can be larger than most formal dinner parties, since relationships and intimacies are long established. There is no sense that guests will be left out of the conversation. As they got older, John's career no longer required the more formal dinner parties and two of their adult children developed time-consuming health problems. Marion also comments that now, even with close friends, they prefer eating out. "Well, as you go through life, the process changes. 'Cause when you're young like that, you have people in for dinner. [Now] we have a lot less of that, we usually go to a restaurant to meet somebody."

Marion situates their experiences through both changes in their life course and changes in social conditions. She talks about differences in her children and the younger people she knows. "[They don't] go for these kinds of parties. I mean, my kids like it if I do it, especially for holidays. . . . I can certainly understand not wanting to go through all that trouble. Who wants to wash all those dishes afterwards?"

Marion articulates a shift that comes about because of where she is in the life course, but it is also a result of changing social expectations about entertaining. Now that John is well established, they no longer stage the dinner parties for work colleagues and focus only on entertaining close friends. Marion still feels obliged to hold the big neighborhood open house. She and John enjoy parts of it, but they now try to "set limits" such as keeping the good china in the cabinet, using plastic cups and utensils to avoid breakage, and putting an ending time down on the invitations. In the midst of describing the open house, Marion interjected that she was looking forward to selling the big house. She spoke about making choices more related to her own comfort and personal preference rather than occupational or social networking. In general Marion and John appear to do their gender and class performances with close and almost "easy" adherence to a specific normative model.

What's interesting in Marion's stories is the seeming lack of concern about the food itself. Her few descriptions of menus seem to come right out of the etiquette books' recommendations, constructing nonregional "American" food, almost classic New England cuisine—in Douglas's sense the A plus 2B ordered meal. Unlike some of the other people I interviewed, Marion does not use food or her knowledge of it as the source of display and cultural capital. In particular, because the house and the table settings command a high social standing, the food does not signify conspicuous consumption. Marion and John are from a generation and a regional social group where food is not the main delineator of "taste"—the meal itself does not have to be "interesting" to function as a site of commonality for guests. Furthermore, much of the "culinary revolution" that Levenstein describes occurs after Marion and John did the vast majority of their social entertaining. Most likely John and Marion's age and stage in life, combined with their security in their class performance contribute to this. The majority of people I spoke to did not stage the kinds of dinner party that formed the backbone of John and Marion's social and working lives. But this couple has the economic and social resources that *both* allowed and demanded that they create these sorts of social events in their lives. Coming from fairly wealthy families and inheriting silver, china, linens and other necessary luxuries, John's striving for occupational success, and, most importantly in Marion's view, owning a notable house meant that they were able and expected to entertain. When John was striving for prominence they "had" to hold more than they'd like. Today, restaurants are more commonplace as sites for social occasions.

As is clear in Marion's stories, the dinner party is traditionally staged through the labor of women, whose job it is to make the whole process appear seamless and invisible. Although these gender ideologies dictate that Marion and John enact these roles at a particular point in their lives, they do experience changes over time; retirement, caring for sick children, even shifts in who they want to be with have meant that they can limit or give up certain kinds of performative events as part of their social life. For example, now that he is retired, John does more of the preparation work for the open house. According to Marion, he enjoys holiday decorating and setting the table. Although shifts in age and employment have meant that they share more of the domestic labor, from Marion's language one can infer that John still exercises more choice and control over which tasks he takes on.

In her analysis of domestic hospitality Virginia Olesen (1993) argues that the shifts in types of hospitality allow for shifts in the types of selves people can construct within and around such events. The "temporal context" in hospitality is significant for the production of self, such that we need to focus on the "analysis of lived experience with hospitality . . . [with] particular attention to how that experience came about in the specific material context." When I met Marion, she and John were in the midst of a life change that also shifted their definitions of self. This shift also affected their definition of the situation regarding their commensal lives. The intersection of their personal social lives and the larger social world occur in certain ways: First, with retirement they experience a relative freedom from the need to create social networks related to John's job advancement. This means that Marion, in particular, is relieved of some of the gendered obligations and work of her earlier married life. As she happily exclaimed, "Where the condo is, you could eat in a new restaurant every night!" When I spoke to her five years after the initial interview, this was precisely how she and John were living their life. She was still enthused about the choices and the freedom from cooking.

Second, although it's true that their social lives no longer require entertaining in the home, in the last thirty years there have also been shifts in the commercial and social landscape that make restaurants more accessible and "eating out" a more acceptable way of socializing. Since the 1970s, the time frame when Marion and John did most of their entertaining, there are greater varieties of restaurants, more affordable for many segments of the population (especially those in John and Marion's income bracket), and a change in the social norms (see Finkelstein, 1989; Bell and Valentine, 1997; Wood, 1995; Warde and Martens, 2001). In other words, more people of more social classes eat out now than they did twenty or thirty years ago, often for different reasons. Warde and Martens suggest that the increase in women's participation in the paid labor force, a general decrease in leisure time, and the status and pleasurable aspects of dining out all contribute to a rise in restaurant dining.

The illnesses of Marion and John's adult children created another shift in their lives and sense of self that is reflected through their sociability. Chronic illness changes the sense of self for both the sick individual and their family members. One of their children is a recovering alcoholic. A large portion of our conversation focused on Marion embracing Alcoholics Anonymous as a support structure. More concretely, Marion's view of her self and her social world changed with this life experience. She described parties she'd attended since her involvement with AA, where she and John left early after noticing how much of the event centered on alcohol consumption. Her construction of sociability had necessarily shifted, such that she saw these parties at other people's houses as "not really being social"—and her self as someone who had different ideas. In particular, Marion did not like the social form of the cocktail party, partly because of her obvious discomfort with excessive drinking, but also, I suspect, because the sociability of events centered on alcohol are not structured and potentially too intimate for her "tastes." The more formal etiquette of a dinner party manages interactions more and establishes clear expectations of guests and hosts.

Marion and John's experiences with domestic hospitality reflect certain generational attitudes and experiences about marriage, gender, upper-middle-class career development, and socializing with friends. Their social and economic resources as well as the ease of fit with the Emily Post narrative of hospitality seems to insulate them from some of the discourses about food. Having "done their time" with domestic sociability, they embrace a social life around eating in a restaurant without tension. It is probably significant that the time frame in which they actually held formal dinner parties is in the past, prior to many of the cultural, social, and economic changes that have shifted the landscape of sociable meals.

My Creative Outlet

At the time I first interviewed her, Joanne, a white upper-middle-class woman in her late thirties, was married to Ron, who owned a graphic design firm that provided the majority of their income. His job required that he travel frequently. Joanne had a college degree but worked part time in a job that fit around the school and leisure schedules of her three young children.

Like many mothers, Joanne described her interest in cooking as an out-growth of health concerns related to mothering: "I decided to learn how to cook, when was it, when I had my first baby and he started eating, I got really conscious about food and what was in it. . . . I get really angry when I go through the grocery store and you see that Blue Kool-Aid stuff in the plastic bottles."

DeVault (1991) describes how pregnancy and parenting advice support cultural ideologies of intensive mothering that "push women toward thinking about the work of feeding" (114). Concerns about nutritional information are a significant aspect of middle-class mothering, specifically, such that caring work is often about providing children with "good food." For Joanne, although cooking for friends was a creative source of pleasure, it was also rooted in gender expectations about the work that mothers do for their families, insuring healthy meals and providing care through food.

Joanne and Ron prided themselves on having a wide variety of friends and social contacts. She commented,

> I can't stand being stereotyped as one type of person, so we really make an effort to have all different kinds of friends. . . . And we do all sorts of different activities. . . . And plus, Ron and I are so different in that regard. I mean, he's a corporate designer, he's on his way up in the world. . . . So we kind of live in two different worlds, which is quite challenging. . . . Right now it's going to come off as a lot of our friends we meet and maintain are through Ron versus through me because I feel like through motherhood I've lost a lot of the past. . . . But if I think about it, [when we invite people over] I pick who I think will get along well.

Although Ron's public life brought people in, Joanne acted as the "kin-keeper," a particularly important job given the heterogeneous and dispersed group of friends they described. Joanne's effort of connecting them at various moments included deciding when reciprocal bonds need to be reinforced by a dinner party as well as evaluating how people will get along. And yet, in Joanne's description, it's almost an afterthought that she does this work.

Research on kin networks and support suggests that upper-middle-class people are less likely to have kin living nearby and therefore tend to actively create larger, more dispersed social networks of friendship and support than people of lower socioeconomic means (Walker, 1996). Spouses often combine previous social networks to create new "commensal circles" (Sobal et al., 2002). For people of particular socioeconomic and cultural positions, the dinner party represents one significant component of this work. In his study of friendship and class, Graham Allan (1989) supports the insights of Bourdieu and DeVault, who observe that in the middle-class dinner party, the intention of all this effort is not just to demonstrate the social competence and skills of the host, but rather to generate an ambience in which friendship can be promoted and endorsed. . . . In general, while the meal serves as a focus, the chief purpose of the occasion is to provide a relatively open-ended setting in which sociable relationships can be affirmed and expressed. In this respect, the dinner party, with its scope for wide-ranging discussion, argument, and story-telling, is entirely consonant with the broad-based way in which middle class friendships are typically defined. (141)

In Joanne and Ron's case, their shared patterns have been explicitly negotiated to include a variety of people. Although having people over often helps her husband's social networking, Joanne insisted that cooking for people is something she chose rather than felt compelled to do.[5] Joanne also socialized through potluck dinners with other mothers whose spouses work late or travel frequently. Sobal, Bove, and Rauschenbach (2002) suggest that "commensality is an important component of eating that was one part of the ways people 'do marriage.'" In particular, "partners eating networks were blended as they negotiated involvement in extra-marital commensal circles," which included kin, friends, coworkers, and others. Joanne's cooking for friends solidifies those social networks according to middle-class ideas about sociability and food. This discourse constructs friendship as shared leisure but also rests on food work as an accomplishment. DeVault (1991) points out that "the requirement for their social gatherings is that the meal should be interesting enough to serve as a focus for conversation and sociability." In these cases, food is a source of entertainment and pleasure both for guests and host (210). This discourse emerges when Joanne described dinner parties as

> a way to keep my mind active. . . . In the winter months I always buy cooking magazines and find a project and then that's like my creative outlet. . . . So, having friends over and making a beautiful meal was my saying "Yes, I still have a brain and can do stuff besides change diapers."
>
> My winter project was to have somebody over every month. . . . So we make it a point to at least once a month have somebody over. And um, it was usually, I don't know, people we worked with or people from school or the neighborhood. . . . So, I invite two couples that I think will get along quite well. Um, I pour over my cooking magazines to figure out a funky meal I could do so it's not boring . . . and, um, gosh, I mean, I really get into, you know, the flowers, setting the table beautifully.

For Joanne, food becomes a display of self—in contrast to Marion, who also produced such events, but restricted her menus so as not to reveal anything other than what was expected of white upper-middle-class households. For Marion, the rules of such occasions were part of her habitus, a social and cultural inheritance from her aunts and the private schools she attended. Unlike Marion, Joanne was not raised in an upper-middle-class household. In fact, she described her "large Irish family" as "oblivious" to the aesthetic dimensions of her sociability with food. As an adult, Joanne learned to cook and entertain, using work experiences and textual sources that specified how to create styles, account for nutrition, and manage the production of such an event.

> *So you do everything?*
> Yeah, pretty much. I used to work for a catering company and so I learned a lot by watching how they managed everything. And I really got inspired to do things at home in a more beautiful way. So I really love to set a beautiful table. So, then I would go shopping that morning. And you know, buy all my produce and stuff. And just spend the afternoon, you know, making a beautiful dinner.
>
> Usually [I made] the feature article of a magazine . . . oftentimes I would go through and take eighty percent of that menu and then flip around to another book and get . . . dessert. And if there's certain things, like I'm allergic to dairy so there's stuff I won't do. Or if I knew somebody didn't like something really spicy I'd moderate it, you know what I mean? . . . I sort of use [the magazine] as a resource, to spice up stuff because I was never taught to cook when I was little. So this is a project I really took on in a whole different way.

Joanne's normative ideas about the appropriate food and setting for dinner parties come from what she has learned in her adult life rather than through her family. In DeVault's interviews she also describes a similar way of organizing meals based on "textual standards for stylish eating, characteristic of families in professional/managerial class group" (1991, 203). Women like Joanne, whose economic class location was different from her family of origin, often talk about learning to cook as rejecting their mothers' reliance on tradition and embracing food magazines and cookbooks by professional chefs. Ironically, many of these chefs and magazines present a reconfiguration of "peasant" cuisines, geographic and regional foods created by women who were invoked to maintain tradition.

At the same time, the food discourse was often presented as an achievement of differentiation. Both men and women who were upwardly mobile professionals spoke about the development of their tastes and cooking abilities as something that came with their movement into a different socioeconomic bracket, placing them in different food universes than their families of origin. Speaking of his parents, one man said, "I don't want to be snobbish about this, but they don't go out to eat, they don't go to fancy restaurants, they don't have this kind of palate." At another point in our conversation Joanne described her family of origin as "only eating foods that come out of boxes." According to DeVault (1991), the women she interviewed who experienced this found that "cooking was not a practice to be learned imitatively, but a new terrain of study" with shifting styles and codes that had to be mastered as tastes change (205–206). Keeping track of these changes in taste and learning to produce such meals is both a performance of self ("proving that I have a brain") and a kind of status work that Joanne does to help construct her family's class location. Joanne's knowledge of those styles came from a familiarity with various gourmet cooking magazines and cooking techniques learned from working at the catering company. The meals that Joanne cooked reflect a knowledge and engagement with cultural discourses about what items were healthy, popular, and trendy. She used phrases like "funky," or "out-of-the-ordinary, not mainstream." Her menus for dinner parties reflect knowledge of foods that were recent additions to the American supermarket and the white middle-class palate:

> The first course I'll usually do a salad. So like I did, um, grilled eggplant on wilted arugula, something with balsamic vinegar. If it . . . it's wintertime I'll do a soup. And then the main course. For example, I did this, um, it was a white fish, what was it—a sea bass. I did a sea bass with this citrus chutney sauce, like on top of it . . . and I made that part, I made the salsa sauce all day. And it was, you know, the papaya and all that stuff, it was done in my skillet. And it was set aside so all I had to do was heat it up after I cooked the fish that night. So all the prep work I learned, after years, to get everything done in the afternoon and then throw it together right before you're going to eat it. That's a skill.

"Unusualness" and variety are crucial elements of the foods served at upper-middle-class dinner parties. Up until the late 1990s, sea bass, arugula, and balsamic vinegar were items that were not widely known or eaten by a large population of white Americans. They reflect a performance of worldliness and sophistication enacted through food.

"Unusualness" is also often code for foods ethnically or racially different from the guest and host's own background. Salsa and chutney are not familiar to Joanne's Irish Catholic relatives, but are perfectly appropriate for the people chosen from their "eclectic" array of friends whose discourse of food choice posit variety and "culinary tourism" as important elements of enjoyment. Heldke (2003) critiques culinary tourism as a form of colonialism, particularly practiced by those with privilege whose own culture is less interesting. It is fueled by a marketplace that renders certain cuisines exotic or novel and others ordinary, and it is supported by cultural culinary adventurers who help establish these boundaries by eating and cooking the "other." Culinary tourism is also a way of creating boundaries between guests and others, since people who "only eat out of boxes" would not have the knowledge to appreciate the kind of sociability Joanne was creating.[6] Although her social network was "eclectic," it was tied together by shared knowledge about food and aesthetics of taste.

For Joanne, the party and particularly the food were about bringing different people together in their lives and socially bonding them. But it was also about expressing her creativity, demonstrating her skills as a cook, learning to stage this event well, and feeling satisfied that she could do it. The food itself is something she'd thought about a lot, especially in comparison to Marion, for whom the discourse of appropriate dinner party food is established by "tradition."[7] Even though the beautiful table is important to Joanne, and the house is big enough to accommodate people, the food, the cooking, and presentation of a meal are the real items on display, the centerpiece of her event. Simmel asserts, "the socialization of the meal lifts it into an aesthetic stylization that in turn reacts on the former [the needs of the individual]. This is because when in addition to the satisfying of the appetite, an aesthetic satisfaction is also expected from eating, not only can a community of several afford more easily the necessary effort than the individual, but also the former [the community] rather than the latter [the individual] is its [the aesthetic's] rightful carrier" (Symons, 1994, 347).

In other words, groups of heterogeneous individuals become connected through the food. Joanne does the work of organizing and cooking for the event, but its ultimate success depends upon complicity among Ron and the other guests in its form, acting and interacting appropriately to create the sociable moments. DeVault (1991) states, "In this context, food becomes a tool to be deployed with a different sort of skill. It constitutes a common code that can mediate relations among professional and managerial couples, and that these couples bring back into their everyday family lives" (210).

The Social Geography of Homes

The emphasis on the food emerges in a different way when Joanne talks about homes and space for having people over. Historically having a large house with a formal dining room was a symbol of middle-class status, displaying space and goods when people came over for a meal. But Joanne described the ideal house for entertaining in words that echo Visser and Stewart:

> I said to Ron, people want to be in your kitchen when you cook. . . . I would love to have a big square kitchen with an island in the middle or something so people could sit on the other side. . . . In our old house, we never used the dining room. . . . And what I'm realizing now is that people, they want to be

where you make food and hang out where you make food because they have such a comfort feeling—One, watching it; and Two, knowing someone else is making it for them; and Three, they just want to be where it's all happening. So, if I had to design my own house, there would be no dining room, it would be a big area and you eat right there. But people, oh yeah, then they can see the mess. . . . [But] after you've learned to be efficient, it's not messy. It shouldn't be messy because you can't function appropriately. That comes with the art of knowing how to be organized in the kitchen.

The house itself both as a setting for the party and as a display piece in its own right takes on a different form and significance than in the Emily Post model and in Marion's experiences. Because cooking and food are a performance of self, the place where it occurs shifts—in effect, changing the dynamic of individualism and connectedness. Cooking in the kitchen for others, while they watch, is a different staging of intimacy.

Joanne was not the only person who shifts the back-stage–front-stage rules about the dining experience. Many people told me there was truth to a common cliché that "at parties, everyone always ends up in the kitchen." What Joanne described was a shift to more informal rules about friendship through domestic hospitality. Such changes may also be connected to the changing circumstances of women in particular being in the paid workforce. This change translates to different ideas about the use of domestic space. According to Ellen Pader, this is a white middle-class American model that doesn't hold for everyone. In various cultures and historical times many people socialize in the kitchen. However, now it's acceptable in wealthier circles. This parallels the way upper-middle-class people appropriate "peasant" or working-class cuisines as specialty foods—"discovering" informality and difference (Pader, 1994).

Kitchen design has become a lucrative enterprise, where food and home-decorating magazines place a major emphasis on constructing and creating these rooms so that they can accommodate guests. Trends in the last two decades saw American kitchens getting bigger. In 1995, Laura Shapiro captured Peter Connolly, marketing director for IKEA, expressing this: "If you look at new homes today, the percentage of square footage that goes into the kitchen is much greater than it was 20 or 30 years ago. . . . People want center islands and lots of counter space" (Shapiro, 1995).

Perhaps this indicates that one shift is about lines of intimacy and distance, that what is being staged is a performance where guests have the delimited experience of "being family." Joanne ascribed to hospitality as "making people comfortable," which is a different expectation than the Emily Post model, where hosts entertain and are generous to guests, but an air of formal behavior permeates the activities. In Joanne's more modern version, guests are opened to a moderated experience of family life, made comfortable, invited into the kitchen to watch their meal being prepared. People who had friends watch them cook often (but not always) had children who were also present for social occasions. However, it's not clear what they mean by "family"—some people talk about "comfort" and "argument-free conversation," which are, in themselves, idealized versions of what family life is like. Clearly many middle-class families need to construct close relationships with people other than kin because kin do not live nearby, so their social events must embrace guests by "making them feel comfortable." At the same time they also express an ambivalence about the expectations of family, distancing themselves from the specific daily practices of their families of origin.

An alternate way to view such changes is to see the kitchen as supplanting the dining room as the display showcase of a home. Magazines hold regular contests for the "best kitchen" with important criteria being the size and comfort level of the room. In essence, the social conditions and rules of formal interaction about having people to one's home have changed only somewhat, but ideologies about food and cooking have completely changed. For example, Joanne has decided that it makes sense to explicitly invite guests into the kitchen and prepare parts of the meal under their scrutiny. In contemporary American society the kitchen has become a place where both sociability and activity—talking and cooking—occur at the same time, allowing the cooking and the food to become a centerpiece of the conversation. Along with Post, Simmel suggests that this is not conducive to sociability because it brings people "too close" to the organic nature of eating. However, neither takes into consideration the extent to which the disciplining of self has become an internal individualized process in contemporary society. When such concerns are individualized, an "informality" and a closer relationship to the aesthetic are less risky sociable occasions. In this context, more people share Stewart's contention that the shared aesthetic experience of making "beautiful food and beautiful settings" provides grounds for good sociable interactions.

However, when the kitchen becomes front-stage there must be certain adjustments in how one thinks about socializing and food. When the host's skills as a cook become a focal point of the event, there is a boundary shift, such that the invisibility of cooking is lifted. But not entirely. Joanne explains that she's had to learn her part, specifically as a paid worker for a caterer, learning how to give an efficient and orderly performance as cook. People want to see the host or hostess cook and be with them. However, what guests see is a highly staged version of the work, one where the cook is well organized and knows that his or her activities are on display. In the world of 1960s sociability, Julia Child could assert that no one would know about cooking mistakes since "you are alone in the kitchen." In this more contemporary approach, accidents such as dropping food on the floor and "rescuing" it are out of the question. This staging of food preparation parallels the experience of dining in restaurants where foods like Caesar salad are elaborately prepared at the table. Clearly, in both cases, much of the preparation is done before the actual cooking occurs. Cooking for others in the "front stage" is still about class and gender, but as a different kind of performance. People cook to demonstrate ability, the skills that one cannot purchase even in a commodified expanding capitalist market. To shift the socializing from the dining room to the kitchen does not necessarily signify a "democratization" of social relations but rather a change in the geographic terrain around which one demonstrates cultural capital.

In some cases, women in professional managerial households continue to fulfill the hostess role at dinner parties, albeit in a modified form. But Marion's story demonstrates that this is not a performance that wealthier women are always required to carry throughout all life stages. Furthermore, depending on the configuration of class location, various aspects of the dinner party assume greater significance in the demonstration of cultural capital. Marion and John come from families where each generation has had wealth and social status. They inherited both goods and styles of socializing that adhere closely to a traditional model. Their house is the most significant showpiece in their enactment of class-based social interaction. And yet, as retirees, they are happy to jettison this aspect of their social lives and shift to a sociability based on eating out. Joanne and Ron are upwardly mobile professionals. Their life as married adults is different from that of their parents. Their socioeconomic standing is newer and not securely anchored in inherited cultural capital. They lack a local and traditional social network—thus, Joanne uses her cooking and entertaining skills to cultivate the kind of varied, but close, friendships she desires. Further, entertaining in the kitchen shows shifting lines of intimacy and display, the cultural expectation of informality even within a formally constructed event as a hallmark of contemporary American friendships.

Still at the heart of these two stories lies a gender- and race-based construction in upper-middle-class companionate heterosexual marriage. Although both Marion and Joanne exercise a certain amount of choice about what they construct, neither overtly challenges the gendering of food work. They also both operate comfortably within codes of upper-middle-class conduct and sociability. Their social worlds, while broad in some respects, are also restricted by class and race, so that their friends understand the invisible rules of conduct. In both cases, the production of domestic hospitality is dependent on a gendered division of emotional, interactional, and physical labor. I wondered whether the doing and performing of gender changes when the person doing the food work is not a woman and not white.

Pretend That We're Rich

Perry is a thirty-year-old African American professional. Two years ago before our original interview, he moved to the northeast to take a job teaching at a private school. Perry loves to cook and more importantly, he loves to have dinner parties. He explained why he decided to hold his first formal event and how that led to a more recent dinner party:

> It was in Baton Rouge, a bon voyage party for another friend who had just gotten a job in New York. So I decided it would be a great idea for us to all pretend that we were rich and had money and stuff . . . and so we made it this big performance and I would send out invitations, which I did, formal invitations. . . . The invitation included a menu of what would be served. That was a four-course meal, actually five if you include the hors d'oeuvres . . . and appetizers, soup, salad, the main course, and dessert. And I knew that I wanted to cook the food myself but have other people serve it. And I did the same thing for my birthday when I moved up here.

More than anyone else I spoke to, Perry explicitly tried to create a dinner party that held to the standards of Emily Post and the Park Avenue hostess. Of all the descriptions of people's socializing with friends over food, his story of his birthday party dinner comes closest to a traditional model. Perry even hired servers who were, in Emily Post's language, "competent and suited to his needs." However, his parties have more guests and more alcohol than a traditionally formal dinner party. It's also unusual for someone to host and cook for their own birthday, a time when they would ordinarily be the guest of honor at a sociable occasion, free of responsibilities. But Perry claims that labor as part of the pleasure, in fact, asserting it as a performance of self where he garners honor and attention for his cooking. He insists that guests not contribute anything (except presents) so that the performance is more exclusively focused on him. In his description of what he wanted to do, Perry clearly references a discourse about dinner parties as staged events that evoke a wealthy lifestyle. His narrative paints a picture of what such a performance should look like.

> *So tell me about planning all this . . .*
> I started planning, I knew I was gonna do it in December so I started planning [then]. I got the menu and everything together and sent out the invitations by the first week of the month and they had to RSVP by the week before. So, and it really started getting really expensive because I sent out like 25 invitations assuming that, you know, maybe 15—and 16 decided to come. Which meant I had to go out and buy more dinner plates.
> But you know, to be honest, I had enough plates, but they didn't all match. So I had to have matching plates *(both laughing)*. So, I went out and bought—

So did people bring things? Offer food or wine?
They knew that, you know, just bring the birthday presents *(both laughing)*.
Just to come, because lots of people said, "Oh, can we help you?" But I didn't
want any help. I really wanted to do this.

Was it also the same kind of formal [as the bon voyage party]?
Formal, in terms of dress, but also formal in terms of the menu. I got all these
international cookbooks to try and find things that I couldn't pronounce. So
that it would look fancy, like "Potage d'Oignon"—like, French Onion Soup. And
Mai Tai Compote, um, which is really, you know, fruit marinated in some liquor.

Perry explicitly tied the construction of formal occasion to the kind of food
and menu offered. He references textual discourses, but his menu also "plays"
on the seriousness of formal cuisine. Rather than rely on Post or Stewart's
menus of "white food," Perry artfully parodies French cuisine, while at the
same time constructing a menu that suits the tastes of his guests.

So you just picked them out . . . based partly on names [of dishes]?
Yeah, based partly on names, but things that I thought would go together and it
turned out to be more of a French meal . . . because we had "Carrots Provençale,"
and the "Potage d'Oignon"—French Onion Soup. And it was, like, overdosed
with cognac. So, everybody was kind of giddy . . . um, and . . . something (I can't
remember what I called it), Herb Stuffed Chicken Breast. And um, we had, oh,
for the appetizers we had—it was called "Mushroom Duchelle" *(laughing)* which
was—oh, it was "Mushroom Crepe Duchelle"—and um, what I did was I made
these crepes, and uh, stuffed them with this kind of mushroom stuffing and
they were tied—oh, and the name's coming back to me now. It was "Mushroom
Purses," um, "Crepe Purses Mushroom Duchelle." Yeah and so, it was a crepe
with this mushroom stuffing tied in, like, a purse with, uh, the top of a scallion.
And then, yeah, a salad. I think . . . it was a mixed greens—baby greens. I also
bought little—because I know that everyone doesn't like the dressing on the
salad—I bought these little containers where you have your dressing come out
of little separate dishes. I had about seven different kinds of dressing. And then
for dessert, you had your choice of—

You gave people a choice . . . ? (laughing)
There were four choices: Lemon Sorbet, but the sorbet, but I made the sorbet
and then scooped out the interior of a lemon and put it inside of that and froze
it in that. *(laughing)* and um, Cappuccino Mousse, which was a bitch to make.
And White Chocolate Cheesecake with Raspberry, um, Sauce. And maybe it
was only three. Maybe it was only three desserts. Yeah and lots of wine.

The formality of the event is concretely constructed through Perry's use of
invitations, his setting of a matched and attractive table, and his creation of
a menu that references French cuisine. The advance planning and attention
to detail acts as a code for guests about the expectation of formality.

Furthermore, Perry chose to cook foods that illustrate a specialized knowledge of cooking. He "plays" on ideas about haute cuisine and authenticity. For example, other people I talked to were interested in re-creating "authentic dishes and menus" from cultures other than their own, approaching this pursuit of authenticity with serious study.[8] Through his knowledge of cooking techniques, Perry demonstrated that he is, in fact, a "serious" cook, but his food and the construction of this event are both more playful. For example, although some of the foods were simple to make, they were given fancier names, like "Carrots Provençale." His complaint about making the Cappuccino Mousse illustrates how some menu items required careful and extensive effort to create. A number of the dishes demanded some previous experience with particular cooking techniques, like making crepes. Finally, the written invitations and seating arrangements, the staging of courses, and the abundance of foods (three desserts and seven salad dressings) created an atmosphere of formality, luxury, and indulgence.

Even as a parody, the event depends on Perry's effort. In order for him to construct the kind of dinner party he desires, he does a large amount of invisible work in the back stage prior to the party itself. In the narrative that follows, Perry describes the work of organizing and "pulling off" such a performance, coordinating both his own work and that of his hired help.

So when did you start buying the stuff and doing the cooking?
Um, I started doing the cooking the day before. And the sorbet, and the mousse the day before. And the other things I made the day of. And actually what I did, I set up, I had three servers who were students and I set some things up so that they could just, it would be done, they would just put it in the oven. And then serve it hot, because I didn't want it to sit for a long time. And so sometimes, I would leave the table and go in the kitchen and see how things were going

And the chicken, you know, I gave them instructions about when they should put the chicken in, because I was expecting guests at seven-thirty, so I said that since this is such a long meal we probably won't be ready for the chicken until around 9-ish. So don't put it in until about eight-thirty, so that it doesn't get dried out. And so I kind of gave the students instructions and I had to come back. And one thing that happened that really threw me off was—I make place settings, too, so you have your name and where to sit, where I want people to sit because some people don't like each other (*both laughing*). It's true and so some of us I don't want to sit next to- next to whomever so I forget, oh, I didn't make the place-, the nameplates and so I was trying to do that and it was just a nightmare. But I got them made and I arrived around eight o'clock.

Everybody was there except for me. So, I arrived late and people were milling around talking, and eating the Mai Tai Compote.

And drinking, and then we all sat down.

So, everyone sat down and the servers came out and with, um, to take wine requests and I had red, white, and blush wine. And after that the appetizers came and they would clear things and then the next would come.

As host, Perry had to prepare in advance for his guests' needs, both by providing a variety of foods that they would all like and by making sure they were seated in an order acceptable to everyone. In this case, the staging of such an event, the host works to create a congenial atmosphere both by providing an out-of-the-ordinary meal, but also by arranging the setting so that all social interactions go smoothly. The mental labor of whom to invite, what to feed them, and how to make sure they get along, are requisite elements of hosting. Because Perry wants to show off his culinary skills but lacks a partner to assist, it's his responsibility to carry off all the cooking and the socializing:

It was kind of a co-birthday party because Dan's birthday was same day. So, I was at one end of the table and he was at the other end. And, it was kind of difficult positioning people because it was like, well, she doesn't want to sit next to him, but if I do that, that means she'll be across from somebody else she doesn't like so it was kind of like, ooo-ooh. Um, but it all worked out in the end because there was a couple people there other people didn't know so that worked out.

So, everybody had a good time?
Yeah, everybody had a good time, everyone got drunk (*both laugh*).

The repeated appearance of alcohol as a social lubricant for intimacy suggests that Perry's party was, in the end, less formal than parties given by the Park Avenue hostess or Marion. At the same time, Perry's party is, in many ways, the fulfillment of what Emily Post dictates, complete with congenial guests, an amiable host, excellent food, and helpful servers. In its format, Perry's birthday dinner follows a hegemonic discourse about the appropriate staging of a dinner party. But in a profound way it also subverts a historical image of this kind of socializing. It is, after all, a parody, and the guests are participants in this performance. Perry ties their sociability to the amount of alcohol consumed, the drinks creating an intimacy that most formal dinner parties eschew. Furthermore, the quintessential host and cook, is, after all, a woman, and most likely, a white woman. Perry is an African American male. The dinner party is also a kind of commensality and socializing that is traditionally the province of married upper-middle-class couples. Although Perry is an upwardly mobile professional, he is single and he is gay. It's not clear if any one piece of Perry's social location contributes to his construction of these events both as important to his social life and as something to be parodied. I suspect that economic circumstances might weigh slightly more heavily than other factors. Perry's current situation as someone on the fringes of upper-middle-class circles, whose resources are more cultural and social, encourages him to convert those resources in his social relationships. Being gay and single means, perhaps, that such forms of sociability traditionally exclude him. Edward and Ben, an upper-middle-class gay couple that I interviewed, centered their social life around cocktail parties, eating in restaurants and, most routinely, formal dinner parties without the sense of parody or ironic distance that Perry creates. Among the gay and lesbian families Carrington (1999) interviewed, people with more economic resources and greater job and time flexibility engaged in more formal entertaining.

Perry's story prompts me to ask questions about the continued existence of the dinner party as a form of sociability, a way that contemporary Americans continue to use in constructing their friendships. It appears that some people with economic and educational capital still rely on this model when creating a certain kind of social atmosphere. Specifically, they are enacting a performance about social class and the experience of status. Given the persistence of social inequality in America it is not surprising that social practices reflect, reinforce, and continually construct symbolic boundaries. One result of mass culture and globalization is the widespread availability of (symbolically valuable) goods. But perhaps precisely because of these trends, people with economic and cultural means continue to use social practices in their homes as a way of distinguishing themselves from others and constructing social relationships based on class-coded knowledge and preferences. Alan Warde (1997) surmises that for some people in middle and professional socioeconomic circumstances, "Food is a figure of distinction . . . class distinction and cultural capital have to be actively displayed and deployed on occasion. Mannered behavior, facility in conversation with aesthetic judgements about food and drink, an appreciation of fashion in cuisine and a respect for formal eating are characteristic of the professional fraction. Class-based style survives" (186).

While Perry and his friends may not have the economic means to live in a Park Avenue apartment and have a dining room that seats twenty, staging a dinner party allows them to "pretend that we're rich" for a short period of time. But in other ways, his construction of these kinds of events is more complex than a straightforward class performance. What, in the staging of dinner parties, has shifted so that the requisite gender, class, and race performances connected with them change enough, and thus an African American gay man can claim this form as part of his social life? What remains the same? How flexible is this social form and how is its enactment reflective of social conditions?

One possibility could be that, in emulating "the rich," Perry is performing a burlesque or ironic parody of an upper-class dinner party. There are elements in which he is attempting to enact the cultural template—in particular by cooking a meal with ordered courses, setting a formal table, and expecting guests not to contribute other than gracious conversation (and birthday gifts). In other ways, he is satirizing those requirements—for example, by inventing elaborate names for the foods, hiring students as servers, and most importantly, by being the one to cook the meal. The guests, all of whom he described as friends with whom he socialized under other kinds of circumstances, all understood that this was not Perry's "normal" style of life. Celebrating a birthday also lifted the dinner party out of the realm of other events and comparable dinner parties, since it was a specifically festive occasion where attention is intentionally focused more on Perry than on anyone else.

Perry is not rich—but he takes advantage of the various resources available to him in order to construct an event that allows him and his friends to experience class shifting in a temporary way. One distinction between the wealthy and everyone else was, at one point, signified by their ownership of homes, goods, and furnishings that could not be purchased by the less wealthy. Quality as well as quantity distinguished this: For example, in her fiction Edith Wharton illustrated the standing of various New York society families by describing the make and number of different china dinner services they had. In contrast, today, "designer" goods are available inexpensively at department stores. Indeed, Martha Stewart is known for marketing entire lines of home goods that are inexpensive but supposedly mirror luxury and antique lines. The existence of high-quality mass-manufactured goods means that Perry can afford to "run out and buy some extra matching plates" that serve as (perhaps not equal but) comparably adequate goods. He also uses his contacts in the well-funded private school where he works to make use of a house with a large kitchen and dining area so he can host a large dinner party "in style"—which would not be possible in his small teacher's apartment. Just like people who save up and go to high-end restaurants for special occasions, Perry can temporarily buy in to an upper-class standard of living. It is both a fulfillment of an experience and a subversion of it.

In this case, Perry is intentional in his subversion of gender, race, and class expectations around men, cooking, and hosting. At the same time, Perry clearly gains more attention for his performance of self than Marion or even Joanne. He asserts a fair amount of control over the format, food, and interactions, creating an event that is almost entirely designed to fulfill his vision and meet his needs. One reason this is possible is that Perry is not negotiating his sociability with a partner and he is doing all the work. However, we can also see the ability to control the form of the event as a result of gender performance. When men cook, they experience a greater degree of flexibility in their effort and they gain more attention for their work. I interviewed a number of men for whom engaging in such activities was a reinforcement of such performances rather than a shifting of them.

Gender on Display: Men and Cooking as Performance

> Cookery is become an art, a noble science; cooks are gentlemen.
> —Robert Burton

> Men cook more and we all know why. It is the only interesting household task. Getting down and scrubbing the floor is done by women or by the women they've hired.
> —Nora Ephron

One reason for shifts in domestic hospitality is that these events are built on different kinds of interactional work than those in the past so that the role requirements are less rigid than the classic host/guest distinction. These shifts are linked to economic and social changes in men's and women's lives. Virginia Olesen (1993) suggests,

> In some homes, boundaries between cooking and interacting have shifted so that both wife and husband now produce hospitality, for example, husbands doing special cooking—for example barbecues—or manage interaction when the wife is in the kitchen. . . . The form of domestic hospitality, host/hostess with clear responsibilities for management of the occasion and guest(s) as those for whom the occasion is produced, still occurs, but unilateral responsibility for the occasion has weakened to alter this "traditional" American form. (190)

Although Olesen may be correct about changes in form, it is unclear whether this also represents a shift in the requisite performance of gender.

Dina and Gerry are upper-middle-class professionals who have been married for fifteen years. They are white and did not describe themselves as "ethnic" in any way. Gerry is a medical specialist who works long hours and travels frequently. Dina has a master's degree in education and does the majority of the household labor and childcare. They both work full time. When I met them, Dina was also going to graduate school and their three children were in elementary and middle school. They live in a college town in a large renovated old house with a landscaped yard and pool. Dina and Gerry like to have dinner parties about every three weeks, usually for six to eight people, often other couples who are similar to them—people in their forties, with school-age children, who are white college-educated professionals. Dinner party invitations are generally reciprocal among these friends. I interviewed two of the couples they socialize with—Larry and Rita and Amy and Evan.

Larry and Gerry met at a medical conference and discovered they both love to cook. Amy used to work in the medical office where Gerry practices and became friends with Dina when they both became interested in renovating their homes. All three couples spoke about choosing friends who "enjoyed cooking," and they structured their social lives to center around sharing good food with friends in their homes on the weekends. Although all of them spoke about eating in restaurants, they preferred get-togethers where someone cooked a meal. The dinner parties given by Dina and Gerry and by their friends Amy and Evan shift our ideas about domestic hospitality in one important way: both Gerry and Evan are the main cooks.[9]

Gerry and Dina's house has a large dining room that extends into an enclosed porch. There is a wide hall between the dining area and the kitchen, which is large enough for people to stand at a counter or sit nearby. They both described setting a fancy table "even when we invite people with kids" and talked about the preparatory work they do to stage a formal yet comfortable evening for friends.

Gerry picks a weekend where he'd like to cook: he is in charge of the menu and the ingredients, but he delegates much of the planning and organizing, including whom to invite, to Dina. In heterosexual couples women are often the ones who actively create and maintain the shared friends. Gerry relies on his wife's social networks to provide the companions for their dinner parties. His purpose is to expand his social horizons. He said, "doctors are pretty boring. But unfortunately for myself, I don't know a large group of people in the arts or dance. . . . I'd very much like to. It's just that in spite of meeting many people every day, you know, as patients, I usually don't socialize with them. A lot of the people my wife knows become good acquaintances of mine."

Although Gerry wants to use his "free time" to construct close social relationship, he also sets limits on who those people can be. Dina, who is responsible for constructing their social network, cultivates friends with the kinds of people Gerry might like to get to know. She also keeps track of who they've had over, which friends get along, or who might be best suited for the type of party they want to have. In effect, Dina accounts for both their needs as a couple and for the interests and concerns of her potential guests. She establishes the conditions for sociability and, in choosing people according to Gerry's interest, also limits the kinds of intimacy that can occur in these occasions. For example, she described her thinking about why and when they invite people over:

> Well, winter is an especially lonely time for everyone. We're pretty isolated. So
> I think we tend to make more of an effort, but don't necessarily entertain more.
> But we make more of an effort to try and get people together and often times

there's either a sick child . . . or it snows or something. So it seems like there is an effort but we try. . . . I know we use it (dinner parties) as a way to draw people into our lives. It's stimulating and you meet some wonderful people. It's selfish, you know?

Dina obviously does a fair amount of mental work in creating their social networks. Some of this is revealed in the way Dina describes her choices of friends. The people they have over must share their appreciation for a certain kind of event, one that centers on the staging of an elaborate meal. Dina has cultivated a network of "people who like to cook" from neighbors, acquaintances who do artisanal woodwork, people whose artwork she admired, or parents of her children's friends. In one example, she described the details that led to one choice, "I remember walking into her kitchen to pick up her son and the smell of an apple pie. And it was noteworthy that whenever she baked something, you kind of remembered it . . . so we thought they'd be fun to add to this group of friends."

Although Dina asserts, "These are nice people. They're comfortable," her criteria for selecting them among other potential friends is based on things they can do, specifically cook. In other words, it is not a revelation of self, a shared intimacy that creates the sociable bond, but rather potential similar interests. Such relationships are more superficial and perhaps more interchangeable than those built on affective ties.

Like many middle-class professional couples, Dina and Gerry don't rely on kin for sociability, partly because they live some distance from any relatives. They also don't have a built-in occupational network of friends, so Dina is obliged to cultivate their social relationships. DeVault (1991) suggests, "Social meals for professionals are usually meals with other couples outside the family group. In these situations, people cannot rely on family traditions; instead they must search for common interests, often topics of conversation associated with shared experiences of travel, cultural pursuits, training for professional positions and so on. . . . In this context, food itself can be used as a tool to promote sociability" (209).

Because Dina acts as the kin-keeper, Gerry is not concerned about the nature of sociability at these events. He emphasizes material circumstances when describing the decision-making process of whom to invite. In particular he focuses on how many people they can accommodate with food and seating:

It's usually not too much more difficult cooking for four than for six. Once you go above six, one starts to have problems because of the economics of skill. For example, I'm still lacking an eight-quart casserole pot. . . . If you're going to make a chicken casserole: a chicken for eight is usually a large roaster of five pounds and those things don't fit in a small pot. . . . I've done dinners for up to twelve and then you really have to start modifying what you make, based on what resources you have. . . . [T]here are many dishes where it's just as easy to—there's a favorite dish of mine which is scallop and corn potstickers. You know, these little dumplings—and it's easy enough to make twenty as it is to make thirty. . . . But again, you know, there are the simplest things, like we have china for eight. When we start to get more, people have to use odd sets . . . so kind of ridiculous things like that enter into the size of the party. We have a table that's big enough for ten. Twelve is a squeeze.

For Gerry, pragmatic concerns about his cooking abilities and the availability of appropriate tools determine the size and makeup of the party. Although he says this is "ridiculous," he downplays the skill of cooking and emphasizes his lack of a big pot, a big table, and matching china. Ironically, although he claims the food is the driving force behind the party, the "surface" elements of form dictate the size and formality of his events. If the occasion involved family or some other group with greater expectations of intimacy, the form would be secondary to the interactional content of the occasion. This is not to say that the food is unimportant. This is how he plans the party:

The next thing is the menu and I may spend a day or two looking through cookbooks [or] *Gourmet* magazine. . . . So I might come up with some sort of antipasti or appetizer. Those potstickers I mentioned or maybe I'll just make some fresh guacamole and chips or some salsa . . . like the yellow tomatillo or something that's fairly easy to make and you can put in the fridge and do that. So, then some salad and then an entrée which can be crabcakes or something off the grill, fish. . . . And then I don't generally make bread and I usually don't make desserts. Mostly because I don't have the time. . . . [I]f I made dessert, it would always be chocolate . . . [but] we're supposed to be healthy now.

Like Perry and Joanne, Gerry references cookbooks, magazines, and nutritional guidelines as the source of his food knowledge. His rejection of dessert as unhealthy may come from his status as a doctor. For upper-middle-class people, these texts serve as a shared code about appropriate foods, manners of cooking, and ways of thinking about eating.

Dina and Gerry have a clear division of tasks regarding social events with friends. They both conceptualize Gerry's weekend cooking as his "release" or hobby. Dina said, "Gerry likes to cook out of magazines because he likes to experiment on people. . . . [T]he goal for Gerry is he has the day off and this is what he wants to do with his day off."

Although Gerry controls the decisions about the menu, the appearance of the table, and other aspects of the atmosphere, it is almost always Dina who invites people, plans, shops, arranges flowers, and makes sure the setting is appropriate to his intentions. When Gerry has the time and considers it part of the fun, he will do the food shopping himself. But more often Dina does these additional chores along with her regular weekly routines. She spoke at length about helping Gerry by going to three different supermarkets "to find the right kind of crabmeat or whatever." She explains,

> Oh, and it's a pain in the butt, too. He'll say "This week scan the markets for crab." . . . And if you call them ahead of time and say "I'll need . . .," then they'll hold it for you. . . . Well, I was at Whole Foods (an organic grocery store) and crab is sixteen dollars a pound, cracked, and I called him and said, "Do you want me to pick this up?" and he said, "Well, I want to go to the local fish market and see how fresh it is." So he kind of left me to scout around, but he went and got it that day. . . . So he does plan ahead. . . . If Gerry is in charge . . . [for this past dinner, for example], I bought all the groceries . . . and he prepared them all day . . . as a matter of fact, he left a list of ingredients. And exact. I mean, he's the chemist. Three and a quarter pounds. So, of course there I am.
>
> And then in the morning of that day I'll usually set this room up for dinner. I'll put the leaves in, make sure the floors kind of clean. . . . Gerry likes to set the table formal so we usually have like an Italian cloth and pressed napkins. I don't do the linen. He'll do the linen. He'll actually iron. . . . He'll buy flowers. And I'll set the table. I think he likes us to use way too many plates.

Although Dina complains a bit, both she and Gerry describe this division of labor as logical; the demands of his job mean that he lacks time during the week to prepare. Furthermore, since the cooking is his "hobby," it's also seen as deserved leisure time, something fun to do.

In Gerry and Dina's descriptions, there's an interesting tension between work and leisure: on the one hand, cooking elaborate meals and having them ready to serve at the appropriate moment is a complex task. On the other hand, it's Gerry's way of "relaxing." Dina clearly enjoys this way of socializing with her friends—but she also works to create the event and to make it possible for Gerry to experience it in the way he desires. This arrangement, which privileges Gerry's right to leisure, seems reasonable because of the way they assign priority to his financially dominant career. Considering the relative resources he brings to the marriage, he is seen as deserving more of a break, whereas Dina's invisible work is expected and incorporated into her weekly routine. This is reflected in their day-to-day routines, where, although Dina claims that "he's very equitable" so that whoever is home first cooks dinner for the family, she also admits that she does the majority of this work. She went on to say, "If I teach Tuesday nights, he's in charge of food . . . often that's pizza. No, he doesn't necessarily cook for the boys. . . . If I'm working, we'll take in something." Dina and Gerry's situation is supported by ideologies that intersect over class- and gender-based privileges in heterosexual marriage. Karen Pyke (1996) asserts that particularly for high-status men, "its very invisibleness makes the embeddedness of masculine privilege in institutional life become less vulnerable" (530). At the same time, Gerry's choices, while supported, are not uncontested by Dina. Gerry defensively comments about his weekends:

> So I'll be gone shopping and then I'm tearing around the kitchen. And I'm not available to do the things Dina wants me to do, which is, I don't know what . . . take care of the kids—which I do a fair amount of—and obviously things like more recently, we couldn't do any extensive cooking because of basketball. It took up every weekend. Both kids were involved so I wanted to try to be there. But when it does allow, [cooking] pretty much takes up a day. . . . [I make] too many different things. She's always telling me not to make all of these. Because she doesn't want to have to deal with the dishes. Well, I actually do the dishes too.

Gerry and Dina see dinner parties as a crucial way of constructing an interesting social life, of fostering friendships with people who they would not run across in their day-to-day routines, with whom, in fact, they are not "close." The particular way they choose to go about it, marking a dinner party as an out-of-the-ordinary event, reinforces certain gender and class inequities in both their lives and their social world. Gerry's desire to construct cooking as a performance and a stage for his culinary skills means that Dina has additional gender and family burdens. Pyke (1996) elaborates on the social conditions that support these individual accommodations:

> The ideological supremacy of the male career is piled on top of other more deeply seated patriarchal ideologies concerning the essential nature of gender differences. It provides a rationale for husbands' entitlements that obscures the underlying gendered power structure. The logic is this: because husbands are the main providers in their families, they ought to have certain privileges and rights that enable them to perform their duties. Such entitlements are ostensibly not due to their maleness but to their provider role. This ideology justifies husbands' privileges and rights and wives' concomitant obligations as structurally necessary and only incidentally gendered. It permits the reasoning that if the wife were performing this role, she too would be entitled to the same privileges. But because providing is an important way that men accomplish their gender within families, such as the doing of housework is for women. . . . I[I]t does not have the same meaning and accompanying entitlements when performed by women. (533)

Gerry and Dina and their friends have definitive ideas about what constitutes good food and appropriate dinner party menus. Dina talks about how they organized the party:

The goal was to make it portion-friendly instead of homestyle. So we had all our glasses on the table, and plates, and what we did was serve each dinner plate here in the kitchen and bring it in . . . [and] that worked really well. Because it was easy. The salad was easy to do ahead of time. . . . And then he could just serve the plates as soon as we were done with the salad. . . . It looked pretty, too, with that little Napoleon of vegetables, which was really clever. Have you seen it? It's on the cover of *Gourmet*. It's pretty and I think that's why he chose it, because it looked pretty and we wanted to try it out.

Dina makes it clear that this is a highly structured event. Not only is everyone seated and served, but the meals are "plated" for each one. In other words, guests do not even get to choose what they want from among the ordered menu. In a "homestyle" meal, food on platters is brought to the table by servers and can, in fact, be served to guests, but they have the option of choosing foods and amounts. Although it's not inherent to the format, the word "homestyle" evokes a degree of informality that Dina and Gerry avoid. That is, these guests are not being invited in as family, where people might be able to refuse certain foods without drawing attention to themselves. As a contrast, Dina uses the phrase "portion-friendly," to mask a degree of informality that Dina and Gerry avoid, which evokes a discourse of nutrition. Limiting the amount of food for guests is a way of acting as their external guide to appetite and restraint. Pre-plating the meals places the guests under a very severe set of obligations, since one is then forced to taste and acknowledge all the foods provided. In Dina and Gerry's construction, providing food this way gives them control over the act of *service*: it occurs in the kitchen, outside of the purview of guests, and doesn't involve standing and lingering over people as they choose foods.

Even given the constraints on intimacy that Gerry and Dina create, they are, after all, interested in constructing sociability. So, when I asked Dina why they held a particular dinner party, she said, "the goal was to talk, because these were people we hadn't seen in a long time . . . all these people were talking about islands. . . . We talked about politics a lot, too. Everyone chatted . . . you know, you didn't go to bed and go 'oh my god, wasn't she horrible!' Because we've done that, believe me."

Dina was very specific about what made for good conversation at parties and what didn't. Enjoyable conversations were about travel, house renovations, and shared food knowledge. Dina described a party that did not have a balance of sociable moments:

Oh, I think there was a dynamic going on that was difficult. And it certainly wasn't with the four of us because we are pretty much on the same wavelength. . . . I[I]t was uncomfortable. Parts of the conversation were not as easy going.

There wasn't as much fun. James had never met the other two couples and he, you know, started having this conversation with Brian about politics . . . all these side conversations, you know, there wasn't just one dominant.

It's clear that the dinner party is the right forum for Dina and Gerry's sociability because the formal setup allows for some control over the conversation.

Traditionally, dinner parties are entirely the work of the host and hostess (or their invisible hired help) but in contemporary American society, it seems that guests are often uncomfortable about not contributing. In fact, perhaps because people do not generally rely on hired paid help, guests feel the need to contribute, since the labor of the host and hostess is not as invisible as the labor of servants or caterers. For example, Gerry says "sometimes I'll say bring nothing, and people have a hard time dealing with that. So if they insist, I'll say, Well you can bring a bottle of wine because most of the people here are quite capable . . . dessert is the easiest thing." Notice, however, how Gerry's concerns are less about making guests feel comfortable in their contributions and more about making sure such contributions are compatible with his class-based standards for a good meal with appropriate wine. For example, the only exceptions to the "no contributions" rule that Dina and Gerry made were when the guest had a special culinary skill such as making "outstanding" homemade jam. The other exception was for a series of shared gourmet dinners they set up, where all of the other couples were chosen because they had professional experience with food, such as having taken cooking classes in Europe, owning a restaurant "with a good wine cellar," or bottling their own salad dressing.

Dina and Gerry are securely upper-middle-class in their income, their career prestige (particularly Gerry's), and their family background. Materially, they don't need to reassert their class membership, although in order to have similar friends, they must do so socially through such performances of cultural capital. But not all the people in their social circles are as economically or socially secure in their class membership. For these people, having dinner parties appears to be even more necessary for their continued participation in class-based social networks. People in their social group are not heterogeneous, but they are, in fact, chosen among others with similar characteristics.

Amy and Evan also have advanced educational degrees but at the time when I interviewed them, Evan was unemployed and struggling to find a new job in business administration. He spoke about his career worries and concern about having the income to keep their historic colonial home. Amy's work as a health care administrator provided their main income. Because their schedules are fairly flexible, Evan and Amy try to share the daily food preparation for their family of five. However, in their daily routines, Amy does the majority of planning and other invisible tasks. They have negotiated a division in their "special event" cooking. As Amy put it, "Evan usually does all the gourmet cooking and I do the Jewish cooking, Thanksgiving cooking, that sort of thing. Evan does the fancy stuff."

Like Dina and Gerry, they both spoke about loving to cook for friends. Before they had children they belonged to a "gourmet club," where members rotated meals at different people's homes. But Evan said,

> We stopped when the kids [were born] about five years ago. And we enjoyed the people but we really weren't . . . the food was not very good. So for a gourmet club, for the food not to be good. . . . The rest of the people were not gourmets. People looking for a night out. My mother says if it's got more than eight ingredients or three steps, she won't do it. And there were a fair number of people in the club who were that way. . . . We weren't that excited about the food. . . . And a lot of the times we'd rather eat [at] home than go out and not have good food. Because we can eat better at home.

Evan asserts that the social event is not entirely about intimacy—or perhaps, that such intimacy cannot occur unless the participants share ideas about "good food." Amy and Evan talked about Passover Seders and Thanksgiving dinners but their real enthusiasm was for dinner parties where Evan would demonstrate his cooking ability. He described how he likes to have people watch him cook in the kitchen and talk about what he's doing, mentioning that their friends have even suggested that he give cooking lessons. In line with many of the upper-middle-class men who cooked, he talked about acquiring specialized knowledge of cooking in the same way one acquires specialized knowledge as a professional. He emphasized his ability to adapt techniques and recipes to suit his creative needs. To explain his approach, he compares himself to other people and names jobs he's had that give authority to his experience:

> Oh, my mother was not a gourmet cook. In retrospect, she did a few dishes well that I enjoyed, but . . . I've cooked from a very early age. I don't exactly know why. [I] worked as a baker's apprentice, doing cooking, and the following year I worked as a cook and a restaurant manager. And I worked with chefs. And I became very interested in pushing the envelope. . . . One of the things that I have done, and Amy gets kind of upset with me at times like this, is there are certain things that she'll have a recipe and she'll ask me to do—and I tend, even if it's a fairly complicated recipe—to change it. Other people don't do this, but I've done enough so that . . . there's a lot of stuff that I throw everything in all at once. You'll come in and even if I've got two or three dishes that I'm making, you'll find glasses or plates that have everything all done, all the spices measured out. . . . Amy is also much more in the structured thing. . . . Whereas . . . I took

a lot of cooking classes and worked a lot of different places so that I'll walk in and see something [in the refrigerator] where she sees nothing. [It's also] my familiarity with a wide variety of recipes.

In the same way Joanne critiqued "food from boxes," Evan distances himself from the food of his family of origin and asserts the primacy of "expert" discourses of food. More than other people I interviewed, Amy and Evan distinguish themselves from others by the quality and the type of food they enjoy. For example, Amy said, "Most people don't like food as spicy as we do." By "most people" Amy is referencing their social universe of mostly Euro-American whites, who she presumes have no cultural referent for "spiciness." In fact, although Amy and Evan claim to have great interest and knowledge in various cuisines, their social circles do not include people who are racially or ethnically from any of the cultures they admire.

Evan's cooking skills and culinary knowledge serve as the focus of the couple's sociability, acting as the social conduit for shared class-based understandings of food as novelty and entertainment (DeVault, 1991, 211). Although Amy and Evan were less financially and professionally secure than many of their friends, the specific kind of knowledge of food and cooking they demonstrate at their parties acts as cultural capital that secures their membership in their class. As expertly unpacked by Bourdieu, "taste" is socially constructed and stratified. Access to "good taste" is limited most powerfully by cultural resources: "taste" is constructed as "natural" so that people do not often question the class-based criteria functioning to guide their preferences. People's expression of their cultural capital, the ways they display their knowledge or preferences, acts as a reinforcement of class distinction. Margaret Visser (1991) has said that, as a society, we are no longer interested in conspicuous consumption since western society is democratized enough so that elite cuisine is too widely available to serve as a marker of distinction. Rather, she suggests, people engage in "conspicuous competence," where the ability to cook complicated cuisines that are not of one's native ethnic or regional background is itself the most important demonstration of socioeconomic success. On this terrain, both class and gender combine, such that upper-middle-class men are the ones most likely to participate in this process.

Although they often used "we" in describing activities, it became clear through their descriptions of specific events that only Evan cooks when entertaining friends. He said, "I like to have friends watch me cook. But I'm not terribly tolerant of Amy in the kitchen. Amy tends to get in my way; other people I put up with. I tend to tolerate other people. . . . It depends on who they are."

His statement positions cooking as a desirable activity, such that their shared acknowledgment of his skills provides him with justification for dominance and control over that activity when he chooses it. As DeVault (1991) and others have pointed out, even when men do a share of household labor, they exercise greater flexibility and choice in where and when they do so, generally without the guilt or "morally charged ideal of deferential service that appears in so many women's reports" (149). Furthermore, Evan implicitly invokes the notion of cooking for friends as performance, and in particular a performance he does not wish to share with his spouse.

As a gendered experience, it's interesting to compare Evan and Joanne's construction of their experience and their role in creating dinner parties. They both speak about cooking as a skill, and about opening up the kitchen for guests to watch them cook. Joanne, though, presents it as something related to the desires of guests and their ideas about comfort: "People want to be where you are . . . because they have such a comfort feeling." For Evan, people are in the kitchen to watch him perform and admire his skills: "One of the things that people tend to be amazed at here is that they can come in and everything's all set and things are not cooked, but I can get in there and pull out two entrées . . . and have it all come out boom, boom, boom."

There is a subtle but significant different in their language. Although Joanne talks about Ron being "intimidated" by her cooking skills ("so he never goes in the kitchen"), the semantic emphasis is on his choice rather than her needs. In comparison, Evan comments that "Amy gets in my way." Both Joanne and Evan share the class-based experience of doing these parties as an acquired skill, something that allows them to construct a social class solidarity through marriage and friendship. However, Joanne's work is also an expected performance based on gender. She learned to cook in order to create healthy food for her children and friends. Her goal, at a party, is "to create healthy and beautiful meals for people," which one could interpret as a form of caring work. Evan, on the other hand, speaks competitively about the cultural capital he has acquired and can demonstrate to others. It was striking how little of our conversation focused on caring for guests or the construction of friendship, except when he resorted to citing textual information about commercial hospitality.[10]

Like many couples, there were some discrepancies in the way Amy and Evan talked about the division of other tasks besides the highly regarded act of actually cooking. Amy said, "Either one of us will go shopping. It doesn't matter. I used to do most of the shopping. I enjoy grocery shopping. Evan sometimes does it, not that often." Immediately Evan chimed in, "Whoever is doing the main part of the cooking usually ends up doing the shopping." At the same time, Evan acknowledged that Amy's ability to keep track of a "mental list" of what he needed and do a large share of the prep work allowed him the freedom to cook more spontaneously.

Like Dina, Amy did a lot more of the invisible, less glamorous food work that made her husband's performances possible. Amy was also responsible for activities that could be labeled "caring work." One example of this effort is the way she used the dinner parties as socialization for her children. She described how guests often comment on her kids' manners at table. The family is a key site where class-based cultural capital gets conveyed to children, often by the women who are responsible for their socialization. Training her children to use plate liners ensured their ability to function in social settings that demand upper-middle-class attention to details of formal etiquette. Since Amy and Evan are less economically and socially secure than many of their friends, it's extremely important for them to instill appropriate upper-middle-class cultural capital to their kids so they can achieve upward mobility. Amy's efforts on behalf of her children constitute status work, born out of what Barbara Ehrenreich (2001) calls "fear of falling."

Amy's responsibility for the invisible labor meant that she exercised some control over the format of their parties. For example, she explained that it was her recent decision that they use paper plates when entertaining because "we don't have a dishwasher." In Amy's estimation, there is a balance between the construction of the appropriate setting and the amount of work she must take on. Expensive, coordinated paper plates are a compromise, but one that allows her to cut back on the unpleasant labor while maintaining her aesthetic standards. Because she does the dishes, this is her decision. The importance of informality and comfort permeated Amy's descriptions of what makes for an appropriate event with friends. At the same time, there were limits to what constituted "informal." For example, other than the Passover seder, where family and guests insisted on contributing, events were never modified to buffets or potlucks. Dina and Gerry and Amy and Evan were among the few people I interviewed who did not create other kinds of sociable occasions. Even their barbecues were formal sit-down meals. As if to compensate for the paper plates, Amy talked about the various ways she tries to make the house beautiful when guests are coming over. In one breath Amy said, "I want people to be comfortable" and yet she went on to speak at length about setting a formal table because "it's a matter of presentation." Within the common discourse of "comfort" as sociability, these more formal settings are styles, the "visible signs that constitute class as an everyday phenomenon" (DeVault, 1991, 207). Built into these arrangements are rules for what is to be served, how, and with what effort. In this couple, Amy does the majority of the work, negotiating between class-based expectations and the limits of their resources.

Performing Class and Gender

Dinner parties in these contemporary households are certainly less formal than the ideal image. Who cooks and serves has also changed, so men are more likely to be involved, most often as cooks or helpers in the production of food. Still, the dinner party remains a stage particularly for the performance of class and status distinctions. One shift is that men as cooks are engaging in a different performance of gender than we traditionally associate with hosting guests. In these narratives, as women do gender by cooking for their families, men do gender by cooking for friends. These differences invoke a gendered construction of cooking as an activity which, when done by men is high-status, often paid, and publicly acclaimed. It is the traditionally male terrain of professionally trained chefs with technical knowledge of "other" cuisines that require a complex discourse of cooking skills and information about ingredients. This stands in direct contrast with the daily cooking in the domestic sphere associated with women either as wives and mothers or hired domestic help, which is a taken-for-granted normative activity that is presented as an extension of women's caring work of constructing family life. The dinner party acts as an appropriate, indeed perfect, stage for men's gender performances as skilled cooks, engaged in an activity coded as more complex and special than preparing the daily meal. The key to the dinner party as stage is the presence of guests as observers.

In describing what they liked about cooking for friends, many men specifically described their activities in terms of a performance. Perry said, "I like to have an audience." Gerry said he began cooking out of necessity as a teenager in a single-parent home, but notes that his shift in interest in cooking came in his forties, "since I had a bigger audience—meaning Dina and the kids—but it's also about having more money, having more time." Conceptualizing cooking as gender performance also explains the varying comfort levels people had with having guests watch them cook. Although he and Amy carefully prepare and arrange ingredients ahead, Evan wants people to see him actually cooking. Gerry works to get everything on the table before guests arrive, preferring to have people see his performance through the setting and finished product. In talking about why they cook dishes that don't require a long stint in the kitchen, Larry described an unpleasant experience at a friend's dinner party, "when you get there, he's working furiously getting stuff done and it's clear that he can't even engage in much conversation until it's all on the table."

Cooking as gender performance varies but still cuts through lines of race and sexuality. In our conversation, I asked Perry for his reaction to the stereotype that "lesbians do potlucks, gay men do a whole dinner or brunch by themselves." He laughed and said, "It's true. And I think it's about having the attention focused on you. I mean I really do." Although the stereotype plays on both sexuality and gender, the experiences of upper-middle-class heterosexual men echoed his sentiments about being in the limelight. For example, in response to a question about whether people dress formally for their dinner parties, Dina said, "[Last time] Amy had on like evening pants. So she looked kind of neat. But she knows when Gerry cooks, it's kind of a real big deal so she really celebrated for him, you know?"

This description draws upon traditional notions of guests demonstrating their appreciation of the host's hospitality. It also invokes a gender ideology, which suggests that women do gender by making their appearance pleasing to men. Amy dressing up is seen as an appropriate accolade for Gerry's efforts:

> At an event where the food is served, where one person is responsible for the production of the event, where his or her performance as a cook is being highlighted in some way, the presentation of the food becomes an important matter: how it looks, when and how it gets served. As such, many of the men who cooked dinner parties spoke of a certain amount of conflict or stress around getting the meal organized and produced at the right time. The dinner party is a performance that depends on timing. For example, when asked what he liked least about cooking for others, Perry said, "I hate to be rushed. I hate to be still, like, in the middle of doing something and the people are here. And it's like, I know, I hate waiting for stuff. And sometimes I do underestimate how long it's going to take to cook something and that can be really nerve-wracking."

Some men complained that they have to adapt their menus to their guests who are always late, suggesting that this compromises their experience of the event. The men pinpointed this as a crucial area. Marion and Joanne and the other women who handled dinner parties made very little mention of these kinds of problems. Gerry said, "My ideal time is to have everything prepared in advance so I don't have to cook while my friends are over. That I think is a necessity but it's the worst part of cooking for friends . . . knowing you have to cook while friends are there."

In my interviews, I found that regardless of race or class, when women cook for family and friends, they are still doing what is normatively expected. For men, it is special, a choice rather than a requirement and men who choose to do so are celebrated.

Women do in fact, get social attention for hosting and cooking. There are gender differences in the performance of self that occurs while cooking for others. Paula, a thirty-year-old married musician, described dinner parties with two other couples with whom they rotated dinner parties. The cooking became competitive among the women. Paula said, "I felt like we tried to outdo each other in how fancy we would get and I did basically all the cooking for those things. . . . It was my idea. . . . About every two weeks we'd have somebody over. . . . There was kind of a rule—you could bring wine . . . something that can't infringe on someone else's display here, you know? I would do Pad Thai or Mu Shu Pork. . . . It couldn't be something simple like spaghetti, it had to be something really fancy like pork buns."

Insecure about her role in her marriage, Paula learned to cook elaborate meals from a variety of cuisines and organized a social life in contrast to her husband's informal barbecues for his musician friends. However, the reciprocal dinner parties only lasted for only a few years because Paula found she could not sustain the effort. She complained about being tired of the competitiveness and the need to acknowledge each other. This is highlighted for her especially when the effort was not shared by her partner or, as she started to feel, adequately reciprocated by the friends. She described a turning point when they invited one of the couples over, and they forgot and didn't show up: "I never forgave them because I gave up two days and made Vietnamese duck or something." Although Paula enjoyed some of the attention she got for her skills, she was ultimately unwilling to sustain the gender performance in a situation without adequate recognition for her work.[11]

Similarly, Joanne articulated the way cooking proved that she's involved in "more than dirty diapers." However, her performance is seen more as an extension of her daily gender performance, part of the job of being female rather than something extraordinary. As DeVault clearly demonstrates, feeding work in itself is not inherently gendered, but in its contemporary configuration it does contribution to the construction of inequality. According to Warde (1997). "The association of care, love, family, and provision is intricate and inextricable, and serves largely to confirm the subordination of women in society more widely" (131). Furthermore, the performance of gender exists even in environments where both men and women are doing the same work. Elaine Hall (1993) examines restaurants with mixed-gender waitstaffs and finds that men and women are held accountable for different performances of table service based on gender ideologies of care and status. How people interpret caring as labor is a key aspect of both paid and unpaid food work.

Sociability and Caring Work

Although many of these men seemed concerned with maintaining kin and non-kin ties, in the descriptions of their activities and knowledge of people's needs and preferences, it became clear that women do more of the actual interactional work. Issues that women handled more frequently included negotiating the planning and actual menu in response to people's preferences, initiating friendships by inviting people over, and making sure guests got along with each other at the event.

Even though Evan's desire to cook motivated their parties, Amy often decided which friends to invite over. Her reasons for inviting certain people invoked knowledge of different people's ability to get along, their food preferences, their social likes and dislikes: "That's why I specifically called them up to invite them, because I remember a year ago she said she loves raspberries, and Evan makes a great raspberry dessert, so I called her up."

Although the dinner party is often part of marital commensality, it also serves to solidify friendship networks among people outside heterosexual unions. For gay men like Perry, Edward, and Ben, it becomes a way of creating kin. They were among the few men who spoke of making sure they invited guests who got along. People who stand outside the ideological expectations of normative households may need to be particularly aware of the active work it takes to construct alternative forms of family. Perry said, "I do look at my friends as family. Because I am the only person in my family that doesn't live in my hometown. . . . All my brothers and sisters live within ten minutes of my mother. And so, wherever I go, food is one way of bringing people together and creating a sense of family."

Perry distinguishes between blood ties and constructed ones, yet he sees them as equally important in his life. Although part of his need to create kin may be due to his experiences as a gay man, when describing his ideas about friendship, family, and hospitality, Perry focused more explicitly on growing up as a southern African American. Some research that focused on gay and lesbian families suggests that, for people of color, "notions of kinship were bound up with their own sense of racial or ethnic identity," which stood in contrast to notions of constructed kin (Weston, 1990, 36). However, Carrington's study (1995) found more specifically that for gays and lesbians of color, "all of those families who blur the distinctions between biological and chosen families possess baccalaureate degrees, work in professional careers, and earn higher incomes" (34). Perry fits this profile.

Although Perry spoke about accounting for people's food preferences, his tone conveyed humored annoyance rather than accommodation. The women I spoke to, both those who cooked and those whose partners were the main cook, tended to evaluate social events based on the quality of the conversation, whereas the men spoke of the food and how well the food itself went over. When asked what they like best about having friends over one couple responded simultaneously:

She said, "The people. Can I say that? Conversation."

He said, "I like to cook. I get to do a lot of things that I wouldn't normally do just for the two of us. . . . I often feel that I don't get enough time with the people that I'm too focused on the cooking. . . . The trade-off is: do you want good conversation or good food? For me, I think I'd rather have the good food in some respects."

The upper-middle-class men and women I spoke to describe differences in what they think is a successful occasion. For women, it was often that they got to see friends they liked or that the guests all got along. Although men often mentioned these things, they generally focused on whether the food was good or if the conversations about food were enjoyable. "Talking about food" is itself a way of creating bonds of class and gender.

Talking about Food

> I can only say in my defense that there is no snobbery as intense as food snobbery and I had lots of company.
> —Betty Fussell

> Eating takes a special talent. Some people are much better at it than others. In that way, it's like sex, as with sex, it's more fun with someone who really likes it. I can't imagine having a lasting friendship with anyone who is not interested in food.
> —Alan King

Cooking, sharing food, and talking about food figure prominently in the social lives of many Americans. Indeed, as King jokes, food is often a cultural marker of friendship in contemporary society. As Roger Abrahams (1984) comments, "Perhaps even more significant is how the enlarged repertory of cooking and eating has entered into the dimension of the civilizing process—the dimension of talking through and about the most important distinctions of civility. . . . One is overwhelmed by the sheer amount of discussion in Middle American culture of cooking, of different diets, of new restaurants and specialty stores that have opened and of the great meals one has eaten" (23).

Since the 1980s, it appears that the cultural conversation about food has only increased. In particular, talking about food is as ubiquitous to our culture as is talking about television. This talk is gender- and class-based.

While Amy focused on stories, descriptions of situated events as examples of their practices, Evan often digressed into more abstract and general principles of entertaining and cooking, such as what the French consider a good gift for a host or how to make cream-based dishes low-fat. This was interesting given that Amy came into the marriage with a fair amount of culinary knowledge from her ethnic-religious background as the daughter of Eastern European Jews, whereas Evan insistently situated what he knew about food in the world of commercial hospitality.

Men like Evan and Gerry often described their cooking using a technical, text-based discourse when talking about food preparation, tools, and techniques; referencing famous chefs and restaurants; and citing food magazines and specific cookbooks much more than women did. In comparison, although Joanne clearly had a lot of culinary skills, she mentioned magazines and other sources in an offhand way often explaining the culinary processes she used rather than relying on a technical term. Paula described making extremely labor-intensive complicated foods from a variety of ethnic and international cuisines and she pointed to her shelves of cookbooks, but she spoke about the skill of it in a kind of offhand manner, as if it was fun to be good at it; it didn't matter where—or from whom—she learned to do it. When I first encountered this "name dropping" while interviewing, I experienced it as a test of my legitimacy as a researcher talking about food. Eventually I began to see it as these men's assertion of *their* legitimacy as men, constructing a way of describing themselves that attempted to rescue their interests from the stigma or negative gender identity that would be associated with men doing food work in the domestic setting.

However, there were some differences among men. Some, like Evan and Gerry, shared the accumulation of culinary skill with women like Joanne, as a class-based learning, referenced ethnic and regional foodstuffs as knowledge gained, and often articulated a set of rules about what is appropriate, healthy, or trendy. This is, as Heldke describes in *Exotic Appetites*, often connected to a disavowal of a "boring" white culture, negating whatever regional or ethnic foods they might have had as children in favor of the exotic and new. In contrast, Perry's descriptions of cooking and the skills it takes are slightly different: he elaborated on specific recipes from magazines, describing mushroom appetizers in phyllo and Asian soups that he'd tried. But he talked about the difficult things he'd learned how to cook from his mother with the same kind of awe since "she doesn't use recipes anymore . . . and I still haven't mastered her Red Velvet cake." For Perry, the southern African American cuisine of his family is equivalent to the Thai and Italian foods he experiments with in cookbooks. He recognizes the cultural capital in each of them, particularly since serving southern food to his friends in the northeast constitutes a food discourse with which they're unfamiliar and which they value. Perry's approach to food was very similar to the one B. Smith asserted in her books and television programs.

Professional men often focused on people's ability to talk knowledgeably about cuisine as a hallmark of good conversation during the dinner party.

Conversation is a crucial aspect of a dinner party. In dinner parties, the group is responsible for talk that is more orchestrated simply because of the physical limitations of being seated together in, generally, a prearranged manner. Comparatively, in more informal gatherings, simultaneous conversations can occur: at a buffet, guests can sit with whomever they please, or avoid discussions by excusing themselves to get more food, or move about freely from one group to another. But the dinner party that starts in the kitchen and involves watching someone cook for others invokes a different physical and spatial performance of conversation, so people are freer to move about, but with an activity that serves as the focal point of discussion. In particular, watching someone cook highlights the food as an important centerpiece to conversation. In events that I observed among upper-middle-class people, a portion of the conversations tended to be about demonstrating culinary mastery and knowledge and comparing resources such as where to get certain hard-to-find ingredients or important cookbooks and restaurants.

Talk functions to secure friendships, particularly along class lines. Respondents talked about the difficulty in constructing friendships from their workplaces, for various reasons—and this seemed to occur regardless of social class. As Gerry's comment about "boring doctors" demonstrates, people do not necessarily draw their social networks from occupational groups. When people do not have the shared experience and language of work culture, there needs to be other kinds of inscribed interests—talking about food is a language, a discourse that transcends the specificity and specialization prevalent in the workplace. In fact, the construction of social boundaries around class-based cultures seems more about finding people who share a habitus, the different dispositions, attitudes, and abilities to use cultural objects and practices. The dinner party is a social activity that involves demonstrating material skills and knowledge of food, providing the stage for the construction of social relationships based on distinctions. Thus, people act and create class boundaries within specific local social and economic conditions.

Men and women of the professional-managerial class spoke of finding friends with like interests: a knowledge of food and the ability to "talk food" was key. Describing their friends, one couple comments, "all these people are chefs and cooks in their own right and so we're always comparing notes." A number of people said, quite deliberately, "we got interested in finding friends who like to cook," but they elaborated on this by distinguishing the *quality* of food they were after. For example, one man spoke about looking for friends who appreciate food the way he does because "I think that one of the things that does distress me is the low level of expectation that most people have on food."

Different groups have rules about palatability and permitted combinations, such that "control and manipulation of the symbolic aspects of class help maintain class boundaries" (McIntosh, 1996, 23). Sometimes guests *not* talking about food was crucial. Larry said, "Frequently people are very impressed by the food and they mention it. . . . And I don't think it's anything special . . . to me it's kind of an expectation that it will be at this level, and that people will comment on it disrupts it and I think, gee, what are their standards at home?"

In essence, a participant must know when and how to talk about food in a way that creates a performance in sync with that of the host or cook and the other guests. One woman described the experience of attending a dinner party of work colleagues at the home of their supervisor, "and this one woman kept going on and on about how good the food was and how she liked it so much, and could she have the recipe—I mean, she really took over the conversation with this, you know, so that other people were getting embarrassed for her—and later on, kind of to the side, I overheard Jean [the supervisor] say to her, 'I got the food ready made from [a catering service] and brought it home and heated it up.' So that shut her up! But it was awful to sit through."

Although both men and women talk about food and cooking, my interviews suggest that there are differences in the type of talk, its meaning and purpose. For many of the upper-middle-class people I spoke to, it was clearly important for there to be a shared understanding of "good food" among friends. One man captured this well when he said, "I dislike it if I make something and people don't understand . . . don't get it . . . this is really good food and they may be wolfing it down . . . they just may not be interested."

For some men, talking about food is the equivalent of talking about sports, a way of demonstrating membership and competence in maleness. For middle- and upper-middle-class men, it is a piece of cultural capital, the ability to create distinctions based on taste, using cultural knowledge as a marker of class, and in this case also of gender. Knowledge about class-based food tastes is a resource that can be converted into social and economic capital. The talk about food is connected to travel, to familiarity with "high-end" restaurants and "important" chefs, all aspects of these men's experiences through work in upper-middle-class professions.

Both the gender and class performances are intertwined. The men doing the performance are a crucial part of the whole staging of an event, creating the atmosphere for talk, and constructing their identities as upper-middle-class men because their professional identities don't operate to do this for them in the domestic sphere. Although they reap some rewards for being breadwinners, they have to create their social role outside work differently. When intimacy is circumscribed through formality, the topics of conversation become the crucial social glue for interaction. Affect, emotion, physicality, and embodiment are filtered through a discourse of food that takes the place

of more informal forms of self-revelation and exchange. In contrast, one reason why Perry's event and menu parody elite dinner parties is because he does
not want to engage in such formal restraints on sociability. His invocation
of southern hospitality, the happy consumption of alcohol, the pleasure and
jocularity he describes at his party, all suggest comfort with a more intimate
set of sociable relations. For example, he invites people even though they
don't all "get along perfectly" because he constructs a format where people
can avoid uncomfortable interactions and still be close. In comparison, Dina
has to work hard to construct a guest list of compatible people because she
actually knows very little about them beyond the specific activities that draw
her interest.

Blurring the Boundaries

The dinner party is a gender- and class-based performance filtered through
what Omi and Winant (1994) refer to as the racial formations that structure
American culture. When women cook and host a formal meal for friends,
they are fulfilling gender expectations as caregivers and constructors of affective ties. Although women also experience accolades for their work, when
men cook and host, they are engaging in a different but equally gendered
performance. This holds true for men of upper- to middle-class backgrounds
regardless of race or sexuality. In all these cases, the construction of class-
based sociability is a primary operator. A key component of that is the creation of affective non-kin relationships.

I wondered if there were people who held dinner parties who subverted
or shifted these requisite performances in other ways. One example comes
from Cindy and Mary, a white lesbian couple, both in their mid- to late twenties, with a solid middle-class household income. They invite both friends
and family over for food at their house on a regular basis—in fact, one key
difference between Cindy and Mary and all the other people who held dinner parties is that family were often included among the guests at Cindy
and Mary's parties. Like many of the people I interviewed, Cindy and Mary
construct an array of social occasions—not just dinner parties—but I analyze
their story as part of the universe of formal dinner parties because they do
all the labor themselves and, despite their welcoming comfortable manner,
have a seated, formal meal with many of the people who come over.

Cindy does the majority of cooking but the couple shares some parts of
the planning and food work. Like Amy and Evan, they describe a division of
labor based on their shared perceptions of each other's skills and preferences.
According to Cindy, "I'd say at least every two weeks there's somebody that
comes over for dinner. . . . I usually do the cooking. Mary's the baker. . . .

That's the other thing Mary is good at—she's sort of my prep cook. I cook and dirty dishes like crazy and she just kind of keeps them cleaned up. . . . (Afterwards) Mary is the washer and I am the putter-away of stuff as well as dishes, you know. . . . It's perfect."

Cindy, as the cook, is clearly in charge of the menu, although the couple collaborates on deciding who is invited and what kind of event it will be. They have local friends from volleyball over at least two or three times a year. They also host parties of work-related friends, have some spontaneous meals with their neighbors, and do the majority of holidays and other family celebrations that are centered on Mary's biological kin. Among all these events, an important facet for Cindy is her ability to be somewhat flexible in her cooking: "If we're having company over—generally they're people we both know, whether it's our family or friends—so we both have an investment. . . . So I'm lucky that I'm not doing this all solo, because then I probably would have to write down a menu."

Cindy centers on spontaneity as what makes cooking pleasurable rather than work. Their division of labor seems comfortably worked out but not completely free of disagreement. In responding to what she liked least about these events, Mary talked about how, having no prearranged limits, Cindy will keep cooking until guests arrive: "[I think that] what I don't like is Cindy goes overboard so I get nervous. . . . And her line is 'you can never have too much.' . . . [I]f people are late, then one or two or three more things have been added to the menu. . . . She'll just keep cooking."

Mary does not articulate exactly what she finds stressful, whether it's the additional work or concerns about the overlap between "back stage" and "front stage." One possibility is that by worrying, Mary takes on some of the invisible planning and emotional labor so that Cindy can continue to construct cooking as a pleasurable leisure activity.

At the same time, Cindy's comments about why she cooks are different from those of Evan and the other white upper-middle-class men. She focuses on cooking as something she's drawn to, rather than as an acquired skill, saying, "I just have this need to feed people. It must be some Italian in there." What's intriguing is that she invokes ethnicity rather than gender as an explanation for what feels natural or instinctive. The majority of white people I interviewed underplayed their ethnic backgrounds, choosing an optional identity based in whiteness rather than ethnicity. Here, however, it's interesting how those marginal positions weigh against each other as explanations for caring behavior. For Cindy, describing her caring work as emerging from gender expectations would suggest that by not doing the same work, Mary was somehow not fulfilling those obligations. Cindy also often deflected attention away from herself by minimizing the amount of effort she puts into cooking and by emphasizing the pleasure of her guests rather than her own performance as chef, cook, or host. When I asked her what she enjoyed most about cooking for special occasions, she said, "Actually having everybody sit down and eat it. I think that's my favorite part of this actually. Sometimes . . . I set everything out and I stand over there at the stove and I watch everybody go through it, you know? . . . Just having them eat a lot is like feedback."

Creating close social relationships with both family and friends was extremely important to both Cindy and Mary. They talked about the recent deaths of Mary's father and sister as further reasons for their desire to keep biological kin close. Because support cannot be taken for granted, issues of biological and created kinship are an active area of concern for many gay and lesbian couples (Weston, 1990). For Cindy and Mary, this means trying to provide social occasions that are not severely limited by physical and economic constraints—and by creating some events integrating both their chosen friends and given family.

Even though she acknowledged the work they do to make it possible, Cindy almost seemed surprised that Mary's biological family and their friends gravitate toward their house: "Everybody comes over here and it's kind of, you know, this is a small house. And they all have houses but they all want to come here." Thus, for some of the very large parties and Thanksgiving. they work around the lack of a dining room by serving the meals as a buffet. But for the most part, Cindy wants to have "sit-down meals" where everyone can be sociable together. As Queen Victoria asserted, it is quite possible that things *do* taste better in small houses.

Although Cindy is reluctant to claim gender as a reason for her feeding work, she cannot avoid doing gender as caring work because she and Mary see kin and fictive kin as extremely important to their daily lives. Cindy expends a considerable effort, both in her thinking and her actual cooking, attempting to meet people's preferences: "I used to make a turkey, remember? And we don't eat meat. I mean, that's the funny thing. . . . But you know, it's not like a stressful thing." At the same time, Cindy relied much less on cookbooks and magazines than Evan or Gerry. She talked more about getting recipes from friends and/or handed down by tradition. DeVault (1990) suggests that women from different social classes draw upon discourses of food work differently, such that women from professional and upper-middle-class households are more comfortable and more likely to rely on text-based sources like cookbooks and food magazines. Although Cindy and Mary owned a comfortable home and both had good paying jobs, their combined incomes put them on the lower end of the socioeconomic spectrum of people

I interviewed. In describing their friends and family, it seemed clear that although many of them were professionals (nurses, physical therapists), they described themselves as "working people."

In general, the women I spoke to demonstrated a high level of concern about making sure family and friends had food they liked, even if that meant subordinating their own tastes. To accommodate Mary's family, Cindy suppressed her own desire to make creative and spontaneous meals. She described the "required traditional holiday dishes" as repetitive and less interesting to cook, but "there's certain things you've got to make, like I said, sweet potatoes for Anne Marie . . . and Mary's dad loved my dinner rolls so I have to make dinner rolls." Rosenthal (1985) and DiLeonardo (1987) argue that women play a central part in "orchestrating family gatherings and ritual occasions" (DiLeonardo, 966). In contrast, I suggest that gender privilege allows men like Evan and Gerry the luxury of passing off this less desirable work to their partners while gaining social recognition cooking for friends.

Dining Together

The dinner party still exists as a social form because people continue to use social events with food as a way of creating boundaries between groups and also within them. In particular, these stories suggest that class- and gender-based distinctions are inscribed in the material and interactional work of social events that subscribe to the cultural template of a dinner party. The performance of gender identities plays itself out in a variety of ways within these events, but no less significantly and certainly more flexibly than those performances expected in the workplace or even within the family.

Although in staging dinner parties, both men and women act to produce domestic hospitality for their friends, they do so along lines that generally do not disrupt expectations for doing gender. Men who cook are doing public display. Women are more of the interactional and emotional labor regardless of whether they are responsible for the food work. In such settings outside the family and occupational structures, as they create social lives, men and women are still held accountable for particular kinds of gender and class performances.

Regardless of sexuality or race, upper-middle-class men did gender through food work most often in what one would call special circumstances—meaning that, in some way, the context had to be modified from the daily routine of everyday life. I suggest that the specialness functions to remove this activity from the stigma of women's work. In essence, men who cook for dinners, get-togethers, and holiday meals violate gendered expectations of cooking as women's domain, but they don't disrupt gender boundaries because the context or setting allows for different meanings to be constructed. Food work in contexts other than family meals is gendered, but in different ways. These stories suggest a terrain outside work and family life where men enact and reinforce certain kinds of masculinity. One necessary component is the designation of the event as something out of the realm of the daily. The dinner party is the perfect staging for such a performance because it carries with it a history and a discourse that establishes expectations of "specialness." Even the very wealthy do not hold dinner parties every night.

At these events, the food itself operates as both a signifier of inclusion and a boundary of exclusion. Familiarity with various cuisines and cultures provides the cultural knowledge that secures class-based performances of sociability. It is in these spaces where the larger moral discourses about food, filtered through expectations about hospitality, enter into the domestic realm and shape social relationships. It creates class and race simultaneously, and is often dependent on the work of women who labor back stage, cook, facilitate interaction, and maintain knowledge of individual preferences and cultural styles.

As cooking occupies an even greater spotlight in the cultural imagination, it becomes a task with greater status, such that men are more able and willing to do it in certain contexts, particularly those that provide them with avenue for public display. At the same time, particularly within couples and heterosexual marriages, men's ability to do so often rests on the unacknowledged invisible, interactional, and emotional labor of women.

It is important to recognize that these performances and relationships are created by people who have a fair amount of economic, social, and cultural resources to make choices about their environment and social life. For a larger swath of Americans, most people don't hold dinner parties. In fact many modify the template in some significant way. Chapter 4 considers whether these modifications also shift the requisite class and gender performances inscribed in the more formal form of sociability.

4. Sweetening the Pot

The Shifting Social Landscape of Sociable Meals

> Modern society has more than enough devices for keeping people
> apart. . . . When we meet, therefore, with the express purpose of
> socializing, we cannot afford to be distant.
> —Margaret Visser

A Few Friends over for Dinner

It was often difficult to categorize people's activities, even when labels like "dinner party" and "potluck" exist. Unless the occasion clearly fit a specific template, most notably as a dinner party or a potluck, people did not use any overarching terms to describe them. Although I was relying on people's own narratives of event, in their telling, they had trouble coming up with labels themselves. Because I was interested in letting people define terms, I generally did not push them to categorize events unless the conversation warranted it (for example, if comparing one event to another, or if they labeled one kind of party and not another). Perhaps people are not generally asked to give accounts about the form of these activities. They talked easily about the people they know, the conversations held, and what the food was like. However, it was less likely for them to describe the form of the events as well as much of the invisible work that went into creating them. This may be reflective of the way contemporary Americans rely on a discourse of friendship that considers it a "voluntary institution," less subject to rules and definitions (Jerrome, 1984; Allan, 1979, 1989; Rawlins 1992, 2009). Given the place of such events and relationships, having friends over for food is an activity that lacks a consistent vocabulary of motives. I found that even through my own participation and observation, there were times when such events defied neat categorization. I dissect the following example to illustrate how the symbolic nature of such events and descriptions are not fixed and are often complicated.[1]

Not long ago, my family and I were invited to dinner at someone else's home. Gina and Sam are a married couple with two small children. They are, by observation, middle- to upper-middle-class. One mentioned going to school for a master's degree, the other runs a small business. We met through our children's activities and so our talk often centered on being parents. These conversations often touched on what could be characterized as upper-middle-class cultural capital, discussing books, films, and articles in the *New York Times*. Both are knowledgeable about local politics, make frequent business and family trips to Boston and New York, and are, in their own words, "interested in food."[2] At one point, Gina said, "We want to have a few friends over for dinner" and mentioned that they were inviting "some other people we haven't had over in a while," as well as my family, who had never eaten at their house.

The week of the dinner I called Gina and asked if we could be of any help or bring anything. I did this unreflectively, but later on, as I wrote notes about the event, I wondered what prompted me to offer to help. My own cumulative experience as a guest and host, aspects of what might be called my habitus, made the action almost a routine gesture. One could say that my response was shaped by some specifics of cultural capital, my own interpretations of middle-class manners from family and schooling, which decree that calling and offering to "help" was appropriate and normative. But from another observer's perspective, indeed from Emily Post's standards, this offer might seem presumptuous or ignorant. After all, in the cultural template of formal sociable events, the guest is never responsible for anything other than gratitude and good conversation.

Perhaps my presumption was based on an implicit understanding of the event as a more informal and intimate gathering. Such an understanding would have to come from a more-than-superficial knowledge of the people organizing the event. However, if asked, I would say that I did not know Gina "well," although during the time frame when this interaction occurred, we saw each other at least twice a week during our children's activities. We shared bits and pieces of each other's biographies, mostly about the transition to and experience of parenthood, but very little of the "before" stories. In fact, I read the invitation to dinner as her desire to "get to know us better" and involve my family in their circle of friends.

Reflecting on this, I realize that I had decided it was appropriate to call and ask for unarticulated reasons, most notably because I was not certain what kind of dinner this was going to be. If it was a formal dinner party, then my asking was a way for the host to signal to me the type of event and the expectations upon me as a guest. If Gina and Sam were people I knew with some greater degree of familiarity and intimacy, perhaps I would have had previous opportunities to learn their normative practices or been comfortable enough with them to assume I knew what was acceptable, appropriate, and appreciated without having to inquire. However, I had no clues as to the social form being created, other than a sense that Gina and Sam had particular sensibilities about food.

Judging from the vast majority of my interviews, offering to help is a normative practice, one that takes the place of more formalized interactions. Historically in western societies, domestic social events required written invitations that indicated the form of the event. In most editions, Emily Post suggests that almost all events warrant written invitations, although by 1969 she concedes the propriety of telephone invitations for very informal gatherings. Although she doesn't prescribe which circumstances demand them, Martha Stewart demonstrates how to create handwritten invitations.[3] Among the people I interviewed, most sociability was treated with less formality. Fancy birthday parties like Perry's and other events celebrating some life course milestone such as a graduation or an anniversary were the only kind that involved written invitations. These invitations explicitly or implicitly inform guests of their obligations. For example, at weddings and bat mitzvahs, events that demand written invitations and responses, guests are generally not expected to bring food or wine or flowers, only gifts for the persons being honored.[4]

But the kind of events people told me about were often announced by the host inviting people in person or over the phone or even, occasionally, by email. Given this way of conveying an invitation, the host has a less scripted means of providing a definition of the situation in his or her invitation. Thus it appears that the practice of "asking what to bring" is a way for people to determine the exact nature of the event and the kind of expectations being placed on them as guests. As in all interactions, there are cases where expectations are conveyed and acted upon in a manner that aligns people's actions. In other cases, people need clarification in order to capture the appropriate definition of the situation. The guest script carries an inherent reciprocity and obligation but without the strict guidelines of a formal event, the nature of that obligation often needs to be negotiated. In talking about events that "did not go well" people told stories about misinterpretations of the host and guest roles. For example, Pam described an in-law who insisted on bringing food to her large buffet parties without checking with Pam. Pam refused to serve "Bernice's runny potato salad" and risked alienating her relative rather than compromise her vision of the event. Cindy and Mary were among those who resisted having guests "helping out with the dishes" instead of enjoying the sociable time they created. Larry criticized a friend who "makes this big production and spends all his time in the kitchen cooking, you know, this big show, and he's stressed, which is just no fun for the rest of us, hanging out in the living room waiting for him."

Margaret Visser (1992) argues that even in casual gatherings "a person cannot be called a 'guest' in a place where he or she has any responsibilities; no obligations, other than respect for the host, can be laid upon a guest while he or she is under the host's roof." However, given the experiences described to me, it appears that Visser is delineating an ideal form of these roles, one that is not played out except in the most formal of occasions. In sociable interactions, people are held accountable even if the historically constructed roles of host and guest are shifting. On the one hand, people generally aimed for an atmosphere of comfort in their sociability. However, such comfort was not always predicated on either a set of clear-cut social guidelines or a kind of close personal knowledge of each other that would construct implicit shared meanings. For the most part, the people I talked to invented practices to guide them through, created patterns through routine interactions, or relied on family traditions. One woman told me, "my mother taught me never to go to someone's house empty-handed." This was often an unspoken rule among people who attended but did not often host parties. However, the question of what to bring is often tied to very specific knowledge and understandings of particular social groups. For example, when I asked Deanna about bringing things to dinner parties, she described the nature of reciprocity when socializing with people who are very wealthy:

> Now there have been some very exclusive parties where I know that this person could buy the world. I don't bring anything. I mean, yeah, what am I gonna do? Give me that, a bottle off the shelf of Liquors 44—[when] they've got a wine cellar down in their basement. And they're drinking, you know—this would be hundred dollar bottles of wine on the table and I'm going to [be able to pick out] and give them a bottle? So on those occasions, I do send a little note the next day saying how much I enjoyed myself and please invite me again. So I can sit at your table and drink wine that I'll never have an experience to drink again. Yes, those, those are fun.

Deanna resorts to more conventional rules about being a guest when, because of economic and cultural capital, she cannot reciprocate in kind. In this case, the status inequality among participants creates a formality of obligations. But in less exclusive occasions, there are no clear-cut rules. In the social construction of friendship, being able to negotiate the terrain of daily interactions and of social moments becomes an important skill and often determines the nature of social networks. Sometimes people express this through geographic dislocation. One woman, a transplant to the East Coast said, "people in the Midwest were friendlier." In another chapter I talk about a similar process regarding time and nostalgia, where people describe memories of childhood and neighborhoods that were more permeable and relaxed. Understanding obligations often involves adjustments with shifts in life stages and social contacts. Often people talked about finding "the right fit" among friends.

When I called and asked Gina if I could bring something, she said, "Oh yes, wait, let me see what I have you down for. Yes, bread."

In that short interchange, Gina conveyed a significant amount of information. First, this was not technically a formal dinner party, since we were being asked to contribute a portion of the meal. And yet, this was not "potluck" in the traditional sense, because it was clear that Gina and Sam had a specific menu—or at least specific categories of food that they wanted to have "filled" in order to meet their definition of a commensal event. Furthermore, being assigned "bread" as a contribution was also indicative of how Gina viewed us in relation to the other guests. Hierarchies of taste often operate through tastes in bread: commercially prepared white bread is generally unacceptable among upper-middle-class groups. Few people today make their own bread: Gina would not have known if we had the skills to do so. Thus, we were not being asked to actually *make* something. In fact, her presumption was that we would probably bring bakery bread, which is precisely what we did. Because they did not know us well, we were assigned an item that did not require cooking skills, only class-based knowledge of the marketplace. I read this as Gina's way of managing the risks of contributions disrupting her ideas about an appropriate menu for guests. Or, similarly, it could be a way to minimize the burden for guests who were unfamiliar to the group.

As my interviews show, guest and host obligations can often be an area of considerable negotiation and a place where there are norms but not universal ones. In fact, the data suggests that very specific but negotiated roles determine membership and comfort in particular social groups. There is a cultural specificity of rules and roles, one that varies by national culture, by region, but also by class and racial groups in specific locations. Gina and Sam's group of professional-managerial friends had different expectations of sociability than the people Dina and Gerry socialized with, and yet both live in the same surrounding towns and share professional class standing. Class, in a rigid sense of a fixed group, is not what determines such boundaries. Some critics suggest that "lifestyle groups" based on individuation have replaced class-based relations (Beck, 1992). However, my observations and interviews illustrate that people wield symbolic power in their social interactions, such that even voluntary sociable relationships operate on "an unfolding sequence of situated strategies, guided by the position of groups in social space" (Wacquant, 2001).

By indicating that she had a list of what was to be served, Gina implied that she had an ordered meal planned, one that was dependent on guests' contributions. What would our experience have been if I had not called? Would she eventually have called me? How would the negotiation then have taken place? It was also interesting that Gina considered it acceptable to assign everyone something specific. Because the other guests were people I did not know, I was unaware of the nature of the conversations with other guests. Perhaps others felt comfortable volunteering something. Perhaps I was the last person to call and bread was all that remained to be delegated. Gina and Sam may have been aware of other people's "skills and specialties" and asked accordingly. For example, one person brought a homemade cake to the dinner. Other guests commented that this person was "known" for desserts and baking.

The dinner turned out to be five couples (ten adults) and ten children ranging from two to thirteen years old. The guests were all relatively similar in age, race, and socioeconomic background: that is, they were white, straight, in their mid- to late thirties, with at least one adult who was a professional. This was additionally interesting in that one fact we did know about Gina and Sam was that their social networks included people of color whom we also knew. The people who were invited all had children and seemed to know each other. Given this conformity of status, the group may not have had to engage in much negotiation about obligations and taste. In fact, my partner and I, being generally unfamiliar with most people there, were the ones who had to determine a definition of the situation.

It was summer. Earlier in the day Sam had cooked meat and vegetables on the grill and made two different pasta dishes, one for the adults, one for the kids. One of the male guests had come over in the afternoon to help him cook. Each couple, respectively, brought wine, cheese, salad, bread, and dessert. After everyone arrived, Sam put out a big bowl of pasta on a table and the children sat and ate first. The adults ate cheese and fruit, supervised the children's eating, or helped Sam set out food. While the kids played outside, under the general supervision of the older teenagers, the adults sat outdoors at a table and ate dinner. The food was set out buffet style on a counter and people served themselves and then sat together. There were no assigned seats, although Sam and Gina ended up at the head of the table. After dinner most of the men cleaned up the food, the dishes, and the chairs and tables so that there was very little left for the hosts to do. No one left before this was done: this obligation was unspoken, even though some of the younger children were ready to go home. The format may also have been related to the seasonality of the party. Although it was not a barbecue, it was a "summer party," meant to be experienced outdoors on the deck. Again, although they had a table large enough for everyone to sit, the food was indoors. This arrangement reduced labor by eliminating the work of serving the adults.

Later on, I asked myself: was this a dinner party? A potluck? A buffet? One defining characteristic of events is the division of labor, both the emotion work and the often invisible domestic labor. In my notes after the party, I commented on both. Gina checked a number of times to see that all the children were happy and getting along. She picked out table linens while Sam and another man started putting the food out on the table. At the end of the party, guests made a point to thank the host and hostess and comment on, as one person put it, "how wonderful it was of them to do all this work." I wondered about the nature of such gratitude, given that the guests had contributed a fair amount of the food and the labor of cleaning up. I also noticed that many of the compliments were about the food, praising Sam's cooking. Although people thanked both Gina and Sam, the attention to the food encouraged me to see these accolades as a way of acknowledging Sam's gender performance.

In many ways, this event seemed similar to the dinner parties described by Evan, Perry, and Gerry. But the physical work, such as helping at the party and providing food that occurred by guests before and during the event, was of a greater magnitude than in the dinner parties like the ones I describe in Chapter 3. The guests at this party went beyond the "dessert, wine, or flowers" trilogy of acceptable dinner contributions, but Gina and Sam did not see it as a potluck and never used that term. In fact, while explaining my research to Sam, he said, "Oh, potlucks. They're awful. Who likes potlucks?"

Perhaps this is a modified dinner party, the kind of shift in the social form that Olesen predicts, where the burden of work has to be shared because of changes in the material conditions of people's lives. All the couples at this gathering had at least one child under the age of five. There were many conversations about parenting, touching on the difficulties of juggling work and children, the work of organizing children's social and cultural activities, and the various aspects of development and personality among kids. Both men and women at this event appeared to subscribe to a white upper-middle-class model of parenting as a project involving intensive mothering and involved fatherhood. Indeed, my sense was that whatever closeness or intimacy was fostered at this gathering centered on constructing this view of parenting as a shared experience.

Among people I interviewed, those with children often talked about how being parents had changed the nature of their socializing, making it less possible for them to hold formal parties, cook the way they had before kids, or stay out late. Among the guests, there were at least two dual-career couples. However, a number of the women at the party worked part-time, mostly because, as one put it, "I still want to be available for my children." Among these upper-middle-class professionals runs a discourse that people's work and home lives take up enormous amounts of energy. In particular these discourses suggest that families with young children often have a difficult time organizing social lives with their peers. Sharing the labor of creating sociability may be one strategy for making it possible.

In some ways Gina and Sam preserved some of the structure and form of the formal dinner party. In other ways, Gina and Sam modify it because of their own cultural template, which including ideas about the informal atmosphere of seasonal sociability, the needs of upper-middle-class parents, and the primacy of food that conforms to specific ideas about taste. Of course, these conclusions are just one of many possible interpretations. Although I problematize the organization of this event, parts of the form were, in fact, familiar. However, the underlying formality was not. The less structured aspects of the dinner were reminiscent of other events in my experience, but many of those were more intimate, in the sense that people talked about a wider range of subjects. I never explicitly asked Gina and Sam questions about why they held that event in the form that they did. In participant observations, especially those where I knew the participants in other capacities, I chose only to observe rather than ask people to self-consciously evaluate what they were doing. In some ways, I understand and can interpret the habitus Gina and Sam construct because, in overt characteristics, I share it. In other ways, my partner and I had to work to figure out the social expectations because these were people with whom we shared no great intimacies other than some overt parenting situations. I chose to make observational notes after the event because I found it uncomfortable, an experience where people presumed similar tastes based on superficial characteristics.

I present an extended discussion of this one party to highlight the complexity of social events with food when all the rigid rules of dinner parties are not applicable or desired. For many reasons, the majority of people's social events do not fit into those formal templates, so they must "invent" new ways of doing this. But in doing so, all modifications are fraught with new rules and new ways of negotiating a shared understanding of what is appropriate, what tastes good, and what makes both hosts and guests feel "comfortable," appreciated, and connected to each other. The literature on social capital seems ill-equipped to address this constant negotiation between private and public, formal and informal. As Warde and Martens (2001) suggest, we know very little about the shared understandings that create sociable events, especially those that allow for variations to emerge as a product of interaction and alignment. Allan (1989) argues that "the structural conditions of middle-class social existence lead to an emphasis on the deliberate making of friends: on the transformation of contextually specific relationships into ones whose parameters are less narrow, through purposeful involvement in aspects of life otherwise kept separate. Hence, middle-class sociability depends on establishing social contacts . . . and then developing some of these in a fashion that clearly celebrates personal commitment above circumstances" (138).

The path to intimacy and closeness is not as free of constraints as the ideology of friendship suggests. In fact, people intentionally use these events to create bounded groups whose similarities exclude others. There were many other parents whose children frequented the same activities as Gina's and mine, but among them, she chose people whose age, race, class, and profession matched her own.

Categorizing Social Events

As I began to discover in people's discussions of dinner parties, the labels that contemporary Americans have for socializing with food are often inadequate, lacking enough nuances to capture their real experiences. People may hold an event that fits most of the Emily Post criteria for a dinner party and yet not use that label: for example, many of the couples I interviewed often had "another couple" over for dinner. But in terms of Emily Post and other prescriptive texts on commensality—and in people's own descriptions—this did not "count" as a dinner party. I found many stories in my interviews where people held something *like* a dinner party but varied in some way. Almost all of the couples with middle- to upper-middle-class incomes talked about having small events with one or two other people, usually another couple. Focusing on heterosexual couples, Allan (1989) concludes that cross-gender sociability through marriage often involves friendships between couples. He suggests, "the extent to which the home is used to socialize with non-kin is likely to be the nature of the marital bond itself. Where a couple have a predominantly joint marital role, their friendships are likely to reflect this and to some degree, be shared" (81).

In this chapter I begin by describing some of these smaller couple dinners and then examine other kinds of "modified" and often more informal sociable events. At least eleven people had parties that were buffets—parties where the food was set out on tables for people to serve themselves and seating was not necessarily at one table with all guests together. Seven other people described other kinds of "modified" dinner parties, where guests or friends would bring food to the meal, but the event was not called a "potluck." Some of the variations people describe include altering the size of the event (number of guests); accepting guest's contributions of food or labor; shifting shared ideas about "taste," which often centered on the use of commercial food; and finally lessens the depth of the reciprocal obligation. People create variations based on very specific and often complex circumstances, and the exploration of those differences can illustrate something about the nature of power and boundary-making in a setting that is supposedly less subject to formal rules and social obligations. Improvisation is more normative than adherence, but such improvisation is not free of structural constraints. Social distance among the participants often affects the level of formality. That is, people who were more familiar were more likely to have events that were modified for greater comfort and informality. Among the people I interviewed, issues of time and space were the most pressing reasons for improvising from the dinner party template. These concerns are echoed by Warde and Martens: in their study of eating out in Britain, people described increasingly busy weekends, lack of dining areas, and a dislike for formality as reasons they did not adhere to the dinner party template. Among the people I interviewed, women were generally held more accountable for the interactional work of creating and sustaining social networks. These women employ a variety of strategies for minimizing the amount of labor and emotion work expected of them in creating and hosting these events. Not surprisingly, having more economic resources gave some a greater degree of flexibility about formal norms of hospitality. When men organized and cooked for events that were not dinner parties they were invariably given some other name. Although I don't explore this phenomenon here, it often seems that men barbecue.

Other Couples

> Jane Louise was highly attuned to social nuance. So, for example, the meal she served to Peter and Beth must not be too fancy, but it must not be unfancy. A meal too fancy might be something of an affront—the city person showing off—while a dowdy meal might be an affront as well, the expectation being that if you came up from the city you ought to bring a few nice things to amuse your country friends. Jane Louise grilled a steak and made a chocolate soufflé.
> —Laurie Colwin, *A Big Storm Knocked It Over*

One key strategy for sociability under constraints is to limit the number of people invited to one's home at any given time. Interviewees described this as "more manageable" and also "more personal," suggesting that they have to make choices about with whom they want to spend time and resources. People in long-term relationships describe "having another couple over for dinner" as less work than a big formal dinner party. But the majority of people I interviewed who created these kinds of events did not call it a dinner party. Both gay and straight couples talked about constructing a social life around others who are also in dyads. Sometimes the couple would be drawn from one of the host's workplaces but as equally likely they were not. According to Rawlins (2009), "Despite varying degrees and durations of actual friendship practices between spouses, the 'social unity' associated with the other couple companionate ideal also promotes joint friendships with other couples as a normative corollary" (170). Having just one couple over creates a setting where people can "get to know each other better" without having to negotiate a whole host of others. In Mary Douglas's delineation of food events and degrees of relationship (1984), having someone over to your house for dinner signals a boundary crossed: "The meal expresses close friendships. . . . So, those friends who have never had a hot meal in our home have presumably another threshold of intimacy to cross" (66).

When constructing sociability with just one other couple, it is both easier but more risky to create the balance of uniqueness and connectedness so necessary to sociability. Simmel suggests that in smaller gatherings, people are aiming for "a complete harmony of mood, which is so characteristic of the small group" (in Wolff, 1950, 113). Such events involve conversations with "an undisputed single center" around which people converge. Attention is focused on the needs of only two other people, creating a more intimate occasion. At the same time, if interactions are problematic, there is not a set of other guests to mediate or deflect the difficulties. In some ways, these occasions are easier on the hosts: many people asserted that it is less work to serve four than the eight or twelve people for a formal dinner party. Materially, these events cost less, since they require less food and fewer plates and silverware. Some people described "splurging" on these smaller dinners because they could afford to make something expensive like roast lamb or lobster for four people rather than eight. Smaller events are also easier on guests, since the obligations are of a smaller scale. Other people mentioned that small dinner gatherings were easier to reciprocate. Still other people talked about the limitations of their budget, their leisure time, and the size of their home. For example, James and Cheryl told me that they found it easiest to invite one other couple over to their house because it was "less chaotic" for their small children. In creating "couple friendships" people talked about having eaten together in restaurants prior to inviting them over, part of a process of developing and testing intimacy. Even skirting people's lack of labeling and still considering it a dinner party when two couples share a meal at one home, these events were often modified even further in order to "fit" into the social landscape of people's daily experiences.

"It's Always a Balance"

Nora is a white married woman in her late twenties who lives in a semirural Connecticut suburb. She does freelance work as a graphic designer, which allows her a fair amount of flexibility in her time. Her husband's salary gives them economic resources and the stability of a middle-class household. At the time I interviewed her, she had lived in her current residence for about five years. When Nora first moved to the area, she became part of a circle of about twelve to fifteen friends through her sister who lived in a neighboring town. This fairly consistent group held biweekly potlucks and shared dinner buffets. To Nora, people had implicitly agreed upon a kind of reciprocity that allowed some to host without being burdened by too much work. It was normative for people to bring food and help out at the dinners. At the same time, Nora suggested that, in her particular case, the type of parties they held were determined by her "small house with a tiny dining room and no big table."

When I interviewed her, Nora had been lamenting the loss of that group, since many people had "moved on" because of jobs, a desire for a more urban lifestyle, or simply a lack of time and interest in socializing together. With this circle of friends no longer available, Nora was working out "how to have a social life" that fit her mental picture of what these events "should be" with what was physically and materially possible in her house. She and her husband do not usually do dinner parties, although she would like to, describing her interest in cooking and "having friends over." Nora talked about how, at her stage in life, she had the time to orchestrate such events. She compared her situation to that of her sister, who had generally withdrawn from socializing because she had a new baby. Even with time and money as resources, Nora sees herself as lacking the ideal conditions to create and maintain the kind of enduring social contacts she desired. A "real dinner party" to Nora would properly involve a larger group of people, but for now, it's when they have one other couple over. Doing this kind of small scale event allows Nora to construct a Martha Stewart–like version of hospitality:

What about dinner parties?
Oh, that's like the sky's the limit.
   Now we rarely have people over and it's really, you know, lately we've been sort of thinking, okay, we do know some people still so let's have them over

and, um, our house as it is situated isn't great but it's possible. . . . Yeah, and just have like one couple and you know, it isn't as like festive and grand, but our house really isn't set up right now; we just have like one table that doesn't have leaves and so, it's kind of limited as it is. I pine for a long dining table and a dining room.

Even with her concerns about the limits of her resources, Nora and her husband arrange to have people over for dinner. In her descriptions of various occasions, Nora explains what kind of work she has to do, both in terms of physical labor and emotion work, in order to make guests welcome and establish friendships:

> [The last time we had a couple over . . .] what did I do? I baked like a salmon with mustard and brown sugar and lime and yeah, it's delicious glaze. . . . I made, like, I don't know, some vegetable, I don't remember . . . and a wild rice salad and homemade rolls and salad and then, I think the thing I like about that was she brought something from the bakery . . . and it just worked out really well cause I had made something like a fruit compote . . . and brownies, but I set those aside and it just worked. I don't know, I just felt like, there was a graciousness, oh she brought this, oh well I'll just make it work in my menu and it worked really well and she got to feel like, you know, she had contributed, you know, it's like sort of that balance. It's always a balance.

For Nora, her desire for this kind of dinner party has meant having to find a way to accommodate people's needs—and one of those needs is to feel as if guests have contributed. In this case, Nora had already made dessert, which she modifies in order to incorporate an unsolicited contribution from her guest. Since she recently lost the older circle of friends, having people over and securing this social life is an urgent concern for Nora. Indeed, she answered my ad looking for interview subjects because she said she was "trying to figure it out myself." Even though Nora saw cooking for others and creating a meal as a crucial part of her sense of self as a hostess, she has recognized that she has to adapt in order to ensure that guests feel included. In this case, the balance of individualism, the assertion of personality through food work is subsumed to the guest's needs in order to create sociability. Allowing people to contribute to the event is one strategy:

> *Do people usually contribute something?*
> I always feel like I, I wanna say no, no don't do that, but recently, over the past few years I've realized that people really like to contribute and, even if they don't like to cook as much as I do, they probably like, you know, to feel like they've done something, and so I try to think of stuff. I usually give them the salad, you know, bring a salad cause that's not something that's like, that I'm

putting a lot of stuff into. And so they get to bring the salad and so, that, that is, actually what I usually say.

What about dessert?
Dessert, thought, is like you know, special. I don't usually make dessert [for our everyday meals], so I know, if we're having people over, it's like, oh, I get to!

For some people, dessert falls into the category of acceptable contributions. For Nora, it is an integral part of her performance as hostess and cook. In comparison, Paula and Gerry both avoid desserts since neither finds them an enjoyable item to cook. Paula's husband buys dessert at the bakery. Gerry occasionally allows guests to bring something. Neither would compromise their main menu for an unexpected contribution. Along with others who held dinner parties, Nora articulated her identity through her enjoyment of cooking and other people's appreciation of her skill and the food itself. In some ways, the material work of making the meal is easier than the emotion work of being a good host. For Nora, making dessert is one of the most pleasurable activities and yet in this case, she gave up the thing she likes best in order to make her guest feel included. In stating that "it's always a balance," Nora implied that each of these social interactions is fraught with new circumstances and perhaps, new rules of conduct. Sociability on a small scale fosters a greater degree of intimacy. In doing so, Nora must accommodate changes to her ideal construction of the event. According to Simmel, "a gathering of only a few persons permits considerable mutual adaptation" (in Wolff, 1950, 112). Someone like Pam resists others' contributions partly because her parties are for one hundred or more people. Her resistance restricts the number of accommodations she has to make.

People shift the nature of hospitality at dinner parties for a variety of reasons. Here, Nora is describing how, even though she takes great pleasure in doing the cooking and orchestrating the event, she has decided it is more important to accommodate others. One key way is to accept their participation by having some role beyond being companionable. Bringing something (contributing food, specifically) allows people to redefine (or renegotiate) reciprocity. In this case, the shift allows a perception that the division of labor between host and guest is not so large. What's interesting in this case is that Nora is not really willing to compromise her version of the event: she's still in control of the menu and the format. She takes this woman's contribution into the kitchen and modifies it so it "becomes" part of her original idea. The "balance" she describes is of uniqueness and connectedness, but also of reciprocity and attention. Her guests feel unique because she has prepared and cooked a meal for them—that is, done work on their behalf. At the same time, they feel connected because they have been made a part of the activity. Her work of constructing this event, including the kinds of foods that will be served and how it will all come together and look, has to be balanced with the desire to make people feel wanted, welcome, and comfortable. So, she must find a way to incorporate the dessert that a woman brought. There is both pleasure and tension in her description. In contrast to Cindy, whose flexibility and creativity rest in her ability to construct a menu at the last minute, Nora's rests on her ability to incorporate something unexpected into her own aesthetic production. Not all hosts are able or willing to do this: recall that Pam refused to serve Bernice's runny potato salad rather than compromise her menu. Many upper-middle-class professionals like Gerry, Evan, and Gina and Sam restrict the form of the meal and event by choosing the guests and their contributions prior to the event. Given women's greater responsibility for emotion and interaction work, it is not surprising that the majority of these negotiations take place between women. As guests, women may feel the pull of mutual obligation in a different way than men.

The fact that Nora's guest brought commercially prepared food also affects the way in which it is received into Nora's version of hospitality. There are shifting hierarchies of taste concerning the divide between homemade and commercial foods. Among the people in Warde and Martens' study (2001), a vast majority considered real hospitality to be a "home cooked meal" rather than foods that were catered or from take-out restaurants. In the case of domestic hospitality, foods made "from scratch" are more valued than commercial foods. From Nora's description it's difficult to evaluate the bakery-made cookies, since she does not indicate anything about their quality. What's significant is that Nora sets her own creation aside to "make it work."

From the guest's side of the equation, contributing to the meal lessens the depth of the responsibility for reciprocity, or at least strengthens the relationships. Throughout my observations and interviews this was a consistent theme: people often experienced discomfort if they could not demonstrate that they contributed, either emotionally by constructing an atmosphere conducive to friendship, or materially, by adding their food or labor to the performance. Gender performances often were expressed through this process, in that women were more likely to express concerns about reciprocity and contributing. In their study of domestic and commercial eating in England, Warde and Martens (2001) similarly suggest: "We did not explore further . . . but other evidence suggests that notions of appropriate gender conduct in the kitchen limit opportunities for sharing [work]" (60). Interestingly, they conclude that contributions to a domestic meal did not ease the interactional burdens since "the obligation to reciprocity was not assuaged by gifts brought to the meal" (60). While this was occasionally true among the people I interviewed, I also found that reciprocity itself was an ideal rather than an enactment, especially among those who socialized in groups with varying resources. Perhaps in contemporary American society some people are less comfortable being "entirely dependent" upon friends who are not kin and not paid service workers. Interestingly, upper-middle-class people were less likely to have this concern: they often reciprocated in kind by inviting people over for dinner. The other kinds of events that were freer of these concerns were ones where there was an overarching reason for the event, like a birthday where people brought gifts, or a holiday where guests could treat the hosts to flowers or seasonally appropriate gifts.

In order to feel connected to a social group, even a small informal one, people need to actively do something to demonstrate their connection. Still, in these kinds of performative events, the definitional power is more in the hands of the hosts than the guests. Gina and Sam control the contributions of guests by assigning categories of food items that fit with their prescribed menu. It was probably not accidental that Gina gave the least complicated item (bread) to the guests who were the least familiar.[5] When Nora allows guests to contribute, she gives out a task that she perceives as "less work," such as a salad she describes as "not something I'm putting a lot of stuff into." This is both to limit the guest's sense of work and obligation, but also to keep the main effort, thought, and rewards in Nora's hands. To some people, items like salad are also less significant in terms of skill and effort in the overall menu. Although Nora's interests, knowledge, and cooking skills were comparable to those of people like Gerry, Evan, Perry, and Joanne, she subordinates some of those skills in order to "make friends." Although in this case, reciprocal hospitality is not necessary for economic survival, it is an extremely important hedge against social isolation. Given Nora's recent loss of social networks, the cultivation of these bonds is not a trivial act.

"It'll Give Them Something to Talk About"

Sources that describe a decline in domestic hospitality often pinpoint a key cause as women's increased participation in the labor force, especially those in the upper-middle-class professions. Although this may be true, I also found evidence that socializing with friends and colleagues was extremely important to people in helping them define the time outside of work. The adaptations and modifications that women in particular need to make in order to accommodate the demands of work and family and friendship networks are instructive about the workings of power in interpersonal relationships. In a number of these examples, women negotiate gendered expectations by relying on resources and privileges accorded to them by their socioeconomic class.

Deanna is an African American woman in her late fifties with a thriving career. She has grown children and a spouse who is also a full-time professional. She began talking to me about the changes and continuities in her social relationships over the span of her adult life, particularly noting the changes that have happened as she became more successful and publicly prominent. First, she described a range of social networks in her current life:

> Well, over the course of a year there are about three groups of people, maybe four groups of people, that I would socialize and eat with. One is the staff here at the firm. People that I work with here. They constantly have parties and other social events that I get together with. Then, another group is professional as well. And that includes other [professionals]. Someone will have a dinner at their home, or have a party for somebody who's either coming or going. And, we get together at that type of an event. Then I have family events. Ah, oh, the categories are beginning to extend. It's more than four. When I think about family. I have immediate family, which is my husband and my kids, when they're home. And then, we travel and spend time with other family members, like in-laws, aunts and uncles, cousins. And we usually go out to dinner. Or, have a feast of some kind with them. And then, there are people that I would categorize as my peer group; friends. And usually we will have some type of intimate dinner or a large get-together, potluck type of event. So I've got a variety of situations that involve eating and socializing.

Later in the interview, Deanna described her peer group as mainly African Americans, while some of her other social groups are racially mixed. Deanna's social networks are broad and racially diverse in comparison to the white upper-middle-class professionals I interviewed. This variety is partly a result of Deanna's career, which required a lot of high-profile sociability. At the same time, I found it interesting that many of the African American professionals I talked to placed a lot of emphasis on their desire to maintain networks of friends and colleagues. In her descriptions of sociable occasions, there were some events where these groups also crossed over.

In general, Deanna noted that as her career has "taken off," they eat out at restaurants, especially with more frequency than they cook for people at home. Affluent families, especially those composed of at least one professional worker, tend to eat out more frequently than those who are less socially and economically advantaged. According to Warde and Martens (2001) these differences are not only about differences in income but about the cultural aspects of distinction that arise from educational and occupational experiences (70). Modes of eating out are a key form of class distinction. Deanna said, "the more I got involved in administrating, the more responsibilities I had, the less entertaining I've done. I like to eat out. I don't mind because I do have to think about how I'm going to use my time." Deanna situates restaurant-going as part of upward mobility and career changes but also as less demanding of her personal labor than cooking. Warde and Martens (2001) question "given the way in which domestic food tasks have traditionally been distributed, the benefits and pleasures created from eating away from home might be expected to accrue more to women than men" (11). Implicit in Deanna's description is the understanding that if she and Harvey had friends over, the majority of the invisible labor would be hers, even though they both have demanding jobs (at this time, hers even more so). Although it wasn't clear which of them currently does more of the daily food work, Deanna was the main food person when their children were young.

Deanna articulated how, with a move into a particular kind of upper-middle-class professional life, her experiences regarding "taste" and expectations about social events have shifted as her friend networks have shifted. People often described this through changes in their concerns and knowledge about presentation and the food and wine:

> The best parties were when I was a law student. You know we'd just invite people over for dinner and wouldn't have to worry about anything matching or being interesting or colorful. . . . Now with my set of friends, I not only have to think about what I'm going to feed them but how is the table going to look when they come in.
>
> As a law student I would get a big bottle of Gallo. Put the Gallo bottle on the table and everybody would help themselves. Nobody would raise an eyebrow, they'd say, oh boy what a good price look at all this wine for five bucks. And we would drink it through the night. Now if I don't have a recognizable—if I have a recognizable label I'm worried but it's a—-, I have friends who say do you have Kendall-Jackson Chardonnay? Uh. How about a Robert Mondavi?

> *Do you think that's because of, you know, sort of where people are professionally?*
> I think it's that they're discerning. I don't think it's a sense of pretension. I think it is that they know. You know, it's like if you ask them what kind of wine, they know. They're knowledgeable about wine and so they want something that makes sense. I've learned to appreciate wine [from] traveling and knowing what a good wine can do to enhance the meal. It all comes about in terms of what you're exposed to. My wine tasting would have been limited if I didn't do some of the things I've had the opportunity to do, like travel.

As a result of her job, Deanna has traveled around the world, perhaps more extensively than anyone else I interviewed. She matter-of-factly described her cultural capital and habitus as something acquired and shared among a similar group of people. "Discerning" is a significant indicator of class-based taste. Interestingly, Deanna viewed both her current and past cultural tastes as equivalent: it's not that one is inherently better than the other, but simply, once one knows about a particular taste culture, it "makes sense." This description is different than the kind of complete rejection of prior taste experiences by people like Joanne (see Chapter 6). It is doubtful that Deanna and Harvey buy Gallo wine now any more than Joanne makes "food from boxes." However, the differences in attitude matter in terms of comfort and security of class position. Deanna is clearly more certain about her social, economic, and professional standing than Joanne, who struggles to assert a gender and class identity outside the paid marketplace, beyond her devalued work of changing diapers. It's also important to Deanna not to reject those people and times, because not all of her African American colleagues have had comparable upward mobility.

At the same time, because of the demands of her professional life, Deanna is more willing to use prepared foods at her parties. Many of the professional women I spoke to talked about strategies they had for reducing the amount of labor expected of them for domestic kin-keeping and sociable events. Although entertaining properly is supposed to take more time and effort than everyday meals, one key improvisation came from use of store-made foods. Both straight and gay couples who have greater economic means rely on the commercial marketplace to "buy out" of domestic labor. According to Carrington (1999), "All of this purchasing feeding work in the market place enables more affluent couples to achieve a greater degree of egalitarianism in their relationships. . . . [T]hey purchase that equality in the marketplace" (62). Deanna talked about occasionally buying bakery-made desserts for parties. Likewise, she talked about how some expectations of reciprocity were lighter in her professional life because she traveled in circles where restaurant going was a preferred form of socializing. At the same time, Deanna does not entirely escape from the social demands for her to do gender through feeding work. At one point, she complained about her grown children expecting her to do the work of creating holiday meals the same way every year, a common problem for women who are responsible for the production of such family events. Pleck (2000) points to historical expectations for the middle-class mother who, for holidays with kin, "was at the center of the sentimental ritual, symbolizing tradition and cultural identity" (16). In particular, family expectations for holiday meals often center on elaborate but routinized cooking, one that many cooks found less enjoyable to prepare. Deanna had, in fact, devised some strategies for resisting doing gender for her family:

I think with the kids out of the house I can do more things. I'm gonna sneak some of the stuff in the house anyway, from Whole Foods [an expensive natural foods supermarket]. And so, I mean, they make such good stuff they (the kids) won't know anyway. . . . I'm just going to take it out of the containers, put it in the refrigerator and have everything ready. I'm not going to sweat that anymore, standing at the sink all day, fixing those string beans and cleaning the kale!

Deanna claimed that her children's complaints are not about the tastes of commercial foods, but rather about their need for her to maintain the traditions from their childhood. Although in this instance she is describing a family meal, Deanna generally referenced the commercial marketplace as a "good consumer" who knew where to get quality bread or pies. Such foods were not homemade but from the gourmet, artisanal end of the commercial spectrum acceptable according to the standards of her family and upper-middle-class guests. Deanna has the economic and social resources to buy herself time and freedom from some aspects of domestic labor. However, in the case of her grown children's desire to hold her accountable, she purchases such freedom by deception, retaining the misleading impression that she can easily juggle the demands of professional life with unpaid domestic caring work. In fact, Warde and Martens (2001) conclude that "not only has restaurant-going failed to reduce women's domestic obligations for food preparation but it may even have made the burden more onerous by raising expectations regarding quality and variety of dishes" (277). This is true for many of the women I interviewed, who must be discerning both as consumers and as cooks.

Deanna has made some other adaptations to her socializing, emerging, as she says, out of her security in her professional life now. One of the things she talked about frequently was how little time she has to relax by herself, wishing for an hour in the evening to read. In constructing her social relations, Deanna wanted to make sure she has the power to define "free time," outside of the constant and very public demands of her professional life. She told me about two interesting strategies that make it easier for her to entertain and feel like she is in control, particularly of the temporal sequencing, while still making sure her guests feel connected. Here is one example:

Just most recently, I had a party at my house. And it was a lot of fun because there was a mixture of people there. I think the whole meal and the whole evening becomes fun when you let people do things. I mean I think, you know, it, it's hard to get up from the setting, and you're off in the kitchen somewhere fixing stuff and everybody else is in around socializing. So I have learned now to give people things to do, for part of the evening meal. So, yeah, I mean, I let some people set the table. I know how I want it set but somebody could put the plates out, somebody can do the glasses.

So it's not like they're walking into circumstances where everything's set.
No, I let that . . . I give, I give 'em each an assignment. I give—I have these things for people to do. And that sort of breaks the ice, too. Once, you know, before getting to the table everybody is helping and I mean, even if it's just finding the napkins. I mean, find 'em. They're in the cabinet on the left. . . . I'll tell you where they are, spend some time finding 'em, I don't care. But it does, you know, give people an activity. And they're occupied and it's a nice dinner conversation for awhile. So that was fun.

Deanna has control over the form of the event ("I know how I want it set") but again, she "opens it up" so that guests feel useful. The contemporary discourse about food and socializing sees the food preparation itself as a useful tool in creating connections by giving people something to do while they listen to someone else talk. Deanna provides the same kind of activity, where guests participate in a way that eases some of the sense that they are being waited on. Constructing comfort in sociability means easing the reciprocal obligations for the guest, such that any contributions that they make to the event at hand lessens the sense that they have placed a large burden on the host that can be repaid in kind only at a later date. The rigid formality of the host/guest roles may be discomforting to many contemporary Americans. Although people in Warde and Martens' study shared an understanding of formal entertaining, few attempted to achieve it and many associated such occasions with discomfort and inhibition (59). One possibility is that, in contemporary sociability, there is more visible awareness of being served and cared for by someone who is not a paid helper or kin.

On the host's side of the equation, Deanna finds ways to ease her own work by subverting the host role. She describes these shifts as coming out of her "age and experience." In this case, her strategy is unique because a seemingly unalterable rule for hosting is that one must be physically present:

And then the other thing and I think, this has taken me a while to do. I can't stay up late. If I've had a cocktail, a couple glasses of wine, around eleven o'clock I'm ready to go to bed. Yeah. And so this last time I had the dinner party and people were still sitting around my table. I got up and gave each one of them a kiss goodnight and said, if you want to stay longer you're welcome. I'm going to bed. Ah, good night. And Harvey's there, and Harvey likes to stay up if he's got people there to talk to he'll talk to them in the morning. I said no, I looked at myself and I said I'm a little tired. And I'm—I was fading. So I said, I, you know, I just gave 'em all a kiss goodnight and said see you tomorrow. Thanks for coming it was great. And I said, oh don't rush, you don't have to leave. I said, Harvey will still be here talking to you, so oh yeah. He did.

So you know they stayed for about another hour. But these were good friends. These were people I've known for a long time. There was a couple there that were new but they were nice. I said, well, that's just the way it is. It'll give them something to talk about when they leave.

It's important that some of the guests were intimates who have an established relationship with Deanna and Harvey. There's a presumption of interpersonal knowledge that would not make Deanna's act a breach of manners. For the other couple, such a gesture represents an initiation past a more informal and close boundary. Although guests may shorten the temporal sequencing of the event somewhat—for example, if they get tired—it's very difficult for a host to excuse herself from her own event. Women are supposed to be indispensable for the emotional and interactional work of caring for guests. Deanna manages to subvert this expectation through a combination of factors: one, because Harvey fills the role of good conversational companion; two, because some of the guests have the status of intimates who they've "known a long time"; and three, because, as Deanna herself says, she's secure enough in her social position to feel comfortable at that point in the evening asserting her own needs above those of her guests.

Although they are held accountable for gender performances in sociable occasions, women with greater social and economic resources can challenge and change some parts of the expectations of doing gender at these performative events. The women who were most able to do this were paid professional workers with established careers and high incomes. Those changes do modify or shift the nature of sociability.

"You Just Watch People Soften to Your Potatoes"

Creating sociability and friendship networks was a big concern to some of my respondents, even when their work and home lives put constraints on the time, energy, and resources available to do this. This need is highlighted for people when, as in Nora's case, their social circumstances change and the work of constructing social life is made more apparent and visible. In Rawlins's examination of friendship across the life course (1992), he commented on the nature of adult relationships:

Adults cultivate reasonably stable configurations of relationships of self with others, termed "life structures" by Levinson et al. However, inevitable periods of flux, questioning and critical reflection trigger and reveal changes within oneself and in relations with one's spouse, family, friends, work associates, and/or the larger society. Consequently, individuals find themselves facing or avoiding the requirements of negotiating alternative internal and external arrangements. Viewed in this way, the daily events of adulthood continually present both incipient and undeniable practical and emotional challenges. (159)

These changes are even more difficult to negotiate when individuals do not fulfill some expected part of their gender performance. In the case of some women, not being able or willing to cook was an issue when constructing social networks. For example, one woman told me she hated cooking and described having people over her house as "sheer hell." Since her divorce, she said she organized all her socializing around eating out. But what of people who firmly ascribe to ideas about domestic hospitality even as their social and material circumstances constrain its enactment? Helen is a teacher and administrator in her late fifties with a secure professional income. A single African American woman, she emphasized constructing community through food. For most of her life Helen lived in Boston where she had a close network of friends and family. At the time I interviewed her, she had been living in the Midwest in a medium-sized city for about six years but she still described it as being an adjustment. Even so, she had made many social connections through work (both colleagues and students), involvement in church, and in her neighborhood. In fact, her sociable activities and contacts were fairly wide-ranging in comparison with some of the people I interviewed. Helen talked about cooking as something she couldn't do—and yet she used food effectively to make these social networks. She joked to me, "I don't cook. My friends cook. I think I pick them on the basis of whether or not they can cook. Do you cook? Good. You can be my friend."

Even though she was joking, it's clear from Helen's conversation with me that she saw food as central to making social interaction easier and more possible. She told me about book groups she'd been part of and how she tried to "facilitate" making these groups happen. She went on to say, "The hard thing is to find the right book. Then the hard thing to do is to find the right day. And then, the hard thing to do is to get the right kinds of people together. So, I can sweeten the pot by making something nice and having nice things for them when they come."

Helen makes visible the emotional labor of constructing community because she does it frequently, overtly, and competently. Like Perry, as a single person, Helen has more of an overt awareness of the work of such events because it's not shared. She viewed domestic hospitality as central to her social and work lives here in this "new" place. The significance of food as

social lubricant comes up when she talks about helping new students ac-
climate to school: "I don't think of food kind of as a discrete thing. . . . [P]art
of the process is that a lot of kids just feel alone, they just don't seem to have
someone to listen to them. You know one of the nice things about food is that
you can listen to people, you can just chew away and go 'um-hum' and nod
your head and you know, just watch people kind of soften to your potatoes
and stuff like that."

In some of these cases, there are status differences between Helen and
some of her guests: the informal format is a way of putting them at ease.
Having people over to her house is a crucial part of her sociable activities.
At one point Helen wished for a larger house but she said she likes her current suburban neighborhood where she knows all her neighbors and there's
a fenced yard for her dog. Many although not all of Helen's dinners are buffets, partly because of the size of her house and partly because, to her, it feels
"comfortable":

> Well, it turns out to be that usually, the maximum around here is twelve, believe
> it or not, twelve people can fit very comfortably kind of moving around this
> area, and I, I'm really surprised you know, 'cause I push all the furniture back,
> I turn the table so it's either up against the window or this wall here so people
> can get at the food and talk to each other . . . you know, there's lots of space in
> front of it and it works.

Making the events informal buffets also means they can be a bit larger
than the traditional formal dinner party. Although Helen claims, "I don't
know how to cook, but I know how to pretend to cook," she has developed
a repertoire of what she calls "simple dishes" that she provides. The menus
she's worked out make it possible for her to "have folks over and not worry
about feeding them well." At the same time, she doesn't sacrifice "taste," as
she talked about finding recipes that met her standards for "good food" but
that she could cook without worrying if they would turn out ok:

> I can cook chicken in rice with cut-up vegetables all around in one big pan.
> I'm a one-pan cook. I can do a beef stew, not the way my mother does (more
> complicated) but where you stick it all in a casserole and put a cream soup, a
> cup of wine, lots of veggies, and you cook it for like two and a half hours. And
> you season it and put it in a nice little piece of pottery and you put it on the
> table with salad and fresh bread, nice wine.

To Helen, people can relax and have a good time if they don't have to worry
about the work of feeding themselves. The presentation and the food itself
serve as social lubricants. In order to make this happen, Helen has learned

to cook. Additionally, like Deanna, she's comfortable relying on some commercially prepared foods (note the canned soup in her recipe) as long as they fit her criteria for "good":

> Sometimes I buy those big [premade] trays of—what do you call that pasta when you have stuff inside it—lasagna. And I make mixed salad, all the usual kind of stuff. And well, here's the dessert thing. Either I go to Dusty's (a bakery) and I buy those little things or now I'm learning you can buy these little boxes of pirouettes and stuff like that. Like sometimes in summer I make fruit compote and I buy ice cream and then I put those little cookies on them.

The relationship between domestic hospitality and commercial foods is highly problematized in our culture, particularly as the resources used to promote commercial foods are vast and the critique often ignores the ways in which people's choices are limited despite a seemingly endless variety of options. Discourses about commercial food often criticize its use in family life, resting on some implicit biases about the nature of women's caring work and ideas about national culture. Coded into this discussion are issues of gender: no matter how advertising tries to convince people otherwise, women who use commercial foods are often seen as deficient in their caring work. Commercial foods may get represented as an extension of women's caring work, but such discourses operate against others that suggest a hierarchy of taste and caring with homemade food at the top in domestic sociability. Such ideologies are at odds with the realities of most contemporary women's lives, where time is a limited resource but caring work is still an expectation.

Canned soup as an ingredient in a homemade dish carries some cultural and historical meanings. On the one hand, Campbell's and other industrial food producers pushed their products to women as labor-saving, tasty alternatives. On the other hand, they used a rhetoric of care to get people to buy those products. Levenstein (1988) and Parkin (2001) suggest that advertisers historically played on a contradiction between "portraying cooking as an interesting, nurturing and creative pursuit and their claims that new processing techniques and packaging would free women from this boring, unpleasant task" (108).[6] However, among some "taste cultures," using canned soup is like eating white bread, a sign that the person doesn't know the correct codes of palatability. For example, Gerry, Evan, and Joanne would probably never admit to using canned soup in their daily cooking much less for guests. At the same time, Levenstein (1988) claims that in the 1950s, use of processed foods in daily meals often crossed class lines, citing the *Vassar Alumni Cookbook*, with recipes that included canned tomato soup and corn soup. Such trends are echoed in contemporary times. In 1995, Laura Shapiro suggested that

Americans enjoyed the "certainty" of commercial foods: "Campbell's soup is the fourth most widely used ingredient to prepare dinner in this country every night," says Kevin Lowery, of Campbell. "It's right after meat/poultry, seasoning/spices and pasta/rice." According to Campbell's research, more than a million cans of cream-of-mushroom soup are used in dinner recipes every day. "America has a fear of failure when it comes to cooking," says Lowery. "To be frank, that's why we've been successful."

Today, people's relationships to these foods are still problematized, since commercial foods are seen as the source of health and weight disparities, class differences, and capitalism unchecked. Warren Belasco (1993) illustrates how convenience foods like canned soup were the target of the whole foods movement, which encouraged "slow food—instead of the bogus warmth of a can of Campbell's soup—that camp symbol of the 1960s—take time to make soup from scratch" (52). The inheritors of this food discourse are today's middle- and upper-middle-class adults who view nutrition and whole foods as purchasable commodities necessary to class-based ideas about taste. At the same time, processed foods get reconfigured as nostalgic reenactments of childhood culture. Food writers such as Jan and Michael Stern sentementalized:

> Forthright food like meat loaf and instant mashed potatoes, Jell-O salad . . . Rice Krispies cookies. . . . Perhaps as the camp/pop artists of the early 1960s had known, the best way to resist kitsch was to embrace it wholeheartedly. Like Andy Warhol, the Sterns idolized Campbell's soup. . . . But the spirit of *Square Meals* was more 1980s than 1960s, more fundamentalist than mod. . . . Maybe Campbell's soup really did make "the perfect tuna casserole." (Belasco, 238)

As Belasco points out, such nostalgia is selective. Igor Kopytoff (1986) reminds us that all commodities have a biography and are best thought of as in the process of becoming rather than in an all-or-nothing state of being (73). If relations of class and gender get enacted and created around home-cooked meals, it stands that a comparative process operates with commercial foods like canned soup. Even so, this does not mean that people passively accept the cultural meanings imposed upon them by outside forces such as corporate advertisers and food "experts." The power to bestow meaning is not always a function of the power to determine availabilities.

In Helen's use of canned soup, she articulates a hierarchy of taste—her beef stew is "not her mother's" but it's acceptable for certain guests. Her professional career and her professed lack of cooking skills combine to make canned soup and store-made lasagna acceptable within a range of foods. Helen negotiates the terrain between convenience and care in a way that makes sense given her specific circumstances.

Despite the increasing public rhetoric for and against commercial foods, the history of industrial food production in the United States and the variety of consumer experiences of and with commercial food products suggest that not all Americans approach commercial foods in the same ways. Whatever detrimental impact commercial foods have had on our lives, Jack Goody (1997) reminds us that they have "enormously improved, in quantity, quality, and variety the diet (and usually the cuisine) of the urban working populations of the western world" (338). Given this, research on the use of commercial food products needs to consider the ways that people from various social and economic circumstances incorporate commercial foods into their lives. Alan Warde (1997) suggest that scholars of consumption are often remiss in

> recognizing the way in which mass-produced commodities can be customized, that is appropriated for personal and private purposes. . . . Groups of people buy a common commercial product then work on it, adapt it, convert it into something that is symbolically representative of personal and collective identity. That it was once a mass-produced commodity becomes irrelevant after its incorporation into a person's household, hobby, or life. In one sense, all cookery is of this nature: labour is added, and by transforming groceries into meals social and symbolic value is created. That is the currently legitimate labor of love. (152)

People like Deanna and Helen find that these commercial alternatives do fit into their lives, allowing them to engage in caring work while not compromising the amount of time they need to spend on their professional careers or their boundaries about what constitutes "good food." For the most part, both Helen and Deanna have the economic and cultural means to buy food from the "high end" of the commercial spectrum.

For Helen, it was a learning experience to discover and master a few dishes that function as tasty but simple dinners for friends and students. This learning process is a part of her adult life, a new performance of self as she approaches sixty. Helen also talked about finding interesting foods in the commercial sphere with the same happiness of a problem solved. Her sources for cooking information are eclectic and nonhierarchical—in other words, she'll take useful information from whatever source she can: "Like I learned something the other day. That you can cook carrots in, cinnamon or some kind of, what is it, cloves in your water with the carrots and it makes it taste good. I learned it, we had breakfast with some people on Sunday and I learned it from Celia and Celia learned it from having dinner at someone's house. She's like I am, so she's, you know, whatever you can get. Right, cloves in the water, I got that one."

People like Gerry, Joanne, and others who distinguished themselves by their "taste" in food were equally likely to learn new techniques from friends, but they talked about that learning in a very different way than Helen. Other people with similar social and economic capital spoke with precision distinguishing "good texts" and bad, preferences for certain magazines, cookbooks, or chefs as a sign of "taste." Helen did not feel the need to legitimate the sources of her knowledge. However, this doesn't mean Helen lacked a sense of cuisine or distinction in food. She develops a form of cultural capital that functions in both her old and new communities. As a single professional woman from an urban area she is very comfortable eating out and lamented the lack of good restaurant in her "new" home. She recognized "the unfairness of comparing the city to out here. I ought to be quiet, I know, I'm starting to annoy people with my complaints. But the food's all the same at these places." Although she acknowledges a regional bias for the East Coast, her comments can also be read as an interpretation of a taste culture.

Serving the meal buffet style makes it more informal, since guests can mingle and pick their own menu of foods. Helen is also willing to let guests make small contributions to parts of the meal, usually a bottle of wine or something they make that she feels comfortable accepting. Given her disclaimer about "not being able to cook" we can surmise that her gender performance is not as deeply tied up in her success as a cook. She is happy to be able to provide "good food" but, especially when entertaining students, neighbors, and other close friends, her social standing is not at risk. In one case, she did talk about being nervous about cooking for newer friends who she knew were "good cooks" but she did and "it was fine." From her descriptions, it seems that the kinds of "good cooks" that Helen cultivates as friends are of a different sort than those of white professionals like Dina and Gerry who use cooking skills as an exclusive boundary for sociable relationships. Although Helen joked about making friends with people because they're good cooks, her real impetus for closeness is situated in other less extrinsic characteristics of the individual.

For Helen, learning to cook as an adult was an adaptation to a new place without her older network of friends and family and without her established resources for socializing. Before moving to the Midwest she had a network of family and friends who cooked for her. ("When I go home, my mother always cooks.") In Boston she frequently visited with her family and older friends and talked about her family and extended kin, including a brother and sister-in-law who have nine siblings. She pointed out that this network of blended family and friends, are all "extremely close" and always get together for holiday gatherings of forty or more people. "They cook a lot. Even the guys know how to cook. . . . No one has ever asked me to cook. None of my other friends. They just don't. They know. I'm not the only one in the group that can't cook. I don't feel offended by that. We all sort of volunteer [for clean-up tasks] and you know, everyone works."

In this social network from her earlier life, the division of labor and the performative events are worked out along well-established lines. At home, among kin and fictive kin, Helen's gender performance is established over time and therefore not at stake through her food work. Based on a long history together, the group is already intimate and meals are informal. For much of Helen's adult life, these patterns existed in a way that seemed "natural" until she had to establish a new one in a new home. Similarly, she felt she could rely on the commercial alternatives and her friend's hospitality: "When I was in Boston, I used to kind of run around to everyone's house, you know, nine o'clock with this one, twelve o'clock dinner with this one, and so one of my friends said, 'why don't we just invite all your friends here and we'll have a big dinner.' But I don't cook, I call up Empire House, it's a Chinese place, and we order a truckload of Chinese food and go out and buy a lot of wine and beer and stuff like that."

Both her cultural and social capital are centered around Boston. Like other people I interviewed, a number of whom were single professional women over thirty, Helen's priority is creating an environment where people can socialize without feeling as if they have to contribute materially and socially, and her professed lack of cooking skills do not get in the way. Using foods prepared by restaurants, delis, and catering services is acceptable alternative—although, as Helen herself says, homemade food is "best."

The success of Helen's and Deanna's efforts rests on similar conditions. They are both secure in their economic and social standing and therefore take a more formal template and modify it to create the kind of sociable moments that allow for greater intimacy. To have people "soften into your potatoes" is to aim for and create a close sociable bond where food facilitates rather than mediates distances and status differences. However, as both Helen and Deanna's stories illustrate, such modifications do not radically undermine gender performances and accountability.

Buffets: From à la française to à la russe and Back Again

The buffet is, historically, an older style of dining than the formal dinner party. Margaret Visser (1990) describes "Baroque and Rococo dinners à la française" as the dominant kind of event, where people sat close together around a large table and were expected "to eat from the dishes placed in the immediate vicinity of their places. It was permissible to ask a servant to pass a helping of something placed some distance away, especially if the host had recommended it as he spoke his 'menu' at the beginning of the feast, but it was not done to ask too often" (201).

In what was also called "the old English style," the food was already placed out on the table when guests arrived. The role of the host was more direct in assisting guests, by serving and carving. Guests had more freedom to choose what foods enticed them without feeling the necessity to try everything (Kasson, 1990, 205). But dining à la française was gradually replaced by a new style in the 1800s, one that more closely resembles the dinner parties of the contemporary imagination. Margaret Visser (1991) recounts,

> The Russian Prince Kourakin was credited, in the 1830s in Paris, with first introducing an entirely new way of serving feasts. . . . Dishes began increasingly to be served in succession. After the soup followed by the entrées, a joint or large fish was typically brought in. . . . The arrival of feasting à la russe made extravagance a matter of the number and quality of dishes appearing in succession; it also enormously increased the number of the personnel needed for the last minute preparation and serving of all the dishes individually to the diners. The more servants you could provide, the more impressive your dinner à la russe—and the more different from normal everyday eating. . . . Under the new system every course had to be a culinary triumph, because all of it was offered to everyone. Variety now lay in temporal juxtaposition and range, the decoration and presentation of each dish, and careful attention to overall structure as a sequence. (202)

According to Kasson (1990), this style was particularly marked by the fact that it "drew a sharp line between diners and servants" (205) and, because of the bringing in and taking away of courses, increased the amount of dinnerware (cutlery, glasses, and plates) that a host had to have. Dining à la russe was more of a temporal performance where the meal "assumed a dignified and stately progression, a drama in which guests were recipients rather than actors and in which even host and hostess assumed roles as understated as possible" (207). Like the dinner parties described in Chapter 3, such meals require greater bodily control, careful displays of manners, and regulated appetites. For example, the guests at Gerry and Dina's dinner parties, whose meals were pre-plated, were restricted to a highly structured occasion and meal. Kasson details how this shift regulated appetite and changed the temporal nature of the meal:

> The old English style emphasized the display of plenty rather than order. Although soup and dessert marked the meals beginning and end, the interim was

relatively unstructured; diners simply followed their appetites in choosing what to eat. This freedom, however, became redefined as disorder, even slovenliness, according to the rising standards of middle class refinement. Appetites were no longer to be freely satisfied, but to be disciplined in accordance with sanctioned notions of taste and ceremonial forms and rhythms. (207)

Historians of manners suggest that such a shift was in accord with a greater demand for behavior at the table to reflect social and cultural distinctions in social class. As abundance became more generally available to the larger masses of people, particularly in the United States, quantity no longer operated as a crucial distinguisher of class. According to Visser (1991), "At formal dinners today, no one may take a second helping: dishes are passed but once. The emphasis is on speed and variety. Eating a lot—of one dish, anyway—is not elegant. This was not the case at dinners à la française, where, just because everything was laid out on view, diners were thought to be especially polite if they ate—repeatedly if they liked—from only one or two of the dishes standing near their seats" (223).

Visser concludes that today's buffet dinners are contemporary versions of the older style of dining: à la française being more like a buffet, à la russe being more like a dinner party: "A 'buffet' meal foregoes table, immobility, and precedence, but partly compensates for loss of formal eclat by means of the display of food; it is a return to some of the principles of dinner à la française. But ceremonial intensity need not be commensurate with the quantity of the food consumed: it is possible for a meal to consist of very little . . . where the simplest elements bear all the ceremony of a huge banquet" (204).

Given this history, one might expect to see buffets as a response to the formality and class divisions of dinner parties. In some senses, this held true in my interviews. People held buffets for a variety of reasons—the most obvious was that they do not have a dining room or a table big enough to accommodate everyone invited. Buffets are often the solution for people who hold large parties but don't have the space for many guests at a seated dinner. At the same time, lack of material resources were not the only reason for buffets. Sometimes, as Helen illustrates, the buffet is more suited to an informal mode of sociability. Buffets allow for a more relaxed interchange around the food: without the formal seating, guests can stand and talk in groupings of their own pleasing rather than being seated next to someone for the entire structured event. Helen described the "happy mingling" that happens when she pushes back the dining room table and makes room for people to talk. Others describe buffets as easier because the food is all prepared in advance. As one woman described it, "If they're all mingling and talking and eating, folks are less likely to notice it if I run off for fifteen minutes to finish off the whipped cream. If we're sitting around the table and I disappear, it's noticeable. The whole time I'm in the kitchen I feel rushed to get back out to the group. It's not like they can't live without me, you know, but there's that empty chair."

Who holds buffet events? Often people who invite friends over for particular events, where the food is supplemental to watching sports on television or playing cards. When men cook, barbecues are also often buffets, since buffet service takes some of the stress off the timing: there's food out already for people to eat while they wait for the other items to grill. Buffets can change the nature of space that people use in their household, creating less distinction between back stage and front stage, but also how guests can interact with each other, how people have the freedom to serve themselves—there is less visible concern that the host/hostess might be offended if individual guests don't like a dish. As Kasson and Visser suggest, buffets allow for a greater variety of food, too. The emphasis in buffets returns to quantity as much as quality. People who do buffets demonstrate hospitality by sharing abundance: more people can afford to do this than to have a dinner party. For example, although Cindy prefers to have dinner parties, some times her exuberance in cooking many dishes at the last minute means that their parties have to evolve into a buffet. Holding a buffet is yet another strategy used by women who struggle with gender expectations around sociability and caring work in a world where they are also engaged in the paid labor force.

Comfort and Informality: The Hosts with the Most

The quintessential buffet was described to me by Tom, a research scientist who works at a high-tech company. At the time I interviewed him, he had just finished his professional training and was describing changes to his social life as he moved into the work world: "At home, I only eat at restaurants now." Tom did not host parties: both his graduate school and current urban apartments were very small, the first having no dining area at all. As a single man with a professed inability to cook, the majority of his social experiences were at restaurants, or as a guest at buffets, potlucks, and informal shared meals with other friends. In talking about hospitality, Tom focused on his friends from college, Rob and Laurie. Laurie is a public school teacher. Rob is an engineer. They are a white married couple in their midthirties who live in a suburb of a medium-sized city close to where they both grew up and went to college. According to Tom, Rob is a "down home working-class guy even though he has a Master's degree." He and his wife both enjoy sports: Tom joked that the back of Rob's truck is always filled with balls, bats, and racquets. From Tom's experience, Rob and Laurie's social networks include college friends (who visit from a two- to six-hour drive away), local friends from childhood, work-related friends, and family. This group is mixed in terms of gender and race but not age. It was also not exclusively "couples." Because Rob and Laurie live not too far from their families of origin, their social events often include one of their siblings or cousins:

> Well, Rob kind of calls me up every couple of months or something and invites me out. And basically that's like a weekend of food. . . . Sometimes it's a big thing like a Super Bowl party where there's fifteen people and I don't know half of them, but sometimes it's just like Laurie says, well, I'm going to make lasagna. Like for the Super Bowl, Rob invited friends over and Laurie as well, friends from work and Laurie's sister and her family and stuff like that. . . . I knew some of them and didn't know others. There must have been about twelve to fifteen people there.
>
> So, you know, Rob calls me up and invites me out and basically Laurie cooks for the entire week prior. I mean, she likes to cook. And the funny thing is she never eats what she cooks. She makes all this food.! And they have this kind of 1950s arrangement where he does all the manly stuff and she cooks and cleans, but it works, I guess.

Unlike a number of the professionals described in Chapter 3, Rob and Laurie are not either geographically or socially distanced from their families. The foods Laurie cooks for their parties are of a different style than many of the professionals I interviewed, Although potentially "ethnic" food, lasagna, nachos, and cheesecake are standard American fare in many working- and middle-class households, regardless of ethnic or racial history. Furthermore, Laurie cooks but also provides commercial foods like chips and candy. Tom knew that her cooking was based on tradition since she talked about cooking "her mom's lasagna" and other dishes that were family recipes:

> What happens is we kind of assemble there at some point and for the mealtime Laurie is just yanking stuff out of the fridge and she always makes this nacho platter with guacamole. And there's always a cheesecake. . . . It's a grandmother's house, in the sense that, you know, there's just bowls of M&Ms in the living room and a bowl of cashews on a table. There's like candy and nuts everywhere and two cupboards in the kitchen that are just filled with cookies and crackers. You know, food that [my] Mom never had in the house. Junk food, I guess.
>
> If there's a barbecue, Rob does the barbecue. And Laurie just makes everything else. She's the kind of person who just like, is always rushing to clean everything up. She just zips it up without [anyone] noticing it.

Tom describes their house as "like your grandmother's or something," with cheesecake and junk food symbolizing a lack of pretensions and a celebratory release from nutritional restrictions. The mixture of homemade and commercial foods are ones that Tom categorizes as "comfort foods," because of their association with indulgence and childhood. According to Tom, Rob and Laurie eat "healthily" on a day-to-day basis since they're both athletic and concerned about keeping fit, but there are different rules for special occasions and social events. The foods Laurie serves mark these events as celebratory:

> It's basically a buffet kind of thing. They have this gigantic new house and they have a very big kitchen with a big table in it. And Laurie will kind of spread everything out. . . . It will always start with the nachos and appetizers kind of stuff.
>
> Everything's put out on the table. The candy bowls are always miraculously filled, you know. It's basically a buffet kind of thing. It's not sit-down or anything. We fill up plates and go somewhere and gorge ourselves.
>
> Most people are kind of casual, you know, jeans or something. Ok, yeah, fine, sometimes we do socialize around the TV. But [on other occasions] we all kind of stood and sat around the kitchen. [They have a room with a pool table.] That's usually kind of after everyone's done eating and everything's cleaned up and you know, like before bed a lot of times we'll go down and play pool for an hour.

The mix of people at the party might suggest that the sociability being constructed is more diffuse than at a dinner party. In some sense this is true, because people have a choice about who to talk to, what to eat, and what to do. However, from Tom's description, the gathering has a certain intimacy of family to it. The number of guests is higher than at a dinner party. The house is large so the centers of focus are spread between the television, the pool table, the food, and various conversations. Simmel suggests that at parties, "the more persons come together, the less it is probable that they converge in the more valuable and intimate sides of their natures" (in Wolff, 1950, 12). However, the presence of food, "a point that is common to their impulses and interests," and an ongoing familiarity of participants suggests that informality and size of a party does not completely restrict the possibilities for closeness. Although in theory the labor may be more evenly distributed among the household members, most of my interviews demonstrated that one person was usually responsible for the majority of the buffet. In this case, Rob and Laurie's events are almost entirely Laurie's production. So what makes it different than the dinner party? In a more relaxed format, Laurie and Rob can accommodate more people who know each other to varying degrees. "And we sit around talking," Tom adds. "It's extremely relaxing. It's great to see them. We're just not going to do anything exciting. But I found that I really enjoy doing that, relaxing and hanging out."

Do you bring stuff or do other people? Food? Flowers?

No, I really can't. . . . They both work . . . so money is not an issue. And they're just exceedingly generous. So I kind of go, "can I bring anything" and Rob's kind of like, "No, no, we're all set. Don't worry about it." Not even like soda or drinks. . . . I would feel like it was, not an insult, but I would feel like it would be noticeably out of place for me to bring food into that house. I think at the big parties sometimes people bring beer. Now I don't know if Rob told friends to bring it if they wanted to drink beer, then they should. But Rob and Laurie don't drink beer! There's always a joke about how, when Nick is there, he drinks beer. And it would be left in the fridge like, until the next time he's there. . . . I certainly don't remember anyone bringing a plate of food. Laurie was like responsible for a hundred percent of the food.

I mean, the food is sort of one facet of what I enjoy about being out there. What I enjoy most is just that Rob and Laurie are like . . . the hosts with the most. Not just in that kind of host, but in terms of friendship. . . . I used to get kind of apprehensive about going out there, because I thought, well, they're really. . . . I mean, they live this kind of simple happy existence and I'm (intruding). . . . But every time I went there I enjoyed myself immensely. They were so friendly, so obviously happy to see me and we just had fun.

Informality and intimacy emerge from the format of these events. Unlike Perry's dinner party, which was also a celebratory event prepared by one person with an abundance of food and an atmosphere of intimacy, Laurie and Rob's buffet parties achieve close sociability without alcohol, formal roles, or shared labor. Tom connects the generosity about food events to Rob and Laurie's ideas about friendship centered on relaxation and comfort: "They treat friends like family." At first Tom talked about being uncomfortable with an arrangement where he has no obvious material reciprocal obligations. However, after a number of occasions like this, he accepted their version of hospitality. Perhaps also, he became more comfortable as he adjusted to his role as someone akin to family. The buffet allows the lines between family and friends to blur. Unlike at a dinner party, there is no necessity for everyone at a buffet to interact with all the other guests equally and continually. People "mingle" and are not obliged to sit for any required length of time with others they don't know. The television with the football game on and the pool table downstairs provide additional activities around which people can center their conversation.

Although Rob contacts Tom and invites him to come visit, it's clear that the constructed comfort of their parties is a rigidly gendered production: Tom even calls them "a 1950s couple." Because Tom is Rob's friend from college, he's responsible for kin-work of keeping in touch. However, once the guests were invited and at their house, Laurie assumed a much greater responsibility for kin-work than Rob. This gendered labor for friends is similar to the invisible work of creating family: Laurie makes the food appear "like magic," and yet Tom knows she spends all week cooking for the events. Because Laurie is doing caring work equally for friends and family here, the more formal norms of reciprocity do not hold. People who are family are the recipients of caring work and are not always expected to reciprocate in kind. In fact, caring work is often a one-sided equation. I did not interview Laurie directly so it's not clear how the division of caring work operates within her extended family. However, given Tom's description of her production of domestic hospitality, it seems that in this case, caring and comfort are still gendered productions, such that women create this environment for friends as well as family because caring is coded as women's work. Intimacy, informality, and closeness are still dependent on women's labor.

The question that Rob and Laurie's story raises is related to deference—if women who do invisible feeding work for both family and friends are doing gender and doing deference, are there any contexts in which this can be resisted, subverted, or changed—even in small ways? When people create fictive kin out of friends, the obligations to friends are different from those to family. How do women resist the construction of deference embedded in these performances?

"I'm Not Serving Anyone!"

Pam is an African American woman who is married, has teenage children, and holds a professional job. I interviewed Pam along with her childhood friend Kendra at the home of Celia, who was also their "sorority sister and friend." Kendra is younger than Pam, single, and a professional in a big company that does hotel and restaurant management. Kendra and Pam have been friends for most of their lives. Like Joanne, Pam talked enthusiastically about cooking for friends and family as a routine feature of her domestic and social life. And again like Joanne and Helen, while her descriptions often mask the amount of work involved in creating meals, she did describe cooking as a learned task:

KENDRA: We grew up together. She could not cook.
PAM: I am, I've always been a tomboy . . . so if there was something to be done in the house, I was as far away from indoors as possible, but if there was a tree to climb I could beat anybody climbing the tree. . . . My father's big joke is, please, whatever you do, don't send the one that can't boil water to take

care of me. . . . And to this day that's the official joke. So I don't really know
how I ended up cooking because I never. I don't cook like my mother that's
for sure, because my mother is into buying.

KENDRA: When she got married. When you got married. Her husband is a big
eater. And that's when you tried to get creative because you really . . . I could
tell that you were experimenting.

Entry into marriage, like motherhood, is a key avenue for women's recruit-
ment to feeding work, such that even a "tomboy" like Pam participates. Her
marriage to a man who enjoys good food encouraged her to experiment and
learn to cook:

PAM: Oh I was experimenting! You know, my nephew, what my nephew re-
members most of all when I cooked the chicken and I knew I had read
somewhere that you could bake it using corn flakes. All I had was raisin
bran, what's the difference? I thought the chicken was fine with raisin bran
on it, a little sweet, a little different. They didn't appreciate it, you know. I'm
that kind of cook: I will mix up anything. . . . Nobody ever told me. It's like
I think I can put this in here and this in here. I am not a rule person at all.
I use a cookbook for cake and that kind of stuff but not for meat dishes or
vegetables. . . . I think at some point Kendra probably told me four ounces
is a serving (of meat).

KENDRA: Well, you know, I've been in food service all my life so a lot of stuff
sometimes just comes to me. . . . But there are certain recipes she would
need and I would just run them off for her for that amount of people that
she was going to serve.

PAM: But everything, I figure, is four ounces. And then I cook six.

Today Pam's planning and feeding work include daily meals for her family and small parties for her work colleagues. She talked about how, before
her oldest daughter left for college, she'd cook dinner for whatever teenage
friends might drop by: "I did a lot of it for me, yes, but also a lot for any kid
that is a part of me, you know, like Rachel and her friends come over and I
cook. . . . And even for work, I mean, my staff expects me to cook for them,
for different occasions. Either they come over to my house or I take food in."

Pam does feeding work to create bonds both at home and at work. She
and Kendra both agreed that she really enjoys cooking. Her enjoyment is
most vocally focused on two events. For the last twenty years she's held two
annual parties, one on the 4th of July and the other on Christmas Eve, where
she hosts and provides a buffet of food for more than one hundred people. In
many ways, her parties appear very boisterous but in line with the expectations of hospitality that B. Smith suggests in her books.

Kendra explained why Pam handles the majority of the work herself: "She just has to be in charge." Pam laughed and said, "I'm not a potluck person. I can't run out of food. I don't want people bringing stuff if you can't count on them to cook enough. And if it looks funny, I'm not putting it out on the table."

Pam had definitive ideas about what was appropriate for each type of party and for what constitutes "good taste" in food:

> I like the traditional food but I like to cook with a different flare, If I'm cooking string beans, I don't do a ham, I don't do smoked legs or whatever, I'm gonna do string beans with garlic. I love garlic—to me that's not a traditional African American kind of thing when it comes to adding ingredients, for our generation, but certainly not for my mother's. It's like garlic, your breath's gonna stink. And I'm like, hey that's gonna taste good. So at least in small amounts, I think it's different.

She also has a repertoire of cooking skills. Each year the annual parties have different food themes: she described menus that included Chinese, Mexican, Italian, Cajun, and barbecue. She talked about cooking these varied cuisines in a matter-of-fact tone, suggesting that none of them required more skills than another. In defining her expertise, the famous African American cook and author Verta Mae Smart Grosvenor argued that "It seems to me while certain foods have been labeled 'soul food' and associated with [us], Afro-Americans could be associated with all foods, I would explain that my kitchen was the world." In her comments about learning to cook, Pam sounded "relaxed" about the "rules" of learning to cook. Although the relaxedness is part of her self presentation, it's also clear that Kendra helps her be this way. She relies on Kendra to provide the technical information and to ease the mental work of "making sense" of cooking. Their description of food and friends is different from people like Joanne, Paula, or Gerry, who used a very different kind of language to describe "ethnic" cuisines as difficult cooking tasks, something they had to work to pursue and then demonstrate for others—creative "accomplishments" that carry status because the foods are exotic. Pam is engaged in something different—she cooks some foods that connect her to a racial community, although she modifies them to suit her own tastes.[7] At the same time, when she cooks cuisines that are "other" to her, they are simply incorporated into her menu. Pam's approach is reminiscent of an oft-quoted phrase from Grosvenor, who opines, "White folks act like they invented food and like there is some weird mystique surrounding it—something that only Julia and Jim can get to. There is no mystique. Food is food."

However, cooking *anything* for one hundred people or more is a monumental task. Both Martha Stewart and Emily Post suggest that parties of one hundred or more are best catered (although Stewart will go ahead and show you how to do it yourself, if you have the resources). When I asked Pam if people helped out before or during the party, she said, "I don't mind people in there talking—but if you want food, you need to set me free and get out of the way." Even though this is clearly Pam's creative terrain, she did agree to a certain amount of delegating and help. Kin and fictive kin who over time had proven they could be trusted are expected to bring certain items and they're "known for that." Pam doesn't bake much so one sister-in-law brings rolls. She talked about a friend who always makes "excellent coleslaw." As they both mentioned, Kendra helps Pam figure out how to adapt recipes or decide on the amount of food per person. Kendra occupies a special role in Pam's life, more like extended family or fictive kin. A single professional, she regularly stops by Pam's house for dinner on her way home from work. Their close "chosen kin" relationship as well as Kendra's knowledge of Pam's routines suggested that she probably assists Pam in ways that neither of them articulated. Sharing this work of caring, doing gender may be an extension of their sorority sister ethic.

Pam, like many of the other women, does gender by extending her caring work in the family into the realm of caring work for friends and colleagues. Like Joanne, she exercises a fair amount of creative control over the type of food and the presentation. While doing gender, all these women also draw on constructions of class and race in creating a form of socializing with food that fits their experiences and needs. For example, Pam's economic means allows her to throw such large and undeniably expensive parties without expecting most guests to contribute. She told me that no matter the size, she only does parties buffet style:

> I have never been willing to . . . there's something about serving somebody that is extremely objectionable to my personality, so like a lot of women fix their husband's plate, and I'm like, I'm not fixing nobody's plate, you need to get up and get your own plate. And I think that's one of the reasons why I do more buffet style because it's clear at that point that everybody's obligated for their own plate (or should be!) And if you think about old formality and hospitality, like you (Celia) prepared all of our desserts, that is really, well, for a small group like this I probably would have done it to control portions, but I won't do it for anything else.

Although she does not explicitly mention race in this context, it was clear that as an African American woman, she was resisting the historical association of black women and domestic service. Alice Deck (2001) suggests that in the United States from 1905 to 1953, images of African American women as cooks and housekeepers appear with persistence in novels, films, television sitcoms, and advertisements. To Pam, hospitality as comfort is about food, not service. She also said, "If you've been invited once (to Christmas Eve or 4th of July), it's *your* job next year to call me and check what time to come. If you don't call, I assume you're not coming." Pam's approach removes the work of having to invite people. The performative event is understood and implied, and maintaining group membership is now the guest's responsibility.

In order to manage these large parties, Pam adjusts the rules and expectations to fit her needs. She likes to be in charge. "I've been doing Christmas Eve since 1986 and my sister-in-law is convinced that I should do potluck because you know it's too much work, but that's my business."

In some contexts, women receive public recognition for their skill and effort at producing food. Kendra described Pam as "the person everybody knows can do it up right." Gloria Wade-Gayles (1997) connects black women's identities and cooking to their community's recognition of talent and skill:

> When the subject was a kitchen achievement, they were more generous with their compliments than they were if cooking were not involved; and the wording of their compliments focused on the talents of the cook, not simply on the good taste of the dish. Instead of saying, "That was a good cake," the women said, "You *know* you can cook a good cake." In other words, go ahead and be vain because you know you are good. (97)

Kendra went on to describe Pam's activities in language that invokes her connection to a community: "As a cook . . . she is, in some ways, a traditional African American woman, you see? She's not typical in that the food isn't fatty, but she uses [certain] spices. . . . And she overcooks. Everybody has to take a plate home. That's traditional. They expect it."

Despite the fact that many people of both races did this, both Kendra and Pam talked about Pam's tendency to cook way too much food and send people home "with a plate" as coming from her racial cultural background:[8]

KENDRA: Even though she is not a traditional cooker, she's not like her mother at all, she does have one thing in common with traditional African American women, she does overcook.

PAM: Oh yeah, no question. And my expectation is, see, my heathen cousin and she's planning on eating the next day all my leftovers. And if she doesn't show up then I have another relative that's going to eat them. So I'm not going to worry about having too much.

KENDRA: And what's typical of African Americans is we do take a plate home.

Women of different racial and class backgrounds exercised varying degrees of flexibility in how they constructed such events and gender performances. But even with public recognition, gender performances are structured in such a way as to make women's activities the fulfillment of an expectation rather than a source of surprise and special attention. Even Pam and Deanna struggle with how to exert power while doing an activity that constructs them in ways they'd prefer to resist. As an African American woman of economic means and with educational and cultural capital, she is constructing social space through arrangements and events that "make sense" to her rules—but also to her performance of self. And that "self" in order to do food work, works to control some of the racial and gender meanings that get applied and must somehow be distanced from the historical image of African American women as domestic servants and cooks.

On "Cultural Time"

When I asked people about how and why they structured their social events certain ways, they often referenced "social group" as a cultural entity—and such cultural entities have informal rules about the nature of time, of setting, of the symbolic weight and value of material things like foods. For example, although I don't include much of this data here, I did a few participant observations (POs) and interviews with some Latino/a couples who talked about how "Americans" have totally different ideas about time, eating, and parties. Indeed, at one of the POs set up for me, one of the couples arrived almost two hours after dinner had been served—and the hostess accommodated them by just setting another meal; one of the hosts sat and had another plate with them. At another event that was set up for me in order to interview some of the guests, I was trying to figure out how I was going to manage structured interviews while simultaneously participating in dinner. Dan and Lisette invited everyone for six o'clock but I was the only one who arrived at that time. Over the next hour, people arrived and the host cooked while we noshed on appetizers and did the structured interview. For many, this would be a very late dinner but the participants all seemed comfortable with the temporal sequencing. In fact, as outsider to both the specific group of friends and their interpretation of racial-ethnic culture, I was the only one who didn't recognize the structure before the event began. Deanna describes this, in terms of her African American friends, as "cultural time."

> So tell me a little about your peer group.
> It's interesting and I don't know how this comes about but I go to some parties and let's say they're predominately black. And it's expected that let's say the party starts about eight—first of all most people don't get there till ten. And by that time those of us who are not on cultural time are soused because we

haven't had anything to do but sit there and, you know, drink. So, when, you know, when the majority of the folks get there around ten o'clock, you know, the dancing and the socializing continues. And then around eleven people bring out big spreads of food and people will just eat and expect that food to be there. I'm, I, you know, I have an appreciation for, you know, people wanting to eat and drink. Eat after drinking to have some food in their stomach. But I like to eat and nibble at the same time so I like to have the whole spread there while I'm there on time. Eating and drinking, yes. I don't want to go to bed on all that food. But it's not unusual. Yeah. Yeah, But it has happened quite a bit.

Pam also talked about how she orchestrates time at her events to fit cultural expectations. In this case she is referring to an event that is predominantly family, but she extends the same discussion to her other parties:

My sister-in-law, who likes to assist with Christmas Eve . . . three o'clock this is when the family starts at three and it's over at seven. So at three o'clock, she says, "Pam you haven't started putting the food yet." No well, I haven't. "Well you told people three o'clock." Yeah, I know. . . . But part of the occasion is to have social time before, during, and after the meal. Three o'clock is like everything is out at three-thirty, you're cool, everything's out at four-thirty. You're cool. Whenever. This is not just about having the food and going home. This is a social event.

Racial-ethnic performances are also a part of the construction of "social space" that Bourdieu describes. Not all the African Americans, Latinos, or Euro-Americans I spoke to shared the same ideas about constructing events according to a "cultural time." For example, later in the interview, Deanna did a more pointed criticism of "having to eat so late at night." In their social lives people negotiate between the culturally mediated discourses and their own contextualized experience. This chapter demonstrates how gender and class performances converge even in more informal forms of sociability.

5. Potlucks

Observing the Mill River "Old versus Young" potluck barbecue was one of the experiences that prompted me to write this book. For five or six years my spouse played pickup basketball at a local park every Sunday morning. Like most regular pickup games, there were informal but enforced rules about when the games occurred, who got to play, and what protocol for type of play. Although it was like any other pickup game I'd ever watched, it was clear that every court has its own tacit protocols. I began observing because of an interest in the ways in which people negotiate informal behavior. The activities at Mill River had a routinized informality: people knew when to play; what time of year there would be someone there; when someone hadn't played in a while; which girlfriends, wives, partners, or children would be hanging around the outside of the court; when people outside the usual circle could or could not participate. I never saw anyone explicitly asked to leave; through mechanisms of playing time and allowing someone to "play" or vocally ignoring or hassling someone, it would become clear whether someone was welcome or not. In this setting, ignoring someone was more the norm, and in fact verbal hassling often signaled insider status. Compared to other pickup game sites, this one was described to me as "more genteel" in determining acceptance or rejection. Regular participation was also important for being given playing time: a player who hadn't shown up in a few weeks could expect to wait a while to get on the court.

The negotiation of informal and formal rules that structures pickup basketball parallels the same kinds of negotiations that structure potlucks. At Mill River, these occasions come together. One formal mechanism of acceptance for regular pickup play was an invitation to the end of the summer "Old versus Young" Basketball Game and Potluck Barbecue. Sometimes the invitations were photocopies handed out to the regulars, but more often people would extend the invitation verbally, "you'll be there of course." Although this potluck did not take place at someone's house, it illustrates the way informal events both cross and create social boundaries. The event was informal but routine and organized: participants contributed five dollars per person for chicken and also brought a side dish, drinks, or snacks. Some years there were "commemorative" T-shirts printed for players. A few times the game was filmed for viewing on local cable access television. This potluck/barbecue was coordinated around an activity and therefore the food might appear secondary to the game—and in some ways, it was. The timing of eating was entirely determined by the game, such that kids, partners, and observers had to wait to eat (especially when, on two occasions, the person cooking the chicken was also a player). Food work was gendered: men handled the barbecue while wives and partners brought side dishes, arranged the beverages and plates, and watched children.

As a participant observer, I was drawn to the event because general ideas and standards of food, both in terms of quality and quantity, were a significant topic of discussion. The first year I attended, a number of people commented on the dish I brought. Talking about the food became a way of meeting people and bridging differences. The majority of participants were African Americans living in a mostly white community who knew each other from various places outside the pickup games. As an unknown white woman, connected to the games only through my partner, I had to extend myself to start conversations, although at the potluck, food became the topic around which social relationships developed. There was a lot of commentary about people's food, what's good and what's acceptable, both at the meal and in general. Many of the men talked to me about where to get good food, where to buy things, what's good and what's not. Talking about what I brought was a way for people to start conversations. A few of the players were vegetarian or did not eat dairy products, so they were particularly grateful for dishes that they could eat, while everyone else hovered over the barbecued chicken. Conversing about the food became a form of inclusion, a shared interest. Gusfield suggests that at potlucks, the communal form of the meal becomes the source of conversation, the food itself reflecting the identity, skill, or status of the bearer. He writes, "Both the communality of the meal and the lack of clear structure for the evening throw people back upon each other, emphasizing their common levels and their mutual interests and appetites in food" (1994, 303). The presumption is that the food is a common thread. Because the form of the potluck is informal, it releases people from obligations of normative guest and host roles, such that the sociability can center around the food itself as a source of pleasure, entertainment, and achievement. Despite the numerous potlucks and picnics I'd attended in my life, this one stood out to me because of the ease of public interaction among people whose knowledge of each other varied greatly and crossed class and race boundaries. For two years, during and after this event, I informally interviewed some of the participants about their lives outside pickup basketball and spoke to them about food. Some of these conversations were the impetus for focusing on differences in experiences for whites and African Americans regarding the people they spent time with outside of work and family.

"The Luck of the Pot"

Potluck dinners appear in many people's repertoire of social events. The *Oxford English Dictionary* (1999) defines a potluck as "One's luck or chance as to what may be in the pot, i.e., cooked for a meal: used in reference to a person accepting another's hospitality at a meal without any special preparation having been made for him [*sic*]; chiefly in the phrase 'to take pot-luck.'"

This definition describes an event where both the meal planning and social experience are impromptu, but the guest is still partaking of foods provided by a host or hostess. What makes the event more informal than a dinner party or buffet is the nature of the food: guests understand that such a meal was not prepared in advance with special consideration for their needs. In fact, in Mary Douglas's schema of lines of demarcation created by various food events, taking potluck denotes a large degree of intimacy, because guests are being included in what is most likely a family meal.

But the word *potluck* has also come to mean a particular category of commensal events in the United States, where each participant brings a "dish to pass" to create a communal meal.[1] Church suppers and covered-dish dinners are other names for similar kinds of sociable meals, although these often take place in a public meeting place rather than someone's home.[2] In fact, the kind of "drop in and eat what the family eats" meals that the *OED* refers to are more akin to the kinds of meals I describe in Chapter 6, events that happen by chance or by habit, with great degrees of informality and blurred lines between kin and friends as fictive kin. Today, the everyday use of "potluck" connotes shared—but separate—labor for a communal social meal.

At one point in my research, I was interviewed by the food writer for a local newspaper who thought it might make a good column. As we talked,

I described some of the kinds of food events that people had told me about, including potlucks. An English woman who had lived in the United States for over twenty years, she commented with some disdain that potlucks were a "peculiarly American activity," complaining, "You never know what you're going to get," especially in terms of the overall menu of food items. I asked if she disliked the possibility of having too many desserts or not enough main courses, but her criticism focused more on "how things don't go together." At a potluck, the menu is often left up to chance and the desires and skills of the various contributors. In essence, to the food writer, potlucks lacked the expectations of an "ordered meal" with an A plus 2B structure where *A* is a large portion of a high-status food (meat, eggs, cheese), and *B* is a "complementary" side dish, such as vegetables, fruit, or grains. From a structuralist perspective, this format reveals and reflects underlying codes about the social order.[3]

The proper or ordered meal structures both daily food patterns and constructs family but is also reflected in the form of festive and special events, creating a symbolic hierarchy of ordinary and extra ordinary occasions. The structure of one meal depends on the overall patterning of meals. Douglas (1972) writes, "Food operates as a ranker of 'consumption events' allowing for very fine discriminations over a long time. For example, different menus and meal patterns prevail annually or weekly, for holidays and life cycle events, for Sundays and for weekdays" (62). The potluck, in its emphasis on abundance and variety and uncertainty about the overall menu, is, in some ways, more reminiscent of buffets and festive meals that shift the form.

In contrast to the desire for an ordered meal, the "American" attitude about informality is summarized by Angela, who said, "I think the thing about a potluck is you really have to roll with the punches, you know, if you get discordant things it just, that's just part of the nature of it, you know, it can't be this finely tuned thing that a dinner party is. . . . But I think that's part of the fun of it, I mean it took me a while to get used to being loose about it, you know, like, whatever follows, ok. The point is that we all bring and we all contribute and that's you know, what [it is], providing, um, grace and abundance."

Joseph Gusfield analyzed potlucks as a form of collective behavior and encountered a similar cultural dissonance between British and American ideas of hospitality. He writes, "English friends who had been graduate students in California threw a potluck dinner after their return . . . [and] were surprised when the potluck engendered anger and met with disapproval among their more reserved British friends. The dinner was viewed . . . as stingy and inhospitable. What my friends thought would be a casual fun affair was taken as a dereliction of social duties" (1994, 298).

The potluck as a social event represents a shift in both the *form of the meal* and *the normative expectations of hospitality*, away from formality and temporal sequencing. To Gusfield, the prevalence of this kind of informal entertaining in contemporary American contexts illustrates a historical shift in the nature of obligations and assumptions embedded in social interactions that take place in domestic settings. Most notably, the change alters the expected performances of host and guest. Because both emotional and material labor is shared at potlucks, people potentially construct different situated identities through these events than they might if orienting their social lives around more formal modes of entertaining. Furthermore, potlucks are about constructing temporary unities, bounded groups of informal and often heterogeneous people.

But, as a social form, what is a potluck? *Yankee Magazine's Church Suppers* writers claim "Today's New England potlucks follow the tradition of the 'carry-in' or 'covered-dish' supper: you are expected to bring a dish already cooked and ready to serve" (Chesman, 1996, xii). At potlucks, the responsibility for the food work, the social interactions, and the timing are more equally shared among participants. For example, Gusfield's description centers on the expectations between potlucks and formal meals: "The term 'pot-luck' refers in this context to a meal in which the contents—the prepared food—is the contribution of each guest to a common meal. Both the cost and the cooking are the obligations of both guests and hostess [*sic*]. It is not the same as some picnics, where each family brings its own meal. The potluck is a meal in which each guest eats the food that they and all the other guests and the hostess [*sic*] provided" (1994, 299).

This definition is generally what people I interviewed refer to in describing potlucks. Although people talked about meals with family and extended kin that were often potluck in format, they rarely viewed family events as a potluck.[4] Once or twice a family reunion was called a potluck, but the ordinary family, holiday, and kin-related get-togethers were not labeled as such, even when various participants shared in the preparations and cooking.

Like the dinner party, the potluck has a cultural template delineating the nature of the event, the expectations on participants, and the division of labor entailed. However, unlike the dinner party, the potluck is not the subject of numerous textual discourses. In particular, it's difficult to find written information about the history and evolution of the term.[5] Although the potluck is linked to a history of communal festive meals, its format varies somewhat because the food is almost all prepared individually, in advance. In community festivals, people often prepare the food together. Most writings on potlucks focus on church dinners, where the event occurs outside the domestic setting (Sacks, 2000). Potlucks that occur in people's homes are slightly different: although some are organized around group membership and community events, many are simply another form of voluntary sociability. The informality of the form as well as the relaxed rules about food suggest that, in its ideal form, the potluck would indeed be a site of more egalitarian sociability, such that the relationships cross social boundaries and the work is more evenly distributed among participants. However, while heterogeneity and comfort are often goals in potlucks, such events often foster a sense of community *within* rather than *across* social groups.

Bringing People Together

Potlucks are often associated with particular communities such as churches and religious groups as well as other kinds of formal and informal organizations. Judging from newspaper listings and online postings, potlucks are held by a wide range of organizations. Example of groups that hold regular potlucks include Texas Senior Citizen's Club, Pow-wow and Drum Group of Alabama, Folk Dance festivals, vegan activists, church revivals, family campgrounds, a New Jersey yacht club, numerous gay and lesbian organizations (some strictly social, some activist, and some a mixture of both), the Seeing Eye Puppy organization, many runner's clubs, Audubon groups, synagogues, and singles groups. Web sites for academic departments listed potlucks as social events for undergraduate and graduate students, supporting Gusfield's assertion of the potluck as particularly well suited to academic sociability. In almost every Web site that described a potluck or covered-dish dinner, the explicit purpose was to "bring people together" in the community, as in this story about a recent boater's association potluck:

> Essentially a covered-dish dinner, the party loaded every table with the kind of goodies that send dieters into frenzies of guilt (and turn well-meaning physicians into heinous figures from the Spanish Inquisition). In the end, the whole affair turned out to be more like a family gathering than merely people getting together to celebrate. It said something pretty tremendous about this unique club we belong to—that we're a lot deeper than clubs which simply get together once in a while for business. Our WBA primarily exists so that people can work together—cooperate—to solve complex but highly worthwhile problems. And it shows; a number of people commented on it. The chatter wasn't the same sort of bored, artificial small talk you hear at the average cocktail party (and this party was anything but dry!); it was that kind of animated conversation that happens when people who genuinely enjoy each other—people who are interested in each other—get together because it's fun to do so.

In comparison, in talking about dinner parties, no one I interviewed used the phrase "community" to describe the participants. The only exception was Harry, whose dinner parties were often given as fund-raisers for a church. Although the potluck is an informal mode of commensality, it is also associated with and practiced by groups who overtly attempt to create formal boundaries of inclusion. In many cases, the potluck is practiced by "intentional communities" of gays and lesbians, AA, activists, and religious groups, suggesting that a meal structured around shared labor also has a discursive emphasis on shared identities. For example, other groups who held regular potlucks were parents of children with disabilities, Tallahassee Community Friends of Old Time Dance, and the Savannah River Group Sierra Club. One can presume that the conversation at such parties, while potentially wide-ranging, would generally center on the issues and experiences that overtly draws the group together. The most detailed statement about potluck dinners, *Yankee Magazine's Church Suppers and Potluck Dinner Cookbook*, suggests,

> Potlucks have become a standard way for both formal and informal groups to gather. Not only are potlucks a popular time-saving and budget-stretching option for entertaining, they have also become standard practice for community groups that want a little time to socialize. We know of several monthly contra-dances that begin with potlucks. Organizations may start quarterly meetings with a potluck. Hockey players and their families may have a potluck at the end of the winter to celebrate the beginning of sleeping-in season for all those who have faithfully turned out for 5 AM rink time. (Chesman, 1996, xi)

At potlucks, especially those organized around other social activities, food functions to evoke sentiments that help socialize the individual as a member of a community. In this case, the work of food preparation is individualized (generally cooked or purchased prior to the event) but shared because the rules explicitly expect that everyone contributes in some way.

Among the people I interviewed, Larry and Rita were engaged in the widest ranging social networks. They are white upper-middle-class professionals in their forties with three children. More than most of the white professionals I talked to, Rita and Larry stressed their ethnic identities as significant to their sense of self. They talked about Rita's first-generation Italian family as a source of cooking skills. In filling out the demographic sheet for our interview, Larry filled in the word "Jewish" for his racial-ethnic identification (although he was definitely not the only person I interviewed who was). Almost all their socializing occurs around food. They rotate dinner parties with Gerry and Dina. Their cooking skills are professional enough that they were invited by a local gourmet restaurant to be guest chefs for a special fund-raising dinner. They cook together for family meals and attend many potlucks. One of their significant social obligations was as board members of a "spiritual and educational organization that sponsors workshops, conferences, and classes":

> LARRY: What we do with them, actually is much more traditional potlucks because we have to get together for some reason. Like, we have meetings probably once or twice a month, not board meetings, but mini meetings, sort of. . . . And they usually come to our house because we're centrally located. Pasta. For potlucks, we make pasta. Everybody has their developed roles. Mark brings bread. Bruce usually brings juice or chips or something like that. Sonya has become a wild card and has been bringing wild things like chocolate-covered strawberries. She's had a great summer: she's in a happy phase, so she'll bring sherbet, something else. People have their categories worked out. We actually . . . mostly for that—and this is the only time we do that—we have bottled pasta sauce. We never, ever eat that ourselves. But it's, like, we both get home from work, there's a meeting at six-thirty or seven o'clock. And the truth of the matter is that none of these people are gourmands. They don't care.
>
> RITA: In fact, some of them don't like spicy food—aggressively don't like spicy food or anything too highly seasoned.
>
> LARRY: One of the reasons I think people will come and the meetings are bearable is because we do food. But we don't put that much effort into the meeting food.

For Rita and Larry, these occasions are important, but the food is only to draw people to the meeting. The food, in this case, operates as Helen would say, "to sweeten the pot." Since the reason for the gathering is centered more on organizational business, the quality of the food and the effort spent by Rita and Larry is less than what they do for their family and their other socializing. Still, the format of the meal allows others to participate but not feel as if they have burdened the hosting couple. There is no sense that such a meal requires reciprocation, only continued attendance. Larry specifies that "everybody has their developed roles" and "people have their categories worked out" so that negotiating the order of the meal is not a concern. It's interesting that Larry associates Sonya's "wild" contributions to her emotions, her "happy phase." His description of her moods suggests a closeness, an intimacy of knowledge about another through his/her material acts, but not as superficial as the kind of knowledge that is restricted to food tastes. Larry does not see Sonya's choices as inherent to her class sensibilities, but rather flexible in what she brings socially, emotionally, and materially to the group. Because the purpose of the sociability and the focus of interactions is predetermined by people's membership in this group, the form of the event can be more informal than a dinner party. In putting together a potluck, the group takes what is offered, recognizing that people contribute what they can, based on their material and emotional resources. The whole, the group, is constructed from what comes at that moment.

"A Stress Reduction Party"

Many potlucks are connected to organizations and work. For example, Mike, who liked to hold dinner parties, also talked about organizing a regular potluck for the people he works with. He described his job in the social services as emotionally exhausting. Mike works for a nonprofit group that does advocacy services for people with disabilities. He described the office as a small place full of hardworking but underpaid people whose daily schedules include the stress of dealing with clients, other agencies, and bureaucracies. Although Mike also held dinner parties that included his work colleagues, in this case he saw having a potluck as a way of relieving stress and creating a common bond between coworkers:

> The party I had this past weekend, it was a potluck so everybody brought something.
>
> *And that was just sort of spur of the moment, that one, or?*
> More or less. I mean, I invited everyone because we hadn't had one in a while—we used to, at work, once a month, have what we called a stress reduction party. 'Cause working in human services, you know, it's a high-stress job . . . so it was like a week and a half before, I made up notices on my computer and just passed it out to everybody at work. We're getting together at my place, if you want to come, come, if you don't, oh well. And if you come, bring something to eat.
>
> *So what did people bring?*
> Ah, let's see. Somebody brought—it was a—mostly simple stuff, . . . somebody brought a fruit salad. One person did make like an American chop suey. I made, ah, those roll-up sandwiches and cut them into small pieces. I'd even thought of my vegetarian boss and made one without meat for her.
>
> *How many people were here?*
> A dozen.
>
> *That's a lot.*
> Especially when we're all sitting in this room talking. It's not a big room. But it was comfortable and we had fun and at the end it was all people who you could just say anything and it doesn't matter and we all laugh and have fun.

The obligation to attend is loose: the potluck, unlike a dinner party, is not entirely dependent on all participants attending. The success of the sociability is not necessarily dependent on any one individual (other than, perhaps, the hosting person) or a balance of individuals sitting around a table. The size of Mike's home and the number of people is significant because he lives in a small condo. Twelve is Emily Post's outside limit for a formal event, but in Mike's small house, six people barely fit around his dining room table. Mike organized the potluck because, as he implied, it was a regular event that hadn't taken place in a while and he felt it necessary. His desire to hold the party was a reading of the "emotional needs" of the workplace. Another reason why Mike hosted the party is because no one else had a house that was wheelchair accessible. In both his potlucks and his dinner parties, Mike has to take responsibility for hosting simply because it is often physically impossible for other people to host him. The physical limitations of space also place limits on reciprocal obligations.

So the planning from your end was making the sandwiches, inviting people?
And buying more soda then I could possibly have ever drank or use. 'Cause I told people I'd supply soft drinks, if they wanted more than that that's their responsibility. I've got about ten more liters of soda, two liter bottles of soda out there to drink still. I have one thing where I won't let anyone leave my house hungry . . . so I usually cook way too much and plan way too much food for the people and the number of people who are coming. But I don't like the idea of people leaving my door hungry.

Did you do that with the potluck?
Yeah, I had—yeah, I had more sandwiches then I needed.

Do you find that cooking is a . . . difficult factor for people with independent living?
Yeah, I mean—If you poll people with disabilities, a lot of people either, you know, just don't have the arm strength or whatever to do a lot of it, or a lot of people just don't enjoy it, as I do. . . . [T]hen I have a couple coworkers who do cook who may have a disability but not one that they live in a wheelchair-accessible apartment. So, like, I'd love to have you to dinner but I can't. And I'm like, well, come to my house and cook for me if you want to. And we've talked about doing that but we never have. But, I'm also the type who couldn't sit there and watch somebody else cook. I'd wanna be in there helping.

So, do you find when you get together with people that it's mostly here or elsewhere?
Yeah, mostly here. 'Cause I know I can get in it and I know I can use the bathroom. And I can cook here. And I have all my gadgets and tools and . . . repertoire that I need here. And I know I can find—reach everything I might need.

The food at the stress reduction party is deliberately easy to make, where people avoid "complicated dishes" and competition among contributions.

The point is for people to eat and socialize in a relaxing manner outside the demands of the workplace to be able to "just say anything." By opening up his home to his workplace colleagues, Mike provides a comfortable environment for sociability to take place. The potluck form alleviates reciprocal obligations. At the same time, Mike takes on the largest burden in terms of hosting, food work, and household labor. He clearly likes to be in control of part of the activity because he loves to cook. Although his work strives to make everyone relax, there's no real way to know whether everyone experiences the event as a form of stress reduction. More than the other participants, Mike has to make additional effort to make sure he's included. He made sure there's enough food by overpreparing, insuring that even if others don't bring much, it's not a big deal, because he's supplied a main course. The risk of the informal meal with diffuse labor is somewhat controlled by his work. The participants are already familiar with each other from a workplace that demands emotion work. People share status and a degree of closeness. Topics of conversation may be broad-ranging, but by limiting the participants, work-related topics always lurk as the possible centerpiece, a place where people can fall back on familiar terrain if need be. In a more diverse group of participants, there is no guarantee that people will find a common thread. In fact, Mike suggests that even though people enjoy the event, he does worry about the spouses and partners attending, who might feel "left out" of the main conversations. Because Mike is single and because he is attempting to de-stress his colleagues, he can be explicit about engaging in emotion work without jeopardizing his gender performance.

Bridging Differences

In poetry, essays, and fiction, "potluck" is sometimes used to illustrate a cultural "bridge" between differences. For example, in an anthology of essays about cross-cultural intimate relationships, one essay is titled "Another Traditional Arab-Jewish Iowa Potluck," which suggests that the racial-ethnic differences between the author, her spouse, and their respective families could be "bridged" by sharing food at their potluck wedding. In her autobiographical story about gaining acceptance for her Armenian American longtime partner from her southern white family, Martha Ayres uses a "parable of the lamb," an anecdote about her girlfriend's "ethnic" food contribution to the family's potluck reunion (Ayres, 1997). Food is symbolically and materially constructed as the bridge between sexual, regional, and ethnic differences. In many potluck cookbooks and articles, recipes span ethnic and regional categories. Although some of these recipes mirror the kind of "Americanized" ethnic fare that Stewart and Post describe, others involve more authentic ingredients or cite ethnically marked sources for their recipes. Sampling something new, tasting "the other" is seen as part of the fun of a potluck. In many ways, potlucks are constructed as a safe venue for tasting new foods because there are a variety of dishes to choose from. Such sampling isn't possible in the format of a dinner party, especially if the meal is served.

According to Gusfield, the potluck is a functional form of sociability when all or the majority of participants all belong to the same organization or workplace but have different social experiences. Because the informality of the potluck is in distinct contrast to the dinner party, Gusfield suggests that it allows people of different ages, genders, races, or occupational status to interact with fewer social constraints than they would experience at a dinner party. He asserts, "In such an egalitarian gathering, no one assumes the role of management and social authority. . . . [T]he synchronization of food and drink is lessened and the experiences of guests less homogeneous, less similar than in the case in a formal dinner party" (1994, 301).

When guests can move around freely, interacting with different people rather than being seated next to one person for a duration of courses, they can minimize their time with undesirable individuals or situations in a socially acceptable manner. In theory, people can excuse themselves to refresh a drink or get more food, finding new conversations in another part of the room. Because the potluck is a performative event following a diffused temporal sequence, guests can orchestrate their own interactions. Hosts are not expected to manage all the conversation and interactions. However, in less desirable outcomes, disparate groups of people can end up in different parts of the room, not interacting. James and Cheryl generally do smaller dinner parties with only a few people who know each other. One reason they gave was the bad experience of a big potluck. Cheryl said, "Remember that? All of the people from his office hung out in the kitchen and all of my friends hung out in the living room. In terms of everyone getting along, it was a disaster. I was stuck in one room and Jamie was in the other. It was so much work! The whole idea was for everyone to mix and relax. Let me tell you, it was not relaxing, at least not for us."

But more often, the potluck allows for a temporary suspension of such differences, especially when the people attending share some organizational or group membership. Gusfield highlights both the form and the shared food as important to creating connections between people who are often only tenuously and temporarily linked. Marion and John, who did dinner parties for most of their adult social lives, now also participate in potlucks with people who take them out of a comfortable class and race environment. They live in a predominantly white suburb (although the nearby city is more racially mixed), and their friends and neighbors are mostly white and middle- to upper-middle-class. Recently they have joined a support group for parents of alcoholic children, and their social lives have begun to include the other group members, many of whom are poor, working-class, and not white. Regarding her other parties Marion talked about formality as a requirement. With the support group, she chose to do a buffet potluck rather than a dinner party because she wanted to "set people at ease." Participants could comfortably contribute food and not feel a social obligation to reciprocate. Marion felt beholden to be the one to hold these dinners for a number of reasons. Although group members often go out for lunch after meetings, Marion noted that these events are not always inclusive because "some people don't have any money." She explained why she and John are the "logical" people to host social occasions for the group: "We're the only married couple [in the group] who are together, you know no fighting. . . . [Y]ou never know what the [other people's] homes are like, if they even have the space or whatever. At some of their homes, you never know what to expect . . . [someone] might be drinking too much. . . . We always have an Al-Anon holiday party because that's the only time that many people get out."

Implied in her evocation of their marriages and homes, Marion invokes class differences between herself and the other group members. Staging these events was a new social experience for Marion, clearly different than her lifelong comfort with upper-middle-class dinner parties. In particular, orchestrating these relationships steps outside the class and race codes with which she is familiar. These people, however different from her longtime friends and neighbors, are important to her. In our actual interview, Marion vacillated between wanting to talk about these friends yet needing to "protect" their identities. Her feelings about them were ambivalent, recognizing the shared need but concerned about the social differences. "They have become a great part of my life. . . . I've been forced to, I've done all kinds of things with these people . . . They're a lot like family and I don't even know who they are. . . . It's constant support . . . because you can't talk to your relatives about this stuff."

In the support groups, everyone shares the stigmatized identities related to drug or alcohol addiction in her/his family. There is an intimacy of shared problems, knowledge of private domestic situations even without the history and shared status of her other friendships. However, even sharing this one piece of identity does not mean that all lines of distance and intimacy are easily crossed. For example, Marion wants to be close to people but she's also aware that these relationships entail risks to her settled upper-middle-class worldview. For example, to invite people to the potlucks, they often use word of mouth because "there are some really sick people that you really wouldn't want them around." John and Marion are still socially quite different from many of the other group members. Setting herself apart from her guests, she commented that "our parties are like controlled and we have fun . . . and we've never had anything taken . . . everyone was good, I mean, nothing was broken or stolen." The potluck brings them together but it doesn't suspend all their differences. In fact, creating these events reinforces their social superiority by constructing hosting as an act of benevolence. John and Marion construct a temporary shared group to come together outside the regular group meetings. But "bridging" can often go only so far. Still, Marion and John's story illustrates the way that, within limits, the form of the potluck can make socializing across lines of difference less problematic.

Informality and Daily Life

Kristina and George Barstow are a married, working-class white couple with two children who attend a private religious school. George suffered a work-related injury that limits his employment and Kristina works as a secretary. They often shifted who was responsible for the majority of the domestic labor based on whose paid job required more effort at any given time. Although they both cook for biweekly potlucks with "old friends," people they've met through their children's school, and their religious community, Kristina saw any potential dinner party as her responsibility and expressed a strong dislike. She claimed she would do it only if she felt obligated—for example, having as a guest one of her children's teachers or a minister from the church. She said, "I don't like the pressure of saying I'm inviting you to dinner. . . . [I]t's like I feel like I have to, you know, make this fabulous meal. . . and there's this sort of tension and so only occasionally I'll do something like that. But it's more of a double-dutch kind of thing [in our daily lives]—we're going to someone else's and it's a potluck. There's this constant potluck thing going on, sometimes planned, sometimes, you know spur of the moment."

Potlucks serve a need for companionship in a way that minimizes the shared daily labor of having to cook full meals for individual households: mothers whose spouses were away or lesbians making community. Some people held events that combined family and friends. Joanne, who viewed cooking and constructing a dinner party as a "creative outlet," also enjoyed potluck dinners with other mothers of young children:

> My friend Jane will come over by herself. See, her husband works a lot and my husband works a lot. That's another facet too, is that I often have women come over with their kids and we'd eat together because it's easier to make one

shared meal instead of two separate ones. . . . [B]asically I'd bring a salad or they'd bring a salad and one of us would do the main meal and the bread and stuff. . . . It's almost a planned potluck. . . . It was, it was planned. This woman had a husband who's a doctor and he works a lot . . . he works a lot of night shifts. So she really understood that, you know, it was needed.

In this case, potluck fills a need for "family dinner" when some members of the family are routinely absent because of work. The desire for ongoing commensality was described to me by women like Joanne whose spouses were often away. When Joanne's life changed because of divorce and new full-time job, most of the other kinds of socializing she did ended, but the "mothers' dinners" remained a constant over the years until her children were more independent. Others who described similar practices included people in couples, where one partner worked the night shift, and younger adults in their early twemties whose lower incomes prevented them from going out with friends. Lauren, working as a teacher's aide in an urban elementary school said,

> You know, there's this idea that because we're young and all this . . . that's available here in the city, you know the music, movies, whatever, all that is "supposed" to be for us, but my friends and I can't afford it. Maybe some people get help from their parents so that even their shitty entry-level jobs don't matter, but most of us, you know, we're not shelling out twenty dollars a night to do stuff. It works out that a bunch of us live in the house and whoever's home and whoever you want to see will come over and we make dinner and hang out and laugh. I mean, yeah, sometimes we'll go out but it's not as regular as TV shows have you think.

Her friend Beth echoed the relationship between material resources and socializing:

> I get a salary at my job, which is pretty good in comparison to some people who make wages and no benefits. But, you know, I've still got to be careful. And most of my friends, I mean, yeah, once in a while we'll go get a burrito at the Tacqueria because they're just so good and it's late . . . but I'm trying not to do that so often. I like eating what people bring over: Dan works in a bakery so when he stops by he's always got all these baked goods leftover from the day. And last summer Erica would get all this garden stuff from a friend who had extra, so we ate great. . . . I guess it's all new to some of us anyway, so it's still fun to see what people can make.

Many of the younger people I interviewed described social lives that were shaped by these kinds of events. Because media and marketing discourses portray people in their twenties and thirties who do not have children as the main consumers of cultural products, restaurant-going, and general evenings out, it is somewhat surprising to find that so many of the younger people I spoke to had more complex social lives.

Women, Domestic Labor, and Shifting Hospitality

As Gusfield (1994) and Olesen (1993) have noted, a key but not exclusive reason for the decline of formalism in domestic hospitality is the increasing role of white middle-class women in the paid labor force, which constricts the category of people who are historically associated with and most often held responsible for producing dinner parties. For example, Angela, who likes giving dinner parties, also cited constraints on her time and energy as reasons why she and her husband were more likely to do potlucks. She said, "Oh yeah, I'm not working a lot this month . . . and like I went [grocery] shopping all morning, came home, made lunch, cleaned up from that, cleaned the house, made dinner, and that was the end of the day, that was it. I'm always busy and we don't have kids, just two dogs that make the place filthy. . . . I don't understand how people have a career, three kids, a husband."

Women are often more aware of the work that formal hospitality entails. Rita and Larry eat out with work colleagues, cook together with their three kids, do dinner parties with other upper-middle-class professional couples, and attend potlucks with their community groups. Both spoke of the great enjoyment they have cooking *because* it's work that they share. But when it becomes the production of only one individual, it loses its pleasurable aspects. Rita commented, "Oh yeah, we are basically usually good . . . coordinating the cooking. In fact, there's a rare one: A couple of Thanksgivings ago when Larry was on call, I had to do the entire meal, and I was just devastated. I could see why women hate this. . . . I'd never felt it before because I'd always done these either cooperatively with Larry or with other friends."

Among the people I interviewed, Rita and Larry are unusual (especially as people with children) in the degree to which they share the food work in both their daily domestic and social lives. However, their ability to do so is made possible by the backstage labor of a paid nanny who, following a list of instructions left in the morning, does all the prep work for whatever cooking Rita and Larry will be doing when they come home from work. Rita and Larry are both upper-middle-class professionals. Describing Rita's career as equally important and demanding as Larry's, they espoused egalitarian companionate ideas about their marriage and child-rearing. At the same time, they acknowledged that their material resources made it possible to juggle work, family, and a rich social life:

> LARRY: We are also lucky. We have somebody who works for us, who takes care of our kids during the day, and she does prep cooking very well. [During the week] that way when I come home from work and Rita's done with work, we can just put the stuff together; we don't have to start from scratch, and that makes a big difference.
>
> RITA: She cuts up the vegetables, thaws chicken, makes the salad. . . . I write her a list every day and I do all of that, all of the kind of assigning things.

Again, the flexibility of Larry and Rita's sociability is a result of their social and economic resources. Upper-middle-class people purchase time and equality through the marketplace and by paying people to do the less desirable work. This allows Rita and Larry to do gender around their careers and their domestic responsibilities in a more egalitarian way—and have a very rich social life while balancing three children and two careers. Paying someone else to do the less glamorous aspects of domestic labor is one strategy for balancing the competing demands on their time.

"A Place for People to Get Together Afterwards"

Potlucks are performative events where individuals devise many ways of sharing the work and social obligations of commensality. In people's descriptions of their social lives, potlucks tend to be more prevalent on occasions where some activity (other than eating together) is the "real" focus of the event. I found that when a food event was organized around some other mutual event such as television watching, poker games, or sporting events, people's expectations broaden about the kind of food (quality and quantity) provided and brought. Commercial foods are often more acceptable at potlucks partly because the food is not the central focus of the gathering. For example, Greg and Ted are two graduate student researchers who share an apartment. They both love to cook so much that they orient their weekly work schedules around cooking elaborate meals together. They are both deeply invested in learning to cook ethnic and regional cuisines and spend time, money, and energy on home cooking. However, when they host "homebrew beer nights," they get take-out food. "It wasn't ever fresh made food," said Greg, "because we were really about tasting the beer. Cooking would have been distracting."

If variety and "taste" are seen as intellectual achievements in middle-class family dinners and dinner parties, then an event that is more relaxed in form will also be more relaxed in food. The performative requirement is not necessar-

Potlucks   163

ily about food. Allan (1979, 1989) and DeVault (1991) suggest that middle-class sociability is about style, but something more complex emerges when looking at the differences between middle-class people who do both dinner parties and potlucks. Sociability is more nuanced and complicated—patterned, in effect around different social circles and different social needs. Style may be constituted through visible signs, but some contexts do not require as much attention to this as it's mapped by the dinner party discourse. Likewise, constituting class also varies: people do not always hold consistent and linear ideas about class location—in particular, for those members of the middle class who maintain contradictory class locations. A person who holds dinner parties may do class at that event differently than they do at a potluck. Larry and Rita have different expectations for their community group potlucks than they do for their shared dinner parties with Gerry and Dina. In particular, their cooking skills are not central to their participation in the potlucks. Guests may overlap, but sociable occasions are not always about producing class in the same manner. The potluck involves both a suspension and a reinforcing of status.

Still, this does not mean there are no unspoken rules or standards for an informal meal, which must still be pleasurable and entertaining. Sometimes the emphasis may be on the experimental aspects: rather than seeing the event and meal together as an achievement, a potluck can be about variety and uniqueness. Sometimes it may simply be about providing space for people to interact. In contemporary capitalist society, there are very few noncommercial spaces for people to congregate, other than private homes or religious meeting places. The potluck opens up the so-called private space of the house without requiring the host to provide too many other resources for guests. Food is still indispensable for most gatherings that take place in people's homes. When Deanna described an annual potluck she hosts after a tennis tournament, the use of her home for the staging of this event is her main contribution:

For example, a friend of mine has a tennis tournament every August that starts on Saturday morning. On Saturday evening we have a potluck party at our house. And people will get there around eight and they will expect to eat maybe around ten o'clock. I have to have the food out at least by ten. I make a whole bunch of chili and they go through that like crazy. And I'm saying well didn't they have a big dinner? At seven or at six? How can people eat that much more food? I'm really expected, I mean their plates are filled like they have not eaten all day, literally.

So you have to plan?
Yeah, I have to plan there are people who are gonna want to eat a lot of food. And half the people who come haven't ever been playing tennis they just come 'cause it's a party. They still eat that late at night. Oh, it's about fifty people at least. At least fifty.

In this case, the size of the party and the preceding tennis match dictate the form. Although Deanna clearly thinks it's silly for people to need to eat so late in the day, she's offered her house and coordinated the planning of the party. At the same time, she's not going to hold a dinner party because it's an enormous amount of work for one or two people: "I'm not going to prepare for fifty!" she says.[6]

So how'd you get involved in this? Is it just a friend that does a tournament?
Yeah. She does the tournament and she's a good friend of mine and we—after the tournaments over, people still want something to do. So we offered our house and said okay let's have, um, a potluck party. 'Cause I'm not, I'm not going to prepare for fifty on my own. Yeah, have to be responsible for everything. So potluck gives us leeway in terms of food: well, if something's not there or if there's not enough, it's not my fault. So it's no criticism of my party.

Deanna minimizes her own labor by making the event a potluck and by not worrying about the "order" of the meal and food items:

Do other folks bring stuff?
Yes. They bring stuff—they bring stuff like for a potluck and I've never made a list but I—after doing it for, this'll be probably the fourth or fifth year now—I no longer get upset about what people bring. I mean, I tell 'em it's a potluck and to try to think of what goes well with chili. I make the chili and I provide the drinks. And I don't tell 'em anything else. And I should but I'm just so busy I don't think about it. I get—I get ice cream. I get all the drinks, alcoholic and nonalcoholic.
    But it, it works out, I mean, there's somebody whose always has a garden. Last year one of the saviors was the fact that this woman was growing corn and she brought about twenty-four ears of corn and just set that up. So the corn and the chili, and somebody else brought a lot of cheese and bread. Usually some people think about what would—they'll ask me has anybody decided to bring bread? I said no, bring it. So it works out well. And you know by the time they finish eating anyway—I mean drinking, nobody cares what they eat. They just see the chili, the corn, the bread, the cheese, and most people are satisfied.

Deanna does a "real" potluck in that she's relaxed about what people bring and whether it will cohere into an ordered menu. The informal protocol for potlucks often dictates that the meal develop completely by chance, the menu being based on whatever categories of food people bring. *Yankee Magazine's Church Suppers* optimistically suggests, "You may end up with eight desserts, but who would complain?" (Chesman, 1996). Clearly, they were not counting on the English food writer I'd met.
    However, a more common strategy, the one Deanna opts for, is where the hosts provide a main course and either assigns other dishes or expects that

people will fill out the other categories necessary for a somewhat ordered meal. Because it's an annual gathering, it's clear that Deanna has had time over the years to negotiate the form of the event in terms of the control over menu and sequence, as well as people's contributions and expectations. In this case, hosting becomes a form of caring work that is routinized over time.

Deanna's concerns for the potluck are very different from the dinner parties where she has work colleagues or other professional friends over. Because the nature of the event is more informal, "it's no criticism of my party" if the menu is not perfectly ordered or if food runs out. Although having people over and creating this time for people to socialize is important to Deanna's circle of friends, in this case she is not attempting to create the same reciprocal webs of obligation that she is when holding a dinner party. Therefore the performances of host and guest can be more informal, the rules of food and hospitality relaxed, and perhaps most importantly, the physical and interactional work minimized. Indeed, it turns out that Deanna and her husband don't actually *cook* for the party. Furthermore, she shifts the host role by eating in advance of her guests:

> *You don't have to . . . host in the same way?*
> Mm-hmm. That's right. No, I just said, I'm just offering a place for people to get together. And the chili's gone when it's gone, it's gone. I'm not running out to the store and saying oh, you know, what can I supplement with this. I mean, that's my contribution. And it's more than enough, as it is my sister (who comes and spends her vacation with us) takes the whole day and makes the chili.
> She lives in Washington D.C. Yeah, she'll come up vacation. And so she doesn't play tennis. She participates in the road race that goes on over there and so she comes home after the road race and she's exhausted. After some rest she'll pull herself together and start making the chili. So she's—while everybody is at the tennis tournament, she's making the chili. When I come home from the tournament around five o'clock, it's done. It's just there on the stove. Then I've got to wait till about ten to eat. But I usually don't. I get mine. I eat ahead. I've learned. It's so dumb . . . before I used to think I'll wait and then I'd snack on a whole bunch of other things. I said, why am I doing this? Why don't I just get a cup of the chili, sit down and eat at my regular time? And let the others get tires around the waist.

The way a potluck meal is structured, even in its timing, is different from a dinner party. For example, in this case, the party is late in the day so that Deanna can construct the performance as "not dinner" per se, where the menu is relaxed because "nobody cares what they eat," and the host can eat when she likes without ruining the temporal order of the event.

If dinner parties are about hierarchy and social differentiation embodied in the host/guest roles and potlucks are about communality and shifted host and guest roles, the question is whether potlucks minimize or shift class performances? Certainly the informality of the event means that class performances are less uniform, and more latitude occurs in people's expectations of each other. To an extent, some boundary-making has occurred prior to the event, simply by the decisions of which guests to invite. Because her friend is in charge of the tennis tournament and who participates, this sets some of the parameters of who is invited to Deanna's house. Because it is an annual event, participation is most likely patterned. Mennell et al. write, "If sharing food signifies an equivalence among insiders within a group, it simultaneously defines insiders as socially different from outsiders, and marks the boundary between them . . . inclusion implies exclusion" (1993, 117). Not everyone who goes to the potluck is invited over for dinner parties. Deanna's narratives illustrate that we can't assume that certain forms of an event are restricted to different class groups, that formality is a requirement for upper-middle-class sociability, or that people engage in only one kind of activity. However, this does not mean that in informal events class performances are completely suspended, but rather that they shift somewhat based on expectations. The range of uses of sociability is comparable to suspected class differences in eating fast food: everyone can afford to do it, but only those with more resources can also have haute cuisine, exercising the choice to eat either or both as a way of constructing consumption and sociability.

Because potlucks are generally governed by informality, the guest role is often less rigid, often encompassing family alongside friends. In Deanna's potluck, this was one of the few events she mentioned in which both family and friends attended. In response to my comment, she spoke at length about her grown children's resistance to having "outsiders" at events like Thanksgiving that they define as "for family":

> They make me make [cook] the same regular things. But let me say just one thing about this: it's one of the few times that I have to entertain so I try to take advantage of having people over when I'm making all of this food. So I can kill two birds with one stone. But the kids, they don't buy it at all. And so we're sitting there with this big roast turkey. And rice and potatoes . . . because everybody thinks I should do the cooking . . . it's always the same thing! One year I tried to have a goose. No. Nobody wanted to eat the goose. It looked like someone's pet. The same menu . . . can't have another, not another soul there. It's the same ritual.

Deanna exercises a fair amount of control over her social life and the gendered expectations of hosting that come with her social class/professional standing. However, she cannot escape doing gender as it connects to doing food work. As in holiday cooking, gender accountability comes from an interesting source, her grown children, who want her to ritually recreate their earlier childhood where she did fulfill gendered expectations of mothering through food work. She acknowledges this history explicitly when she said to me, "If I had just started earlier with bringing [store bought] food in, I wouldn't be in this dilemma . . . but they get very insulted." Deanna's children restrict the boundaries of holidays, constructing non-kin as "outsiders" to a family event. In contemporary sentimental ritual, Thanksgiving is symbolically constructed as a family holiday, where including non-kin is to transgress boundaries of intimacy. As the person responsible for the food work, Deanna would like to shift that boundary, to make her labor of performing food work all-encompassing, but her children resist. In comparison, the tennis potluck is defined as an event for friends, where her sister, as kin, is "added in" and contributes a major portion of the food to the occasion. Events with both kin and non-kin contend with the preexisting templates of social forms of meals as well as specific concerns about boundaries of intimacy and distance. Adding in kin may be complicated: Angela described a dinner with friends where her sister comfortably got up and microwaved her portion of the chicken that Angela had cooked. Although Angela offers an excuse for her sister "because she likes it overdone—she's afraid of salmonella," no guest would feel comfortable reconfiguring the host's food without some kind of careful reference to etiquette and manners.

You Are What You Bring

In writing about food and sociability, one inevitably contends with Brilliat-Savarin's dictum, "tell me what you eat and I will tell you who you are." It's been interpreted and used in many ways, most notably to demonstrate the link between food and identity. In the case of potlucks, foods brought to a communal table can bear the material and symbolic weight of signifying the moral and social contribution of that particular participant. The joke, as exemplified in Susan Orleans's imaginary riff about Tina Turner's cooking, is that the person is defined by what she/he brings. Angela's potluck experiences, her attitudes about the shared food and the participants, aptly summarizes this aspect of potlucks:

> Yeah, I remember one particular potluck, this guy brought (what did I bring to that potluck? um, stuffed grape leaves and I, I grated them with olives and lemons and it was very nice). . . . But anyway, this guy made a really fabulous cheesecake . . . but there were maybe twenty-five people at this potluck, so it was a big birthday party and I, he was a guy that I didn't know, but he brought this cake and everybody was raving about the cheesecake and so he took the,

he had brought it in the pan and he had unmolded the pan and put that part of it around his neck for the rest of the party.

Yeah it was like his marker, you know. And I mentioned that to my husband, like oh, I noticed he did that so everybody would know the cake was his, and he was like oh, it didn't even occur to me, you know.

As Angela's husband illustrates, it's not necessarily easy to be noted for one's contribution at a potluck, where dishes are placed on a communal table and not labeled. In fact, "how to" sources about potlucks attempt to reduce the chance quality of the experience. One strategy for acknowledgment that they suggest is labeling people's contributions. However, no one I interviewed described doing this, nor did I see it at any of the potlucks I observed.

Food contributions at potlucks stand in contrast to a dinner party, where everyone is aware that it is the host's production and her or his labor that created the vast majority of the meal and the sociability of the event. The "cheesecake man" had to creatively invite some way of indicating his contribution if he wanted to be sure that the social accolades came to him. Angela is clearly concerned with this herself: even at potlucks, she plans in advance and with careful thought about what she's going to make and how it will be received: "Yeah, I really get an enormous kick out of it, I mean, if, if I can, if we have something coming up, the first thing I think of is the food, what can I bring and how can I do, and, I mean, you know, if I have to bring something to a potluck and it's dessert, I'll spend a whole week every night just looking through my magazines. . . . I'm usually happy when they say to me *dessert*, because that is like the shining star, you know."

The significance of food as identity is not only about the individual, though, but about how that individual and the food acts as an extension of self, how it fits with the other people, the other items on the table and the tastes of the particular group. People have specialties and become associated with certain foods. Beth said, "Like my aunt, for instance, spinach pie, everywhere she goes, that's all she, and every time we go over to her house she makes spinach pie and it's really good cause that's what she does."

In social groupings where people don't know much about each other from outside the context, they need ways to situate themselves in relation to each other. One key way is through the food itself. Choosing foods can also be a way of distinguishing people you want to relate to from those you don't.[7] For example, Pam and Kendra talked about why Pam isn't "a potluck person," making a direct connection between the form, the food, and the performance of self. They return to Bernice's potato salad as an example:

PAM: If it looks funny, it's never gonna make it to the table. . . . My sister-in-law hates me to this day. She came for the fourth and she bought potato salad.

First of all, it looked runny. Didn't ask me if she should bring it, I didn't tell her to bring it and my mother, she asked my mother and my mother, who knows better, said yes. . . . I was trying to tell her in a nice way but I know that I bit her head off, like, why'd you bring that 'cause I thought I was saying you know, you don't really have to bring anything, but that was not my way. I did snap. But I'm not putting this out anywhere.

KENDRA: But you have to understand the whole dynamics of that is, with potlucks, you get part of a person's personality in the dish that they bring. She don't like Bernice. Bernice is runny and chunky just like that potato salad. Like at work, at the holidays we have potlucks and there are people, like I said, whose personalities become a dish and there's no way I'm gonna eat that. You have to be careful. . . . You obviously picked it for a reason that, this is probably the best dish I can make, or I'm a very busy person, this obviously came from the supermarket.

PAM: See, people in my office, say, they come up to you and they say, "what did you pick because I need to get in line . . . what did you get?" So we know whose stuff we're gonna eat and whose stuff we're not gonna eat. Or at least whose stuff we want to get first!

Kendra pinpoints the relationship between identity and food contributions. What food they bring signifies not only their "personality" as she puts it, but also their contribution to the group.[8] In dinner parties, the creation of the group, however temporally limited to the event, is orchestrated by the hostess. Her creation of the meal represents the nature of the group, the expectations upon them, and the boundaries of their actions. But in the potluck, producing "community" or "connectedness" is a shared production and, as such, is chancier. The informality of the occasion eases some of the constraints and work, but all the people still must "do their part" to make the whole meal and event come together. In the case of Kendra and Pam's workplace potlucks, because participation is determined by being employed together, they don't have any control over who attends—but they can choose to avoid the foods of people to whom they don't wish to feel obliged or connected to. At Pam's big buffet party, she gains that control—and makes it very clear that her party is not a potluck and that having to figure out what to do with contributions like Bernice's runny potato salad is precisely what she doesn't have to do. When this control is dispersed, what you bring—and what you eat—constructs who you are.

Striking a Balance

In cases where people enjoy potlucks, the food contributions and the disparate personalities come together in a way that creates sociability. Angela articulates this by starting out talking about her own contributions but quickly shifting into talking about how the best part, for her, is "how it all goes together":

> I like the anticipation of having people try what I made and trying, I mean admittedly less so, trying what other people make, although I love that too, you know, but it really is for me partly it's like, because food is a part, you know, sort of an identification thing for me. . . . I guess I like, I, I definitely feel like the excitement of, of having my thing be with other people's things, and then, and then like more sort of nobly I like to think we've created this thing together—I do, I do. I think potlucks really can't go bad, or at least I've never, you know, 'cause if everybody brings something, you never wind up with just chips and salsa, you know, somehow people just manage to [make it work].

When the formal responsibility of praising and thanking the host is dispersed among many cooks, how does acknowledgement happen? The potlucks I described earlier clearly demonstrate the way the form helps foster "connectedness." But what about Olesen's complementary idea, that sociable moments must also foster uniqueness? How does that happen in a setting where people are not being structurally distinguished by their contributions? Angela describes her own strategies and her perception of what others in her circle of friends do:

> I think the beautiful thing about potluck is everybody's sitting down. I'm thinking of one in particular, you know, everybody brought something, it was really neat, and everybody, they really put down their best and, and the host and hostess had, you know, made a beautiful spread and it was really nice, and everybody was like complimenting the food and somebody else would say so and so did it, and it was like this rhythm, you know . . . and I noticed that I, I really look out for, like I pay attention to who made everything because I ask what people bring and I make sure that I see, and then, like if people are saying ooh this is good I, you know, I make sure, or, or if nobody is saying anything about the bean salad, I make sure, even if it's not all that great, I'll say ooh, the bean salad, because everybody's waiting to hear the response for their food, you know.
>
> But I think even when nobody's saying anything, if you bring something, I mean it may be a projection because I do it, I do think that, you know, if you're contributing to something I think people are watching to see, you know, who's eating it and if somebody's thing doesn't get touched, you know, it feels kind of. . . . Yeah . . . and I'm usually the first person to say "this is wonderful," you know, I'm recognizing each element, not too much, that will give it away. I mean you want to strike a balance, you don't wanna make that person uncomfortable, but dammit, it I'm gonna spend two days preparing, I wanna hear it, you know, you know, if somebody does it. And you can tell by how much they eat and, you know, and how they eat it, you know.

Striking a balance, making everyone feel simultaneously unique and connected is no longer the exclusive emotional labor of the hostess. Rather, in Angela's concerns for making everyone feel good about her/his contributions, she illustrates the kind of shift in hospitality, in roles and constructions of self that can happen in this more unstructured social occasion. Among the people that I interviewed and observed, most of the time women were more likely to be the ones to make sure others' needs were accommodated.

In describing potlucks, people often used the word "community" to signify a close group of friends. *Community* is a complicated word in American society; like *family*, it is often a touchstone for nostalgic and ideological impulses. But in their everyday use, people used the idea of community to describe their networks of relationship and the obligations and responsibilities engendered by these associations. Potlucks, like more public community celebrations, are viewed as a way of drawing people together. At the same time, potlucks are often used symbolically as a means of representing pluralism. In its most obvious sense, the potluck dish recipes in cookbooks and food columns are often ethnically diverse, attempting to represent a range of cultural tastes. A popular primer for English as a second language uses potluck as a metaphor to teach about American culture through foods as an amalgam of many cultures. More abstractly, Tierney (1997), writing about queer theory and cultural studies, uses the analogy of the dinner table and potlucks to talk about inclusion, especially for gays and lesbians, in diverse communities. He argues, "I get to the table not because I have proven any similarity to you, but because you cannot do without me in a world that is based on mutual respect and understanding (agape). . . . Rather, [we] desire and demand to be equal partners at the table where we honor each other's differences. In effect, we not only get to the table, but we also have a say in what's on the menu (producing meaning)" (51).

In essence, one interpretation of being asked to participate in the construction of the meal, to "make potluck" together, is as a symbolic construction, a performance of group-ness that retains people's ability to have different identities. People don't all have to like the same food because we are not, by show of manners, forced to taste everything because it is a single-stage production. However, there are no clear-cut unproblematic answers about how to act in friendships; thus, contradictions, pressures, and ironies are part of it.

A Surrogate Family

Wes and Becky Pembroke are a married white couple in their late twenties/ early thirties. They have three small children and own a condo in a moderate-sized working-class city in upstate New York, about half an hour from the university town where Wes works. Wes Pembroke comes from a large working-class blended family. He has a master's degree and holds an administrative research job at the state university. His job allows him a fair amount of flexibility in his hours at the office (although it also means he often works late at night or from home) and brings him into contact with a wide variety of people. His wife Becky was attending school part-time for a library science degree so that she could get a job when the children were older. On top of taking classes and having primary responsibility for the children and domestic labor, she also did some paid child-care from her home and volunteered at the local library. Wes and Becky talked about participating in sports and games. Becky described their three-bedroom condo as a kind of "second home" for many of the graduate student researchers that Wes befriended through work. Many of these people were single or in couples but without children and living in apartments. Because a number of them were students, they were generally new to the area or the United States, and the Pembrokes often provided much-needed social and material support. Becky mentioned at least two men who regularly did their laundry at her house. A number of their friends were on softball and volleyball teams, others were from work, and others were people they met playing sports through town league. The Pembrokes hosted people at their house as frequently as once a week, although during softball season the majority of their socializing would take place after games at a local pizza parlor that sponsored their team.

I interviewed Becky, attended a number of their events, and interviewed some of the other people who socialized with them. In this narrative, I also focused on two of the men, Greg and Ted, because they both cooked and also hosted some potlucks and events, although with much less frequency than Wes and Becky. Wes and Becky have a comparably large friend network. The majority of people they socialize with are white but some of the graduate students were foreign nationals. Interestingly, although there were a large percentage of Chinese and Indian grad students in the science center where Wes worked, it was notable that none of them came to these potlucks. This was striking given that some of the participants prided themselves on cooking Chinese and Indian food. One researcher said to me, "Different labs attract people from different nationalities. But some racial-ethnic groups only hang out together." Sports were a key binder for inclusion.

Events at the Pembrokes' ranged from Friday night poker games with take-out food to barbecue potlucks to holiday parties for thirty to forty people. The space where these events occurred was relatively small, including a living-dining area, a kitchen with a "breakfast bar," and an eating area that opened onto a small deck. In fact, the Pembrokes' tiny condo challenged many of my prior observations about the way space often dictated the amount and nature of domestic hospitality. They were able to engage in a wide range of parties in a very small space. During the warmer parts of the year, the yard connected to a common area where parties extended because people often played volleyball. As Becky pointed out, a majority of socializing took place around the kitchen or outside. A typical party would have Wes cooking the main item—although at times people were asked to bring "grillables"—and everyone brought dishes. The coordination of the potluck (what to bring and who to invite) varied in degrees of control based on who was invited and, as Becky put it, "whatever the excuse for the party was." Ted said, "The Pembroke things are always spontaneous. I don't remember the last time a Pembroke party was, you know, anybody hosting, was planned more than a week in advance."

When I asked them why people congregated at their house more than anyone else's, Becky and Wes suggested that this was simply because they owned their residence. There was a permanence to their lifestyle, whereas many of the graduate students changed apartments during the time they lived in the area. However, when Greg and Ted rented a house together, they began to host more events, partly because their home was closer to where most people lived (Becky and Wes lived a half-hour away) and partly because they both had a pronounced interest in cooking and making home-brewed beer. At the same time, Becky described their home as a place for a surrogate family. Ted and Greg constructed single male sociability, but Becky and Wes created a broader-based group solidarity.

"You're Only a Guest Here Once"

Because they host so many parties, Wes and Becky's ideas about hospitality are interesting. When I asked Becky about having so many people over, she said, "you know I always say, 'you're only a guest in this house once, and then you can get your own glass.'" Not only did I hear her say this at a number of parties, but in all of the interviews I did with friends and participants, everyone cited "Becky's line." Her statement clearly delineates the social expectations and the nature of roles at their gatherings. After one or two times of attending their parties, people know where the glasses were. One woman told me she always asks someone other than Becky where things were because she didn't want to be teased for not knowing. In effect, after a few times, the guest's obligation is to know where things are, as if in your own house. Becky's ideas of sociability suggest that being a guest requires one to be waited upon and served—whereas her expectations are informal: she gives permission for people to make use of her house and things (glasses) as if they are kin with kin-based rights—the right to go into their refrigerator or cabinet without asking, the right to make use of their house (no one knocks usually). But as Murray points out, hospitality involves both rights and obligations. The obligation in Wes and Becky's version of hospitality involves having guests do some of the caring work themselves— Becky resists the traditional formal host/hostess labor by putting it back onto her guests. She is legitimated in doing this by the discourse of potlucks—that is, that labor is supposed to be shared and host and guest roles are shifted. She mentioned to me how they are close to some people and especially how, for some of the single men, their house is like that of a surrogate family: "Hell, they even have keys. I don't want to have to wait if they say they're going to come over to do laundry and I have to go out someplace." As one of their friends, Bill said, "I'm perfectly comfortable at the Pembrokes.' It's like a second home because I've been up there so many times and I have a key and I stay there late and whatever. . . . And it's fun to be up there in that situation, [parties] you know, everyone is generally in a good, kind of happy mood. It's festive. . . . I enjoy Wes a lot more (than at work) because he's sort of, well, goofy, in a fun way. So that's enjoyable."

Bill invoked a difference in Wes, as if in these settings his identity is more relaxed, the way one would be with family members, outside the workplace. Ted said, "Yes, you know even though Greg and I rent this great home now, it's like the Pembrokes' home is comfortable. We like to do stuff at our house but it's just more [often than]—not instead of—going up there." In fact, Ted suggests that the new house that he and Greg live in allow them to hold different kinds of events, ones that don't overlap with those of the Pembrokes.' People's circles of friends overlapped but ranged outside the group that attended parties at the Pembrokes.'

Constructing friends as family raises questions about boundaries, especially in deciding who to include. In Wes and Becky's case, they cast a fairly wide net among the people they meet. Bill commented on Wes's generosity and desire to be inclusive as something antithetical to his own ideas about friendship, but to which he must adapt if he wants to be part of it all.

> It's a gigantic collection. It's like, you know, Wes invites basically everybody he knows, from work, softball, volleyball, and assorted hangers-on, whatever. He's really laid back about it. Wes's approach is like just invite everybody, like sometimes to the annoyance of me because I kind of sit there and I go, "Oh, I don't want to deal with that person." But Wes's approach is like, "Screw it, just invite everybody and let things go as they go." In that sense, he's really laid back about it.

Even though he's critical, Bill accepted Wes's decisions because, in the end, it generally worked out and because participating is important enough to Bill that he'll complain but not risk being excluded by attempting to change it. It's also a statement about Wes's ideas about inclusion: because he's willing to host and create these events, he sets the boundaries for group membership. According to Bill, the group is very loosely held together, politically and socially and even economically, with variations based on regional, national, and personal experiences. At the same time, those variations are mitigated by the fact that it is racially homogeneous.

One could say that a temporary collection of sports teammates and graduate students do not have much shared habitus. Work offered some common ground, as did participation in sports. At one party I noted there was a woman who'd never traveled outside the state, a man from Croatia, two people from the West Coast, one from Pittsburgh, and one from Australia. The work of constructing "groupness" needs both strong reasons to be bound but loose enough not to feel restrictive, still in line with American ideologies of friendship as voluntary and family as a "haven." The reciprocal obligations were not about guests eventually hosting, since it was often physically impossible for them to do this, but rather people exerted a lot of social pressure to attend all events. Wes, Becky, and other regulars would give individuals a hard time if they didn't RSVP in a timely fashion, or didn't have a "good excuse" for not attending. Once or twice an event was rescheduled to accommodate someone deemed important to the mix. Even when he'd had a disagreement with Wes about softball, work, or politics, it would have been unthinkable for Bill not to attend.[9]

Cleaning Bathrooms and Making Family Life Public

Wes was often the instigator for events and, usually through email, ended up inviting people and organizing the potluck. But in talking to Becky about who decided to have the parties, she focused on different issues. When I asked her "who does the planning?" for their parties, we ended up talking about bathrooms:

> Well, it depends. Sometimes these things are Wes's ideas and I just sit back and wait, you know, like, look, I'm not going to be the one to run around and make sure the bathroom is clean if this is his idea. But of course, you know, I either have to remind him or do it myself if I care. But, you know, I've gotten to the point (having small children) and these people know us. And we know them. I'm sure their bathrooms aren't clean all the time. And they don't even have kids! But, you know, unless it's a disaster or, say, like

the holiday party when you know everybody is coming, I can live with it. It's going to get messed up anyway!

In comparison, both Ted and Greg commented that when they have parties, they didn't feel the need to "clean the bathroom" so much before people came over because "it's a bachelor pad. One time Greg's parents came and they cleaned our bathroom. Yeah, so the next time they came, we cleaned up more." In conversations about inviting people into their homes, bathrooms came up often. Bathrooms are back-stage in the domestic sphere, but unlike bedrooms or closets, when having a party, bathrooms need to be accessible and "presentable" to guests. Bathrooms become a key indicator of comfort, of anxiety about domestic labor, and about gendered expectations of hospitality. In Simmel's writings about secrecy, he suggests that in interactions, people carefully select what they want to reveal to others, reporting only fragments of their inner lives. In essence, people "hide the truth" from each other intentionally, in order to regulate the degree of intimacy and personal knowledge in sociable relationships. In domestic sociability, people are not only managing interactional knowledge but material knowledge of how they live. The reality of material daily life is that houses get disrupted and dirty with daily use. At the same time, our cultural constructions of orderliness and manners suggest that houses need to look pristine. The people most often held responsible for the daily domestic labor of cleaning bathrooms are women or paid domestic laborers. The clean bathroom is an indicator of the bottom rung of invisible labor. Cooking, decorating the house, and setting a nice table are tasks for which people receive attention and public recognition for their labor. However, the bathroom and its functions are private: people routinely abstain from discussions of their elimination habits, problems, and experiences. The main exceptions are conversations between parents and small children (who are focused on this as a learning task), between patients and health care providers, and among real intimates.[10] There are no public accolades for having a clean bathroom, but there are social repercussions if one does not. In particular, women are judged by their own appearance and by the sanitary appearance of their homes, even if they are not the ones doing the work. Although Becky resisted some aspects of the domestic labor and caring work associated with sociability, it's clear that the cleanliness of the bathrooms lurked as "her issue" most notably because women are more often held accountable for not doing domestic labor.

Becky went on to describe how she and Wes negotiate the division of labor. These negotiations determine the form of the occasion:

> When it's one of the boys' birthdays, we don't always agree (to a potluck or not): Wes gets this idea that we should provide everything, you know, because people

are bringing gifts. I mean, these kids do get a lot from having all these adults around, you know? But, you know, he invites everybody and you know it adds up! So yeah, at those parties, if someone calls and asks me if they can bring something, of course I'm going to say yes. Even if Wes has something planned, there's always soda. And beer. If they want beer, they can bring it, especially you know, [Greg and Ted] drink stuff from [expensive specialty stores] that's, you know, the new taste from this or that country, smells like raspberries or whatever. We're not going to have that around, unless there were some leftovers from the last time. Some people even if it's Mark's birthday or something, they'll always call or bring something. . . . Most of the other times Wes just decides he wants to do something or somebody will say, hey, let's barbecue after the game and so it's his problem to get it organized. . . . But, you know, I'll go out and get stuff if he asks, and when people call, I'll tell them what I think we might need. But he sees everybody more often than I do because most of them are right there [at work]. And if he's there in town he can just pick up stuff on his way home. There's always someone like Bill we can call at the last minute and say, we need soda or, hey, we need mayonnaise. I have no problem with that.

Because some of their friends are like kin, they were sometimes involved in the planning and organizing of events. In more formal circumstances, it's always the hosts who decide the timing and the format of a party. Greg liked to cook and often generated certain kinds of parties that happened at the Pembrokes' house. Becky and Greg both describe these events as more of a "joint production" between the two of them, without much input from Wes. "The holiday cookie party I do with Greg: we make all the cookies in advance, sometimes the night before with the boys. And that's not really a potluck. We just get a deli tray for people who don't want to eat just cookies . . . but you know, most people, I think, aren't expecting to eat dinner at that one. It's for cookies!"

In those cases, Becky sees the party as her responsibility and she organizes it so that she does only the work that interests her. Minimizing food labor is key here. However, for the majority of events, Wes initiates and is held accountable for how it happens. Because Wes and Becky operate as symbolic family for the disparate group, their domestic negotiations are public knowledge. In describing the parties, Bill links the planning of the event to domestic tasks. It's not only whose idea it is, but what the division of domestic labor—the nature of the "economy of gratitude"—has been lately in the Pembroke household:

A lot of times Wes will kind of initiate some of these things. The more formal it is—like a holiday—the more she does. If Becky's been in on it from the start, I think she ends up doing a lot more—not necessarily formal planning but she'll kind of take responsibility for getting things they need. A lot of the time they'll provide the meat for grilling and then other people will bring side dishes or chips or soda. I think if Becky feels that Wes has sort of orchestrated things on his own and set the ball in motion, (and if he's been bad for a while around the house) then he's the one who has to clean the kitchen floor and whatever. I think the allocation of the work prior to the event kind of varies. But certainly during the actual party Wes is the one doing most of the work in the sense that he's cooking, he's kind of cooking stuff on the grill (or he's making chili in a big pot on the stove). Everyone else is kind of eating and socializing. Though, really, I cannot remember the last time they had a party where they kind of said, "We're providing everything, you don't have to bring anything." I think the general pattern, the message will always say "we'll provide the meat."

Although we generally think of much of the domestic labor of parties as back-stage, prior to the event, in potlucks some of that labor gets highlighted simply because it is divided. But, in this case, because Becky and Wes open up their home to non-kin, the ways in which a couple or family negotiates their domestic scenarios become more public, particularly when it varies from event to event. Bill clearly sees different kinds of labor involved, although he prioritizes Wes's visible cooking during the party. Again, he talks about how Wes manages to do this; he's not a voluble host, but rather, "I think during these parties he gets into this zone. Especially when he's around the grill. He's just in and out doing the grill, throwing food at people. Everyone else is just kind of eating and socializing."

Becky was nonchalant when I asked her how they decide what people should bring, noting that up to a point, she leaves it up to folks. Inequities in food are less commented upon than inequities in shared labor around the party. For example, Becky mentioned how although she never says anything, "there's always some people who come late and leave early and don't really help out, you now, just take their own stuff home, or forget to contribute money" when they decide they're going to buy something communally. Sometimes money becomes an issue, especially when Becky feels that their open home is tapping the family budget. Bill recognizes the costs in how the Pembrokes construct hospitality through shared resources:

How does it work with people contributing food?
Well, you know, they live primarily on one salary. And everyone else, I mean, whether they are or not, they all present themselves as poor starving graduate students. So, I don't think Wes and Becky have a lot to spend (on all these folks) but they're very generous, in the sense that they have a thousand people in their house all day . . . and they're also generous in the sense that that they spend a lot, you know, provide the main course. So everyone else brings side dishes or stuff to drink. Beer, because they [the Pembrokes] don't drink beer.

The easiest thing for me to do is buy a whole bunch of soda and chips, just food like that. On some occasions I can be motivated to make nachos or lasagna, something that's easy.

And there's a whole range of foods—you know, the food snobs who experiment and then people who make potato salad. It's even like that with what's available to drink, you know? It all depends. . . . Most of the time it's like a standard potluck, you know, where everybody kind of brings home their own leftovers.

Hierarchies of taste are expected to coexist. Bill brings commercial junk food while others bring homemade cakes or salads. Greg often prides himself on experimenting with a new ethnic dish for various parties and he waits for people to comment on "his dish," just as the cheesecake man in Angela's potluck wanted to make sure everyone knew her/his contribution. Cost and taste were not necessarily the key factors in ranking the quality of someone's contribution to these potlucks. For example, the expensive beer is clearly not what everyone at this potluck desires. In fact, some participants criticized those who brought only an item like that, which would appeal to only a faction of the potluck participants. Bill pinpoints how these parties are potlucks because sharing the food labor and costs makes it possible for the Pembrokes to be "very generous" without supporting all these folks. Wes and Becky can create the environment (and the relationships) for people to feel as if they have "a surrogate family": in this case, their material resources are space, social capital, and food. Wes and Becky create "home" for the group. They don't have the monetary resources to feed that many people on a regular basis—but this kind of community is important to them, so they literally open up their house—and cabinets and washing machine—for people to use as if they were entitled, like family. In comparison, although informal, Greg and Ted's parties had more of a definitive beginning and end noted in my observations, and although the majority of regular people attended, it did not have the same "homelike" atmosphere. Furthermore, the required attendance was less strictly observed: people had an easier time turning down an invitation to one of their parties than to one of the Pembrokes.'

The temporal diffusion of these potlucks meant that social tensions between people of different status situations could be dispersed. One person said, "You know you don't *have* to talk to everyone, you could just go play with the kids or be outside. Some people sit and watch the ballgame on TV." Another said: "We come early because otherwise I know we're going to miss out on the food. I hate getting there when there's nothing interesting left to eat but chips." Another couple told me, "We never last as long as some people. I can't hang out that late at night. After a few hours, you've eaten, you've played some croquet, you've talked to some folks, you packed up your leftovers and you're ready to go home." In contrast, another person said, "People hang out forever. You know, for some of us, it's not like there's anything to rush home to. I understand the people with little kids or who are married; they have a reason but I don't." These comments reflect the decentered nature of the event, such that participants end up with a diffuse experience, a shared but also individualized version of what occurred at the party and how they fit in to it.

Many people who attended the Pembrokes' parties commented on how much they liked having so many people around, with lots of food to try, and various things to do for entertainment. The Pembrokes' potlucks fit most closely with Simmel's definition of a party. Simmel suggests that the party as a social form is not really conducive to close social relations. Higher numbers of people mean less shared circumstances and less individual effort at creating and sustaining a group mood. Although informal and built on reciprocal ties, these parties are not necessarily intimate for all participants. At a potluck there is variation in how connected people feel. However, even large parties have a temporal order, with smaller gatherings happening within or at the ends of more diffuse occasions. This becomes most obvious when Bill describes a kind of "during and after" sociability. He started out by commenting on his ambivalence about the lack of order in the early part of the events; with all that going on at the beginning, it's hard to decide what his role should be:

> [The last time] John [Becky's brother] had called me at the last minute and asked me to bring mayonnaise. So I brought it. And I came in with this big jar of mayonnaise and instantly Mark (one of the boys) was like, "Bill, oh Bill, play this board game with me!" and the other one was like "watch me!" and I'm getting bombarded with other people asking me "what did you bring for (a gift)" and I'm like, what's going on? I suppose, often, increasingly, I kind of check out of those kinds of things, especially if there's a TV on and a sporting event that I'm interested in. . . . I kind of avoid all that, turn it over to other people, you know. I'll interact more with the kids when everything's died down a little more.

Like family, the kinship obligations as well as the informal format of the event allow the Pembrokes to ask Bill to help out at the last minute without imposing. Likewise, he could (within reason) "check out" of interactions by doing things only a person with intimate rights and access could do. He also talked about liking the later part of the events because the conversations and relationships were more intimate:

> Now, at the end, what usually tends to happen, depending on who's there, kind of after the initial frenzy is over, someone will start picking up paper plates and

kind of put the glasses in the dishwasher, that sort of stuff. Somebody would start, you know, do an initial pass . . . [and] one or two people will kind of take it upon themselves to start picking up. And then, when most people will leave there will be a few of us hanging around, at which point a couple of things happen. There may have been an agreement before the party was permitted that stated, like, Wes was entirely responsible for clean up. At which point we'll leave everything at a certain level of mess and go hang out and Wes will do it the next day. Or, if that's not the case, then one of us will usually go and help Becky finish up.

So there's sort of this five-hour period of all hell breaking loose and everyone consuming food, people talking, a lot of separate groups. And then later, there's that extra period of time when, like there's less than ten people and they sit in that kitchen/living room area, talking about one topic.

To Bill, the close sociability of these times are what the larger, more chaotic party yields. In one sense, he must "put up with" the first sequence in order to achieve the kind of gathering he prefers.

Wes and Becky's events function to construct family and community in a setting where people are uprooted and placed down in new context. The Pembrokes are socially and structurally the right ones in this group to do this work because they appear more stable and rooted than the majority of participants. Among their friends, they are the main SNAF (Standard North American Family) with kids, who own their own home rather than rent and lived there somewhat longer than most others. Wes's job had more stability than the kinds of assistantships of grad students. In describing some of the single men, Becky described herself and Wes as "socializing them as parents." One of their boys was a baby when they did these parties: Becky liked the fact that "anyone with clean hands could hold Mark and put him to sleep." Bill and Ted both recalled sitting on the couch late at night holding baby Mark as he slept, a new experience for both of them. Comfort with such a young child is a sign of intimacy and acceptance.

Snob Dinners and "Beanies and Weenies" Nights

The parties at the Pembrokes' house were a regular feature of their social life for at least six or seven years. Becky, Bill, Ted, and the others I spoke to described two different categories of events (along with the "usual" potlucks) that illustrated some of the underlying tensions and differences among the participants. Greg and a few of the other regulars were, as Greg put it, "into gourmet cooking." Greg's desire to cook certain kinds of foods often fueled a party, although many of these were not at the Pembrokes'. To Greg, who participated, and "what kind of cook they were" determined the nature of the event. But sometimes Greg would organize a potluck at either his house or Karen's that was highly structured, focusing on whatever cuisine he was excited about cooking at that point in time. Becky, Bill, and some of the other participants labeled these meals "snob dinners" although Greg called them "gourmet dinners," where the contributions added up to a menu around a specific cuisine like Italian or Indian. Judy, a regular at the Pembrokes', described a "snob dinner" where Greg not only had categories of food and a chosen cuisine, but gave out specific recipes for people to follow. She said, "oh yeah, well, I'm sure he thought he was being helpful, you know, where are *we* going to find just the right recipe for mint chutney, you know, like, I'm not on a first name basis with any Indian cookbook writers. But then you just feel like you're being given homework. No way was I going to that party. I'll get Indian take-out first, thank you very much."

Similarly, Becky seemed both disparaging and tolerant of the "snob dinners." She made it clear that she strongly disliked some kinds of spicy foods, although Wes often cooked very hot chili and used hot peppers in some of his dishes. Becky said, "As long as there's something there the kids and I can eat, you know, I don't care what he and Karen decide to make." However, Becky described the reaction of some group members to the exclusivity of the snob dinners: "We had a thing called Beanies and Weenies night, where I think the rule was you couldn't bring anything that had more than three ingredients in it. Maybe potato salad was the exception. I remember maybe somebody (John?) brought potato salad and that had like four (ingredients) but you know, it was beanies and weenies so you need potato salad. It wasn't snob food so it was ok."

The "beanies and weenies nights" were a reaction to the fact that some of the snob dinners were held at Greg's or someone else's house and that not all of the usual participants in the Pembrokes' gatherings were invited to snob dinners. In fact, there were a few occasions where the Pembrokes didn't attend. Greg said, "Well, I know Becky hates Indian food, so what would have been the point?" Greg clearly delineated the different nature of the various events. When two or three of the "snob dinner" participants moved away, the dinners ended. Greg moved into a shared house with Ted and they cooked and held parties, but the food was often more eclectic. Within the group, various subgroups, networks, and circles seemed to coexist. Although Wes and Becky invited a lot of people to their home, people who were part of the larger circle but did not attend were often connected through the partner or spouse of someone more directly connected to the Pembrokes from work or sports. Some of the people who participated in the Pembrokes' parties were experimenting with style in food, along the lines of the middle-class people DeVault interviewed, where eating based on variety is an achievement in line with middle-class values and expectations (1990). Unlike at a dinner party, taste in these cases is not a rigid requirement for a social gathering; however, it does play in to the negotiated nature of the events. Although they have moved into a much bigger house, over time, Becky and Wes have remained stably where they were geographically, socially, and economically, whereas the majority of the other participants in the group went on to upper-middle-class professional careers in academics or research. For many, their social lives became more like the ones DeVault describes as typical for upper-middle-class people's socializing around food. This experience is echoed in Deanna's descriptions of the shared meals during her grad school days, and Dina's nostalgia for the potluck dinners they had when she and Gerry were newlyweds, living in the Midwest while Gerry attended medical school. The potluck is an enduring form for some social groups. For others, it marks a transitional phase, where class standing and community are both in flux, so that the form of the event is more fluid and status boundaries can be more easily crossed.

"The Sense of the Unexpected"

According to Mary Douglas (1972), "The rules which hedge off and order one kind of social interaction are reflected in the rules which control the internal ordering of the meal itself" (64). The significance of this statement in relation to potlucks is that the potluck is a definitive shift away from the highly ordered presentation in dinner parties (dining à la russe) and even the structuring of buffets (dining à la française). In many buffets, the food was very often the product of the labor of one or two people; therefore, in partaking of a buffet, one still experiences a kind of "order" orchestrated by the host or cook. In buffets, there is still somewhat of an expectation of a thematic cohesion to the meal, even though guests are given more freedom to pursue their individual appetites. However, in the potluck, the labor is shared and spatially and temporally diffused, mostly occurring in different people's kitchens prior to the event itself. Since one person is not in control of the menu, there is less opportunity for the meal to be strictly and clearly ordered. Even when the hosting people assign dishes, they are still not able to strictly regulate the ordering of the meal, simply because other people's cooking abilities and work are not standardized. According to one person, "the sense of the unexpected is what makes the potluck such a lovely idea."

In potlucks, the menu is not controlled, the preparation is not controlled, the timing is not controlled. Given the temporal diffusion, the social interactions are also less controlled. At a local cooperative farm, the potlucks are a kind of rolling buffet: as people arrive, different foods appear and disappear, such that a person could get a completely different meal on their second trip up to the table. I observed people eating a course, including dessert, and then see some terrific-looking entrée and run back to the table for some, even if it violates the "normal" sequencing of meals.

Is the Potluck Egalitarian?

Gusfield (1994) argues that potlucks are more amenable to American ideologies of egalitarianism and a disdain for formalism. Because the potluck is a cooperative event, "no one assumes the role of management and social authority" (301). He envisions hosts as "first among equals" rather than as venerated leaders orchestrating the event and garnering gratitude and other forms of social attention. However, in Gusfield's analysis, there's the assumption that all contexts are relatively similar due to the structuring of the form and that shared labor minimizes difference. Although my data supports some of Gusfield's contentions, I also found that it depended entirely on the kind of community being constructed. The various resources that people bring to the event determined how the group gets defined. Although we can suggest that the host role may be on the decline, some of my interviews with people who did potlucks demonstrate that the labor of orchestrating even a shared event does not necessarily entail that all participants do equal amounts of planning, emotion work, and material labor. In particular, it seemed that women still do a vast majority of this work.

6. Artfulness, Solidarity, and Intimacy

Easy at first, the language of friendship
Is, as we soon discover,
Very difficult to speak well, a tongue
With no cognates, no resemblance
To the Galamatias of nursery and bedroom,
Court rhyme or shepherd's prose,

And, unless often spoken, soon goes rusty.
Distance and duties divide us,
But absence will not seem an evil
If it make our re-meeting
A real occasion. Come when you can:
Your room will be ready.

W. H. Auden

Once upon a time, I rambled, some neighbors included me
in their circle of barter. They were in the habit of exchanging
eggs and driving lessons, hand-knit sweaters and computer
programming, plumbing and calligraphy. I accepted the generosity
of their inclusion with gratitude. At first I felt that as a lawyer,
I was worthless, that I had no barterable skills and nothing to
contribute. What I came to realize, however, was that my value to
the group was not calculated by the physical items I brought to it.
These people included me because they wanted me to be part of
their circle; they valued my participation apart from the material
things I could offer. So I gave of myself to them, and they gave me

fruit cakes and dandelion wine and smoked salmon and, in their
giving, their goods became provisions. Cradled in this community
whose currency was a relational ethic, my stock in myself soared.
My value depended on the glorious intangibility, the eloquent
invisibility of my just being part of the collective—and in direct
response I grew spacious and happy and gentle.

—Patricia Williams, *The Alchemy of Race and Rights*

In the 2008 election, the Obama campaign's use of grassroots organizing
techniques combined with technology like text messaging and regular emails
was a notable and rather successful feature in mobilizing voters. One technique was an old familiar one—neighborhood house parties, where people
gathered to discuss issues and swing voters—but they were promoted via the
internet. As I followed the campaign, I was intrigued by the possibilities in
these house parties—to what extent would they be mixed in terms of race,
class, and gender? Would people stick to their own neighborhoods or would
they be welcoming to others? How well would this technique work in fostering more activism? And, of course, most importantly, if you hosted a house
party, would you provide food and if you did, what would you serve?

Inviting strangers—or others of any sort—into the domestic environs is
a highly political and personal act, one that connects to citizenship, rights,
individualism, and subjecthood. Domestic sociability operates through ide-
als of hospitality, which is generally defined as the practice of welcoming in
strangers and offering them food, shelter, and companionship.[1] It is, in its
ideal instance, the site where people encounter the other and literally famil-
iarize that encounter through shared meals. According to Murray (1990),
hospitality should be considered a key place to understand both membership
and rights, especially the right to partake of food with a group. This is because
hospitality acts as an ideal instance where rights are created for nonmembers
of a group (17).

In 1960, Riessman, Potter, and Watson suggested that the host was a vanishing role in American culture. While their prognosis was not entirely ac-
curate, their descriptions of the various roles and selves created at a dinner
party captures a large dynamic of sociability that remains consistent. They
suggest that hospitality requires a dialectic where hosts and guests attempt to
balance moments of *uniqueness* and *connectedness*, which, "if well realized at
the party, creates three values which these authors see in sociability—namely
artfulness, solidarity, and intimacy—and links the intimate occasion of the
party to other realms of social life" (Olesen, 1993, 191). In searching for these
values to appear in people's descriptions, I was also looking for changing
opportunities for equality to emerge from these occasions.

Television, magazines, and the popularity of cookbooks suggest that social gatherings of the sort I describe here are culturally supported through a taken-for-granted ideology. People I interviewed shared these beliefs. Even if they did not cook or had small homes, they brought soda to potlucks, adapted their homes to accommodate a few guests, and attended a variety of sociable events. Their efforts—what we could call "artfulness"—demonstrate that this is a kind of sociable work that they felt was important to their everyday lives. By centralizing the provision and sharing food, we reveal just how much effort people are willing to extend in order to ensure these kinds of relationships. At the same time, it highlights the difficulties of describing what Bourdieu calls "the logic of practice" in relation to sociable occasions. The negotiations of everyday life are, in part, shaped by larger discourses and institutional arrangements that give some people more leisure time than others, restrict or enlarge social networks, or make certain kinds of relationships more necessary than others. At the same time, the way people navigate these situations often have unique characteristics that draw upon older social arrangements or knowledge drawn from events shaped by older models of hospitality. Academic analyses diverge in their ability to label such practices:

> The sense of inclusion is described by scholars in different ways. Kurt Lewin and Miriam Lowenberg say that food and eating create a feeling of group belongingness. Hortense Powdermaker refers to the cohesion that eating together creates for group and family. And JC McKenzie uses the terms "community integration" and "social well-being." Margaret Cussler and May de Give suggest eating together implies "a kind of kinship." Whatever we call it, this sense of unity with family or other group members is so important in many cultures that people will suffer some hardship and discomfort to attain it. (Kalcik, 1984, 48)

Bourdieu argues that it is difficult, if not often impossible, for actors to put into words what it is they do, precisely because they are engaged in doing rather than explaining. In some cases there simply aren't words to describe an act that unfolds its logic in a time and tempo of doing rather than a logical explanation. In the case of shared meals, I suggest that people rely on certain labels as shorthand for a process that is often more complex and varied than can be captured by the terms "dinner party" or "potluck." Exploring the actual sequence and experiences of shared meals allows some insights into the kinds of relationships people are constructing beyond the workplace or family. How do people make sense of these relationships, as both voluntary and constrained? What kinds of control do people exercise in determining the meaning and form of such relationships? Intellectually and personally, my own difficulty with labels suggests that this is an area of social life that is both underexamined and subject to cultural and social conditions.

Using both textual analysis and narratives of shared meals, I have analyzed the nature of commensality in people's everyday lives. Springing off of Simmel's concept of the meal as a social form, I suggest that people do indeed draw upon templates of what is possible and acceptable. The particular structure of the meal and event (the kind of food served, the levels of formality expected, the division of physical and interactional labor required) is connected to the kinds of relationships people are trying to create. Such relationships, while affirming people's social ties, also are tied up in contemporary experiences and understandings of difference and inequality. Food knowledge is social knowledge, a resource and a tool that people use to establish membership in groups, solidarity among people who are different in some respects and similar in others.

Sharing meals with people who are not family is, in fact, a significant part of people's everyday experiences, such that these events are part of the larger patterning of meals and sociability that goes on in domestic households. The kinds of meals as well as the format and structure of events that involved non-kin could be described as social forms. However, strict adherence to form was not widespread among the people I talked to, such that the ways in which people varied their commensal practices were connected to the social, economic, and cultural resources they drew upon. While every one demonstrated the extent to which formal rules of self-control had been internalized, they also espoused an ethos of comfort, one that suggested at least a belief in relaxed interactions. Sometimes this ethos of comfort often meant that people adapted their practices to create social situations that suggest more informal forms of commensality. However, this ideology of comfort and informality did not automatically lead to social circumstances with greater levels of equality. In particular, although race often operated as a backdrop to the events—shaping who was or was not included prior to the event's occasion—during the actual sociable events, people's performances of class and gender combined in ways that reflected the more institutionally structured aspects of their lives. The idea of social forms is useful if we see them as necessary fictions, as genres from which people organize their actions.

More significant, I think, perhaps, is the internalization of ideas about the body and self control—of manners and self discipline that allow for ideas about informality to emerge. One interesting speculation revolves around the so-called obesity epidemic. Given the sheer volume of media, government, and scientific attention being paid to people's food intake, exercise habits and the presumed resultant weight gain, one would expect to see this conversation reflected in the types of food served, the events being organized, and the negotiations between people regarding dietary needs. However, it was never mentioned overtly by any of the people I interviewed. At one point, I began asking people, "Do you find that the current concern about obesity in America has changed what you do when you have people over for meals?" However, most people struggled to answer this question and some even seemed to take offense, as if thinking about the weight problems of their potential guests crossed a boundary of propriety. On the other hand, people were willing to bring up "health" in a more general form, especially in terms of navigating a path between indulgence and health in menu items. Often, these discussions focused on a friend or family member who had a dietary restriction based on health needs that would affect the meal planning.[2]

This fits one of Warde's antinomies of taste, where such events are deemed special and social, therefore less subject to the restrictive self-control encouraged for daily practice. Looking at food in magazines, Warde (1997) concludes that the message is: "We should eat healthily. But not if it makes us sad" (56). Given the way most people talked about their everyday meals and health concerns, often very separate from these other events, I suggest that the discourses of food and fat focus so much on individual responsibility that in this particular case, people internalize self-control rather than imposing upon others.

In contrast, discourses about what counts as good food and how it is provided are enacted in these social meals. For example, in its ideal form, the dinner party contains certain concerns about the nature of social boundaries, standing as a reference point from which people continue to assess their own experiences. The dinner party operates as a historical terrain of middle- to upper-class married heterosexuals, usually with paid help. Perhaps, for some Americans, the internalization of self-control means less need for this kind of external structure. Emily Post illustrated etiquette as a restraint on comfort, one that allows sociability along a particular path, an "imaginary middle." However, mass culture and standardized education have meant that people are more widely exposed to ideas about control of body and self in interactions. Prior to contemporary times, the right food itself displayed status and manners illustrated character. Today, talking about the food is equally important and, as embodied by Stewart and Smith, being able to make food beautiful through personal effort indicates the importance of style and personality instead of character. At the same time, for African Americans, appropriate manners, as filtered through the demonstration of "home training," are an embodied and active way to claim the rights and obligations that come with full membership in the social order.

In this final chapter I review some of the themes emergent from this analysis, including insights about non-kin relationships, the role of gender and gendered labor in creating events and relationships, how class resources remain a significant factor in defining people's social practices, and how domestic space is involved in structuring choice.

"Doing Friendship": Creating Non-kin Relationships

Earlier I used the phrase "kin work" to talk about the interactional and physical labor that people extend in creating voluntary sociable relationships. And yet, in some ways, "kin work" is not really an adequate conceptual category. While on the one hand, this labor looks very similar to the kind of emotion and interaction work people do for their immediate and extended families, there are also important differences. Even though sociable relationships operate through and under structural conditions, people exercise a fair amount of choice in who they socialize with and under what circumstances, certainly with more flexibility than they seem to do with workplace or familial relationships. Another key difference is that there are, in fact, specific social forms for non-kin sociability that people draw on in creating these occasions. Although "friend" is also an inadequate label for the range of relationships people create through domestic hospitality, most research that explores non-kin ties relies on this conceptual category (Rawlins, 2009).

As Gusfield (1994) points out, sociability is an important but not clearly articulated aspect of social life. For example, although there is a small field devoted to the study of friendship, research is limited and generally focuses on more psychological questions. Although not everyone who is invited into a household for a meal may be designated as a "friend," most accounts suggest that the majority of people may be loosely grouped under this label.[3] The sociological literature on friendship is a relatively small but growing field. Many of these studies begin with disclaimers, analyses, and insights about the difficulty in defining friendship as a category of social interaction (Rawlins, 2009). In Western society, friendship is a system of relations that is generally seen as "voluntary, informal, personal, and private" (Jerrome, 1984, 696). That is, we have choices about the people we spend time with and what we do during that time. People believe they can end or start friendships relatively free of the constraints posed by more institutionalized types of relationships (Allan, 1989, 47). The norms of flexibility and privacy make it difficult to connect these sorts of interactions to any structural arrangements in society. And yet, as broad as some of my respondents' social networks were, they were often circumscribed by race and class, and generally dependent on the labor of women for their existence and maintenance. People's choices were, indeed, structured.

The relationship between sociability and structures of dominance has been examined in relation to social class and gender but not in relation to race and ethnicity in America. There are many studies of race and kinship, particularly those that focus on African Americans (Taylor et al., 1992). However, most of these mention non-kin only as an adjunct to social support, and not as a central category of social relations. Although it has been demonstrated quite clearly that reciprocal ties have been critical to the survival of economically and socially marginal African American communities, very little research has been done on the nature of sociable ties among blacks of middle- and upper-class socioeconomic standing.[4] Mirroring similar limitations on the general empirical approach to social capital, most of the research that focuses on black Americans examines the obvious generative capacities such as civic engagement, school success, and occupational capabilities. The emphasis on exchange and material resources misses the less tangible effects, such as those described in detail by critical race scholar Patricia Williams. Many of the people I spoke to, both African American and white, emphasized benefits that were not measurable by such standards.

In general, friend relationships have not been subjected to a sociological analysis that contextualizes the reciprocal, combined, and cumulative effects of multiple structural inequalities. Some of my interviews suggest that cross-racial sociability is an area of sociability that needs to be examined in greater detail, particularly since these occasions are voluntary and yet require a shared definition of the situation. The African Americans I interviewed were more likely than whites to socialize in groups that were racially mixed, although they also had circles of friends who were predominantly African American. It would be informative to explore the extent to which close relationships across race are a matter of choice, opportunity, or structural positioning. This also raises questions about the diffusion of cultural ideas about food, whether all groups share a vocabulary of cuisine (beyond commercial fast food, for example) or whether a constant process of translation and transmission occurs between people who spent time together in domestic sociability.

Allan (1989) insists that "the central argument . . . has been that friendship patterns are not solely a matter of individual discretion or choice, but that they are influenced by a range of structural factors which, to some degree, lie outside the control of the individual" (130). This point becomes clearer when comparing frameworks used for analyzing kinship and family to those for friendship. Sociologically, it would be difficult to explore the former without some references to the sociohistorical and structural arrangements that impact upon its form. The literature tends "to view friendship as essentially a personal relationship [which] leads to an emphasis on the psychological and emotional benefits it bestows on the individual. Its role within the social realm is consequently often underplayed" (Allan, 1989, 154). Without drawing a line between tangible and intangible benefits, it seems clear that friends have a social utility, helping others to achieve goals, assist in certain situations, and integrate people socially. In the most obvious sense, shared meals provide opportunities for people to share information and ideas about food, taste, and close relationships. When people make adaptations to more formal social forms, they are constructing specific opportunities for interaction, ones that provide their friends and acquaintances space to create more intimate relationships or, in Olesen's terms, different performances of self (1993).

Rawlins (1992) provides an extensive synthesis of the literature, demonstrating how the dialectical nature of friendship affects the needs and interactions people have throughout the life course. Forms of support include emotional, moral, practical, and material aid. Even upper-middle-class people share concrete resources like food. Friends also provide identity and status. Consider how self-expression is connected to providing food, even at a potluck, such that people can "read" each other's performances for clues about shared sensibilities and experiences.

Another key area of research examines friendship during crisis and change in individual's life, demonstrating how social support acts as a dynamic quality of relationships that changes over time (Willmott, 1987). For example, Rawlins (1992, 2009) describes friendship as operating under a dialectic between the freedom to be independent and the freedom to be dependent, such that friends provide the space for each other to pursue life interests without interference while at the same time depending on the other for various kinds of support (16). Thus, friendship is a process involving ongoing negotiation of these contradictory needs. In the interviews, I was struck both by people's abilities to maintain social relationships over time, but also by their ability to adapt across the life course. Many of the original interviewees experienced major life changes, including children growing up, divorces and relationship dissolutions, occupational shifts, geographic relocation, and even death. Although patterns of daily life often seem habitual, I was surprised by how much people adopted new habits. People engage in domestic hospitality throughout the life course, but in different forms and with different expectations of taste, style, food, and intimacy. Some times hospitality shifts to the commercial marketplace, either through an increase in eating out or a greater reliance on commercially prepared foods. However, it seems that neither of these trends diminishes the significance of domestic hospitality in people's lives. Warde and Martens (2001) counter the contention that eating with friends reduces the number of family meals that people do in any given week. They argue,

> As the number of meal occasions increases, so does the potential for sharing and co-operating with a wider network of people. An implicit assumption on the part of those who feel the family meal is under threat is that the less frequent such meals, the less attachment family members will feel for one another. The impression is of a negative-sum game where fewer family meals mean weaker family bonds. However, the corollary is rarely entertained, that more meals with non-family members have positive effects on social relationships with alternative companions. Yet this might well be so. (217)

Despite ideological pressure to support the primacy of family bonds, most research on the topic finds no evidence that domestic sociability diminishes family life (Sobal, 2000; McIntosh, 1996). In fact, it is often seen as an important extension of family sociability. People socialize their children through their participation in such events. Their kin often provide the context for extending social contacts: Nora's sister introduces her to a whole circle of friends. Upper-middle-class professionals like Gina and Amy make friends through the parents of their children. Couples like Laurie and Rob, Cindy and Mary, and Harry and Kate include family and friends in their buffets and parties. Social networks often build out of and include family. At the same time, people often feel constrained to keep some occasions separate for family: Deanna experienced ongoing pressure from her adult children to keep holiday meals restricted to kin. One alternative is that non-kin can temporarily become fictive family, such as the single men who attend potlucks at the Pembrokes, the people who benefited from Perry's transplanted southern hospitality, and the twenty-somethings like Lauren and Peter whose roommates and other postcollege friends eat in together to save money and have fun.

When we look at the patterns of daily life as including the work of doing sociability, we can see this as a meaningful activity that is both voluntary and necessary for people to feel connected to social circumstances outside their work and family. People create relationships through an ongoing active process, a process that operates through discourses about sociability and relies on cultural templates of the possible social forms of shared meals with non-kin. The design, presentation, and work of the meal express ideas about the relationships being enacted. In particular, the process centers on how much intimacy and distance can be established within formal and informal modes of sociability. These set the boundaries for the enactment of such relationships, but in the process are also shifting and creating such boundaries. People do friendship as a social process, one that involves material and emotional labor. Like much interactional work in our society, this process is gendered and is often tied to constructions of race and class that undergird other social conditions.

Another way to view these relationships is as examples of autobiographical occasions. For example, in examining high school reunions as autobiographical occasions, Vered Vinitzky-Seroussi (1998) suggests that people attend these events in search of "a community in which they can anchor their identities" (4). She concludes that people work to construct a version of themselves for the particular event, one that situates the individual both in the past and present. Commensal events such as dinner parties and potlucks operate in a similar manner, although with more frequency and perhaps less intensity than at a reunion (a low-frequency, high-intensity occasion). Both types of events allow people a bounded setting within which they can narrate their "selves" through voluntary interactions. However, the repetition and continuity of sociable meals is greater than at a reunion. Because an invitation to a social meal often involves an expectation of reciprocity, or at least continued contact, the occasions themselves have the temporal sequence that suggests patterning, a potential for repeat occasion on which to build performance.

It is about the resources brought to the social setting from both the past and the present, the inevitable tension inherent in such resources and setting, the hierarchy and norms by which we are evaluated, the community from which part of our identity derives and to which we relate. It is about the audience through which and in relation to one write autobiography (Vinitzky-Seroussi, 1998, 4).

The membership and rights created by sociability with non-kin is both durable and shifting. Food becomes a common ground when other life factors fail to bind or cohere people to one another. Since eating together implies selectivity, cooking or sharing a meal with people is one way to mark them as special. In essence, domestic hospitality is one way that people do friendship. Simmel argues that the aim of sociability includes amiability, refinement, cordiality, and "other sources of attraction," but he fails to note that these are moral categories. Different practices at table define these various characteristics of individuals and groups. To create and experience "refinement" is to engage in an embodiment of a particular construction of "taste." To be "amiable" is to embody a specific standard of sociability and manners. Manners internalize control and manage democracy. When the code of manners becomes more internalized and less clearly demarcated by rigid practices, then people need to rely on different ways to sustain a shared definition of the situation.

Formality, Class, and Close Sociability

In one sense, many of these stories illustrate how formality often restricts the intimacy of sociable meals, forcing them along a particular template of interactions and behaviors. Marion and John used the formality of dinner parties with colleagues to enhance John's career while at the same time reserving more intimate occasions for old friends. At the same time, intimacy can, in fact, occur at formal events. By controlling who is invited and what kinds of interactions can take place, formal sociability ensures that guests already have a context and other experiences in common, such that they do not need to work hard to sort out interactions. Although Perry is parodying the formal dinner party, he uses the format to make sure his guests all get along and share the experience. In looking at friendship in fiction and poetry, Ronald Sharp (1986) argues,

> I have been trying to demonstrate that concealment can be the agent of in-timacy, that distance can create closeness, and that formality can provide a vehicle for intimacy. My emphasis has fallen here not because I wish to deny the importance for friendship of openness, closeness, or familiarity, but because we have tended, lately, to lose sight of the formal and to deny its value. And we have done so without realizing the extent to which we have made an ideology of the informal, and consequently, the extent to which the informal has now itself become conventionalized and formalized. (62)

Formality may allow for certain kinds of intimacy and should not be dis-counted as a way of constructing close relationships. However, informality is not, in itself, a guarantee of intimacy. At Becky and Wes Pembrokes' potlucks, it was clear that some people found the event an easy way to relax and enjoy themselves, while others found the size of the party and the relative lack of structure difficult to negotiate. Spouses and partners who were not directly connected to the main participants complained about "not having anyone to talk to." In other instances people disliked the informality of parties centered on alcohol, which were "too relaxed" and did not create the kind of sociability they desired. There are still cultural and social tensions between "civilized behavior" and intimacy.

Because these different performances of hospitality are built on different kinds of interactional work, with less rigid role requirements, Olesen argues that people construct a wider range of selves to fit the shifting circumstances. In a sit-down dinner, the roles expected of people are more seamless and clearly defined. In less formal settings, such as the potluck, guests carry a greater responsibility for some of the labor, both in the production of food and the management of interactions. Although she does not enumerate the possible types of roles and selves in these shifting circumstances, Olesen (1993) does connect the contexts to structural dynamics, arguing that "the production and realization of selves in various forms of domestic hospital-ity remain tied to the material order" (192). Class resources remain a crucial aspect, although as I hope to have demonstrated, what we mean by "class" and by "resources" cannot be approached simplistically.

People adapt the formal model in order to achieve different kinds of sociability. The recurrent theme of comfort suggests that people want their domestic hospitality to foster less restricted relationships. At the same time, Sharp's suggestion that informality itself has been formalized speaks to the ways in which people often search for models like Martha Stewart and other food and entertaining guides in order to sort out the various styles through which one could construct informality. If etiquette no longer operates as the clearest way of determining social boundaries, then style and presentation become more important markers of distinctive class cultures. In a world of styles, the obligation to "keep up" means that informal social networks serve an important function in helping people with the ongoing work of constructing class. Sociability is, at one level, about the construction of self in relation to others.

Some analysts of consumption suggest that people adopt strategies of sociability that are mainly oriented toward performances of self that construct highly individualized selves. For example, Bauman (1991) argues that "individualization" (particularly through consumption) has reduced the significance of class as a collective identity for people. Beck (1992) suggests that the "disappearance" of class culture has led to a rise of the "lifestyle" as personal projects, creating new individualization and more temporary group alliances that are not grounded in more durable social or material similarities. Indeed, one could read some of the shifts in people's social networks and sociable practices as indicative of an adaptive process driven out of individual desire. However, as Alan Warde (1997) shows, "Food . . . is a corrective to understandings of consumption which exaggerate identity-enhancing or status-symbolic aspects" (180). Class-based style still exists, since boundaries of "likeness" are often constructed prior to people coming together. Food remains a key arena for the construction of class boundaries regarding taste and ideas about the structure of meals, especially in the ordered form and expectations of a meal, which then structures social interactions. It affects choices, conversations, and meanings given. Reading styles and variety are important signifiers of class. As Margaret Visser points out, "We invite each other not to eat and drink, but to eat and drink together. . . . The point is that the people at the party are more important than the food, but the secondary meaning is that eating together implies selectivity" both in food and in company (1991, 89). In the dinner party, such restrictions are inherent in the form. In modified events, selectivity in food and company is more apt to be negotiated, up for interpretation. In potlucks, there is, indeed, less individual control over both. In all these forms, class operates as a set of voluntary sociable relationships that unfold in a sequence of situated strategies. In general, the resources connected to social class are precisely the ones people draw upon in maintaining or modifying forms of sociability suited to the specific needs of their lives. In his research, Warde (1997) points to particular factors as illustrative of this: "The aspiration to culinary communion is exhibited in the language of tradition, the appeal of regional cuisines, the validation of home cooking, nostalgia for high-quality locally produced ingredients, and endless reflection on the authenticity and coherence of national cuisines. Not only is food rather more firmly socially embedded than other items of consumption, the attempts at its further re-embedding are particularly marked" (184).

All of these issues emerge in the narratives of my interviewees. Sharing food ultimately represented a kind of communion, one in which they exercised a certain amount of control over who was included, at least more than in their workplaces or family lives. At the same time, who was invited to people's homes for a meal generally reflected a group of people who were similarly positioned in the socioeconomic landscape. Although I started by having most of the structured interviews begin with a network analysis of people's social relationships, there were more nuanced questions that I could have pursued regarding class and friendship. The "how we met" question emerged toward the end as a potential site where class boundaries were often crossed, particularly when talking to people who were upwardly mobile. I remain curious about the kinds of interactional labors required to maintain those relationships.[5]

At the same time, people consistently used class-based markers of taste, such as knowledge of certain cuisines or foods, familiarity or discomfort with commercial products, and attitudes about eating out, to determine who they felt "comfortable" inviting in. In my analyses it seems clear that class, particularly as it is simultaneously a project of gendered work, is a significant factor in people's sociability. Even in sociable meals such as potlucks, where the structure and form of the meal allows for greater diversity of participants, class-based styles and approaches still affect who is invited and how people interact. In heterosexual couples and households, a gendered division of labor undergirded much of this work.

Informality, Spontaneity, and Class Differences

Although adaptation was a major theme throughout the observations and interviews, I have also tried to emphasize the ways in which class-based codes of taste and behavior place restrictions on how informal and intimate such sociability can be. One telling example is the extent to which sociability needs to be planned. If the work of friendship is about voluntary closeness, we might expect it to include numerous spontaneous and less scripted interactions. Although not common, some people described meals with others who "just dropped by" around dinnertime. As a feature of daily life, the inclusion of non-kin in family meals signified both the creation of a fictive kin relationship, but also the permeability of the private sphere. Kendra stops at Pam's house on her way home from work at least once a week and eats dinner with the family. Before they go to church meetings together, Margaret does "an inventory of the fridge" and adjusts dinner to include Stephanie. Lavinia, an eighty-year-old Lithuanian woman often "pops over" to the apartment of other widows in her building, and invites them to share the dinner she is about to make "so we all eat a good meal and have someone to talk to." All of these people were single and yet found regular but spontaneous ways to expand their social contacts. Similarly, Lauren and the other twenty-something people I observed had some structured group meals, but many of the weekend events were not planned very far in advance.

However, upper-middle-class professionals who often rely on the most formal models of domestic hospitality describe restrictions on their ability to engage in such spontaneous sociability. For example, Deanna compared her current circumstances to those of her mother and grandmother, associating a more open, informal sociability with a generation of people and where they live. Although she described her mother's experiences positively, she explained how such practices wouldn't work for her own life.

> My husband and I don't have people who drop by our house . . . whereas my family used to have people come in all the time. People would just stop by and sit and talk.

> *Is that because of the nature of your jobs?*
> Yes, but . . . I think people still do that at my mother's house and at my husband's mother's house I mean they're used to having people just come over. And people would see—you know, my mother—at my mother's house. She would be sitting at the front porch and people would just come over and feel that that was an invitation. If you're out there then it's an invitation for us to come over and talk. One thing would lead to another.

> *And she'd be cooking dinner?*
> Yes. That's right. And you know, people—oh, if you were there at mealtime you definitely were expecting an invitation to eat. It would be insulting not to invite this person. But I don't—if somebody comes by at dinner, excuse me! You have to go "I'm getting ready to cook our dinner. Can we talk another time?" And I guess that I just don't feel obliged—sometimes you do. I mean, [it] depends upon the situation but not the way my mother, my grandmother would feel like this was, you know, she'd send people out to the store if she saw five people coming, "Oh my God look who's here. They're here, I've gotta feed them." So, she would run and find food. And feel embarrassed if there wasn't enough still. And these people may or may not know that they were gonna get a meal but she was gonna feed them. I don't have that same obligation. . . . They were family and friends, you know, and if not, colleagues at work, but just, you know, neighbors who would just stop over . . what are you doing? Have some

coffee. Coffee would go from one thing to another. So I find that at least now with my group . . . people just don't stop by and shoot the breeze.

When people talked to me about their memories of a more spontaneous past, I began to suspect that this construction was partly based on real experiences like Deanna's, but partly based on a nostalgia for a more "open" time. Descriptions of family meals from childhood often began with happy memories of sociable moments, but they often traveled over less pleasant terrain, such as difficult relatives, intergenerational conflicts, and rigid family expectations.

Still, spontaneity was not seen as a resource for upper-middle-class-people. Edward, a professional living in Chicago, talked about the extensive planning he and his partner Ben go through in order to hold dinner parties, vary the menu, and keep track of reciprocal obligations. But, after talking at length about the kind of planning that goes into their parties, he said, "People almost never stop by our apartment unannounced. No one in my acquaintance does that, nor can I think of the last time it happened. Is that a difference between large cities and smaller communities? People did that when I was a child, but never these days. In the rare chance that someone did stop by and we decided to eat, my guess is that we would order out rather than cook."

Somewhat ironically, Edward told me this story while he cooked me an elaborate but spontaneous lunch over our extended interview. In order to get up to his apartment, I needed to be "buzzed" in. However, it was clear that some professional's nonwork lives could not support such informal spontaneity. In a sense, this means that the work of doing sociability, of creating friendships, must be an active part of their lives because access to friends is not always easy. The set of opportunities to meet people is not straightforward. Recall Gerry's comment about how, without his wife's efforts, he would not meet many people other than patients. However, sociologists often presume that professionals are embedded in far-ranging and diverse social networks. What these stories suggest, however, is that the social capital of upper-middle-class professionals is not solely dependent on their direct economic and occupational resources but rather connected to other conditions such as where they live, how partners, spouses, or children contribute to social contacts, the kinds of cultural templates of sociability they draw on, and their relationship to other material practices and leisure activities. These factors are also class-based but have a heightened salience for the less constrained pieces of everyday life. This does not negate the significance of differentiation as a key practice among these types of people; however, it does problematize neat correlations between professional status and social capital. Furthermore, the discourse that connects "authentic" or "interesting" food to class-based interests is not fixed as a means toward which white upper-middle-class Americans construct their social identities.

As Heldke (2003) asserts, it's possible to imagine authentic cuisine as "one that responds deeply to the context in which it presents itself," rather than being a function of novelty and exoticism (194).

Gender and Food Work

Feeding work remains an important material site where gender gets constructed and reproduced, even as the context shifts. Most sociological analyses of domestic labor, whether quantitative or qualitative, demonstrate that the majority of daily food work in domestic households is done by women. Furthermore, such work is coded as a way that women do gender. Men, on the other hand, often do gender through food work that is celebratory, special, or out of the ordinary. Although some men engage in daily domestic labor and some women do food work for special celebrations, the gendered meanings of such work remain consistent with larger constructs of gender difference in contemporary American society. Furthermore, among the women I interviewed, the responsibilities and rewards of paid work did not eliminate the expectation that as women, they would be engaged in constructing domesticity, usually through unpaid food work in the home. This expectation often extended into the realm of sociability beyond kin, such that women were more likely to do the work of maintaining ties (and material exchanges) with friends, colleagues, neighbors, and other kinds of acquaintances. Women's experiences in contemporary society have changed much more than men's. Thus, they are often the ones who are held responsible for prior arrangements but also for finding creative ways to adapt older forms to newer social realities. Although Joanne and Marion do dinner parties, they also experience changes in their lives (divorce, retirement) that shift the nature of their commensal activities. Women like Deanna, Helen, and Angela make modifications to the class-based social form, allowing guests to help by contributing food, using commercial products to supplement homemade meals, and adjusting temporal expectations to fit the competing demands on their time. It is not surprising, then, that women negotiate the terrain of voluntary social ties in the same way that they are often called upon to create and define family. This is not to say that men do not actively engage in this process, too, but it is often mediated by gender expectations. Graham Allan (1989) suggests that most prior research on gender and close relationships concludes that role performance is one key reason for differences in men's and women's friendships. He summarizes,

> The argument put forward by a number of writers, including Pleck (1976), Hess (1979), and Bell (1981), is that men's position within the social structure

tends in the main to encourage the formation of sociable relationships with others, but at the same time, to restrict the extent to which the self is revealed within them. Pleck expresses this well. . . . He suggests that a distinction can be made between sociability and intimacy, with men's relationships tending to score highly on the former, but relatively low on the latter. Men, in other words, are likely to be involved in a set of relationships whose basis is sociability and enjoyment, often arranged around specific tasks and activities. However, the majority, though not all, of these relationships are likely to be relatively shallow in terms of the degree to which personal worries, anxieties and other matters of consequence to the self are discussed. (71)

When looking at food-related social activities, this dichotomous contrast between sociability and intimacy becomes too simplistic. For example, the simultaneous and ongoing construction of class and gender differences also plays into the kinds of sociability men are more likely to create. One the one hand, many of the men I interviewed organized their social relationships around activities, including the activity of cooking and eating together. However, women did this too. These activities form the basis of sociable interaction. In many cases, upper-middle-class men focused their conversations and interests on the food. But this is a gender performance limited to some men, one that appears to be a choice rather than a constraint or expectation. The form of the sociability (informal or formal), the presence of a woman in a mediating role, and the homogeneity of the participants are all equally salient factors, often linked to class-based resources and expectations.

There is an enormous and growing sphere of advice and other materials geared toward teaching people about "entertaining" and "cooking." Its aim, if we look at sources like Martha Stewart, is to show people how to "do it right"—applying techniques for constructing the aesthetic and sociable atmosphere. At the same time, when we look at people's actual practices, it seems that sociability occurs for many people despite their inability to match cultural templates. For some upper-middle-class people, there are aspects of the discourse to which they ascribe and aspire more concretely than people of other social classes. However, when we look at the gendered expectations that go along with such performances and constructions, it appears that people, particularly women, often choose to adapt rather than sacrifice the sociable aspects. This is true for guests as well as hosts. Again, Warde and Martens (2001) suggest that "intriguingly, one cannot be a free rider in such circumstances because the participation is itself intrinsically rewarding, as it is only by being generous rather than selfish that the pleasures of company can be obtained. In such scenarios it is unacceptable to refuse to play a part despite even limited competence, because technical excellence is much less important than the expression of sincere participation" (210). Helen uses commercial foods and learned to cook in order to encourage sociable occasions in her life. Tom "puts up with" Wes's desire to include "just about everybody" in his potlucks because it's important to Tom to continue being a participant. "Good food" cannot guarantee a successful and enjoyable sociable occasion. According to Warde and Martens,

> Many potential pleasures which are highly valued are entirely contingent on other people, over whose behavior no individual has exclusive control. There are many aspects of life which require mutuality, where co-operation cannot be achieved by formal and imperatively co-ordinated action, but rather is reliant on mutual sympathy, independently and voluntarily granted, for sustaining the activity. Examples might be teenage gangs, marriage, a good night out, and a successful dinner party. Others have to feel the same, to share the same affective condition, to be in the same mood, to be in sympathy. This constitutes the social context of enjoyment. (209)

Constructing a shared definition of the situation is a key aspect of domestic hospitality. When the production of that hospitality, the food and interactional work, are made more visible, people often have to come up with new ways of negotiating what constitutes an equitable and equally enjoyable occasion. People with greater economic and cultural resources can draw upon those resources in order to adapt circumstances so that the work is less problematic or distributed through the commercial marketplace without having to compromise the "style" of the event. They can also presume that participants will share some, if not all, of their ideas about what counts as good food, be it a rejection of commercially prepared items, a celebration of the artisanal, or the performance of culinary skill.

The question of class-based resources is important because its more complicated than it appears on the surface. On one hand, as Warde and Martens (2001) suggest, "income permits the development of friendship of one of the most intimate kinds—eating with friends in private." (88). However, they find that students and people who are unemployed are also more likely to eat with friends than housewives and full-time employees. Sobal and Nelson's recent inquiry into commensal eating (2003) found that people did very little eating at friends' homes and almost no eating at neighbors' homes. The one exception was unmarried individuals. They concluded that work-oriented society was often the reason people's social networks appeared restricted. However, the qualitative data, both structured and informal, suggests that people do in fact engage in a range of activities but are often unclear about how to talk about them.

Informal modes of entertaining do, in fact, allow more people of different social and economic circumstances to enjoy sociability in their homes. On one hand, my interviews suggest that people with the greatest amount of social, cultural, and economic resources have the greatest variety of experience. At the same time, these people are also often restricted by time and choice to certain experiences. Furthermore, such experiences are gendered. Women of upper-middle-class professions may be able to modify cultural templates of formal sociability by going to bed early, using commercially prepared food, or offering the food buffet style, but they are also the ones who are still consistently held accountable for creating and sustaining these relationships. Indeed, because class-based codes about food shape the construction of meals as a social and cultural achievement, there is some suggestion that these women are under an increased pressure to continually monitor, learn, and enact new standards and codes about appropriate foods, wines, and meal formats. This stands in counterpoint to people with less economic means for whom creating a shared meal is, in itself, the achievement, especially when one must navigate increasing social pressure about the kind of foods one serves in private households. In both cases, it is these women who confront the moral discourses about food most directly in their sociable lives.

Domestic Space and Shifting Ideas about Domestic Hospitality

One significant shift in domestic hospitality has to do with changing ideas about space. As kitchens and the work of cooking become more visible, sociability is moved into a more informal state, simply because people are more aware of the work, even when it is a highly staged version of cooking work. However, some reasons for these changes may have less to do with undoing formality and more to do with cultural meanings attached to various rooms. As Ellen Pader points out, cultural differences also contribute to the construction and display of cultural capital in a household: the very definition of private and public space is affected by cultural meaning. For example, different racial and ethnic groups may view areas of the household in a specific cultural manner: Is the kitchen open to guests? Or is there a front-stage–back-stage division? Pader's study of Mexican and Mexican American homes illustrates that the organization of domestic space is linked to larger cultural ideas. In the Mexican homes, "family and others are not sharply delineated by spatial arrangements" (Pader, 1993, 121). Space affects the experience and interpretation of intimacy and distance, depending on what cultural meanings are given to certain rooms and interior areas. The most notably consistent aspect of domestic hospitality is connected to the expectation and work of keeping bathrooms clean. While kitchens, dining rooms, and living spaces are all visible and acceptable sites for displays of goods and "taste," and in fact, are often acceptable topics of conversation, bathrooms are uncomfortably both public and private, such that in domestic hospitality, they must be accessible for guests and yet they represent fairly intimate domestic space. The work of keeping such space presentable is most often the concern of women. Given the way such spaces are increasingly commodified, it seems important for social scientists to continue to explore the ways in which the uses and maintenance of domestic spaces affect people's larger social relationships.

Pleasure, Work, and Sociability

One of the most notable themes I found in doing this research was the extent to which people will go to insure these kinds of relationships in their lives beyond work and family. Given the increasing demands on people's time, it was surprising how much work people did to establish and maintain sociable ties that sometimes offered instrumental rewards, but more often than not, provided them with pleasurable interactions. For example, Daniel is a working-class African American man from Chicago. He has a clerical job plus, at the time I interviewed him, he had been taking classes and was just completing his bachelor's degree. Every day except Friday, he cooks dinner for his live-in girlfriend and his sister-in-law and nephew who live in the same apartment building. On many occasions, he also makes food and brings it over to his parent's house for dinner. Given how busy he is, it's not surprising that he often views his social world as restricted. He said,

> I don't have a lot of friends, I only have a couple. But, uh, when they come over, say, I'll say, "You hungry? You gonna eat? You know. And there are times where they'll say "No." and I'll start eating and they'll say, "well, fix me something." So, they're trying to be cool, but then they say, "Well, ok, you can fix me some of that too." And you go and you eat together. So, um, that's the way I look at hospitality, is that you treat a person when they come to your house, like I said, you give 'em the luxury of sharing your house with you. . . . And I'm the kind of person that, I believe in having all the things I need around me, you know. I don't want to have to take time to go out and look for it. . . . [So if people stop by] I can whip something up, just something to eat, hot dogs or whatever.

Daniel plans in advance, even for his "very few" friends. In fact, when he went on to describe his social networks, it turns out that he has many acquaintances that, at the last minute, often get included in his barbecues and spontaneous dinners. In effect, he makes sure people will feel welcome without restrictions. Similarly, people who lived in rural and suburban communities made special efforts to make sure they had regular contact with friends. Geographic distances often make it difficult for people to maintain social ties. For example, Carrington (1999) points to the spatial isolation of gay and lesbian families who moved to the suburbs of San Francisco. Similarly, Cindy and Mary said, "Nobody drops by in Cranby. We're like nowhere." At the same time, Cindy put a lot of effort into inviting friends and family over for formal dinners, cocktail parties, and holiday meals. They also had some spontaneous meals with neighbors and local friends:

> Next there's Flora and Mike. They live next door and they'll come over really just spontaneously like, if he plows the driveway or something like that, then I'll invite him in and the next thing you know we're having dinner. And we may not have anything planned, but we're rummaging around the kitchen trying to figure it out.
>
> *Do you ever go to Flora and Mike's house for dinner?*
> Yeah, we did, but we brought about three-quarters of the meal. We brought over a pot of soup and a whole bunch of stuff. Flora and Mike, they're right next door so we just come right over.
> We have another friend Karen. She's a farmer down in Connecticut. Once in a while she'll call up and want to spend the night. That usually includes . . . I mean it always includes dinner. We never actually say "You're going to come over for dinner," but she comes over for dinner.

The shifts in formality and informality in domestic hospitality demonstrate the lengths to which people go in order to have sociability as part of their lives. According to Warde and Martens (2001), "We know that behaviour within the communal mode is itself very varied. What is eaten, with whom, when and under what circumstances is highly differentiated. One defining feature of behaviour in this mode is the capacity for different groups of people to improvise on common social templates to create very different occasions and effects. If the commercial source of variation is specialization, the communal equivalent is improvisation" (221).

In asserting the ways that structural conditions position people to choose among certain sociable forms, I do not mean to diminish the personal satisfactions derived from such activities. Both are, in fact, possible. As Warde and Martens (2001) write,

> Consumption is about strategic individual or collective action. There is no doubt that consumption has been, and still is, used to mark social position, a function even more central to status-oriented societies. But from that point of view, how, and indeed whether, people get intrinsic enjoyment from those activities, is largely irrelevant. Concentration on the competitive instrumental aspect of consumption tends to see the primary satisfaction as the enhancement of social

power, and any expressed or felt gratifications as, if not merely rationalisation, subsidiary. Such a focus cares little for the experience of enjoyment. (166)

The practice of creating sociable meals with non-kin is a process whereby power is inscribed and enacted, creating social connections, reinforcing distinctions, and establishing a hierarchy of practices. At the same time, when we uncover the many ways that people adapt in order to continue to engage in these activities, we have to acknowledge that they are also a source of pleasure and satisfaction. People create such sociable relationships both for the gratification of eating and in, Simmel's terms, "being sociated." Daniel summed it up when he said, "I don't cook for my own pleasure. I cook to watch people eat my food. . . . I like the expressions I get on their faces when they eat my food." Cindy laughingly told me, "I just have this desire to feed people . . . [J]ust having them eat is like feedback. I stand over at the stove and I watch everybody go through it. That's the best part." Again, Warde and Martens (2001) aptly summarize this when comparing eating in and eating out:

> We still know comparatively little about entertaining and the social relationships involved. Nevertheless, private hospitality is enjoyed more, people feel more relaxed and they particularly appreciate their companions, conversation, and food. These attractions depend upon a particular "definition of the situation" of the private host-guest relationship, including, above all, a norm of reciprocity shared by all. One very significant difference between the experiences of the commercial and the communal modes is the nature of social relations and obligations. *What is remarkable is that being a recipient of private hospitality is extraordinarily pleasurable despite the obligations to labour copiously in return at another date* [my emphasis]. (221)

They suggest that enjoying the sociability of eating out is not an individualized act, but rather dependent on the good will of others: one cannot enjoy a meal at which others are not also experiencing enjoyment. Indeed, as my interviews suggest, "the shared affect associated with competent participation in a collectively constructed event gives some of the highest of social rewards" (Warde and Martens, 2001, 210). Many people, perhaps, experience what Patricia Williams (1991) describes as the opportunity to be spacious, happy, and gentle (230). This voluntary cooperation and coordination is taken for granted unless it doesn't go well or if it's difficult to achieve. Perhaps such work is also more apparent when the invisible labor is no longer invisible.

Among the other questions raised in this study, these stories also draw attention to accepted ideas about what constitutes "work" and "leisure," to where the lines between public and private are drawn, and how consumption and production are intertwined within the space of group life and individual households. Scholars of gender and race who focus on interaction and social construction point to daily practices as the arena where structural inequality gets inscribed, created, renegotiated, or reinforced (West and Zimmerman, 1987; West and Fenstermaker, 1995; Glenn, 1999; Omi and Winant, 1984). The study of domestic hospitality demonstrates how the ongoing construction of difference and inequality is an organizing principle for contemporary social life.

In sum, people create bonds of intimacy with some degree of choice in non-kin relationships, using food and the household as material sites for its enactment. At the same time, the form of the event, the kind of food served, who prepares it, and how it is served indicate the nature of the relationships being created. While there appears to be a discourse of comfort and informality that governs contemporary sociability, it appears that people still use such occasions to draw boundaries around like others, a process that often mirrors geographic and social segregation by race. The work of creating sociability is often about constructing social class. More often than not, it is also about constructing gender, where women are held accountable for the interactional and emotional labor of such events. More generally, it appears that sociability shifts across the life course, where people's material and social circumstances require shifts and adaptations from earlier practices. At the same time, it appears that even these shifts involve performances of gender and class.

People engage in commensality with friends and others who are not kin for a variety of reasons. They find pleasure in it and gain both tangible and intangible rewards from doing it. Such activities, while often lumped into the study of leisure or friendship, are more important than superficial gloss on the real work of family and paid labor. Despite my critique of the concept, for lack of a better and more all-encompassing means of talking about social value, we can see that since social capital is such a significant aspect of class-based resources, maintaining social networks is not a trivial activity. Ultimately, as Simmel argues, the main point of sociability is for people to "feel sociated," to experience the connection to others—and with food, it is a more concrete experience since people partake in a shared experience. As M. F. K. Fisher so aptly put it, "there is a communion of more than our bodies when bread is broken and wine is drunk."

Notes

Chapter 1. Feeding Friends and Others

1. Using personal experiences reflexively is a hallmark of feminist sociology. I embrace Dorothy Smith's call to see everyday life as a problematic rather than a phenomenon, in order to uncover the power relations that often cause a disjuncture between people's lived experiences and the legitimated cultural discourses that shape them (Smith, 1992, 110). In this way, one hopes to preserve the presence of real subjects in our work without neglecting the "relations of ruling" in and through which they work.

2. See Belasco, 2008; Avakian and Haber, 2005; Heldke, 2003. Like the study of sex and gender, the study of food and eating has been legitimized by activism and scholarship, although within mainstream social science and humanities disciplines, scholars are still asked to justify the choice of topic, especially when the analysis takes material processes seriously. On the flip side, the "hard" sciences are only just beginning to consider the full range of food's uses in social and economic contexts. In terms of meals specifically, Belasco points out, "Given that modern meals themselves are so ephemeral, it is not surprising that it takes some effort to see food as a subject worthy of serious analysis" (2008, 5).

3. More precisely, she states in the opening of her study, "Nutrition as a biological process is more fundamental than sex." A. Richards. (1932) *Hunger and Work in a Savage Tribe: A Functional Study of Nutrition Among the Southern Bantu*, Second Edition, 2004, Routledge Library Editions, U.K. In the introduction, Malinowski writes, "[it is not just linked to preferences and taste but to family structures and the bonds of kinship and sentiment, to economic production and technological accomplishment, to marriage, authority, and power, and ultimately to political organization, religion, and symbolism" (2004, vii).

4. Some examples include Neustadt, 1992; Pleck, 2000; Long, 2000; Camp, 1989; Belasco, 2008; Ray, 2004).

5. For a discussion of how cooking is or is not invisible work, see Julier, 2009.

6. From Charlotte Perkins Gilman to Robin Morgen, feminists have questioned women's association with the stove. For a good summary, see McFeely, 2002.

7. See, for example Brett Williams's explanation of why Mexican migrant women feed their husbands tamales, a labor-intensive but highly valued food whose distribution is often used by communities of women to signal approval or disapproval of male family members.

8. For examples, see Witt, 1999; Avakian, 1997; Beoku-Betts, 1995; Counihan, 1999; Goldman, 1996; Ray, 2004; Williams, 1984.

9. See, for example, C. Lashley, P. Lynch, and A. Morrison (2006) *Hospitality: A Social Lens*. Elsevier Publishing, Waltham, Mass.

10. Despite the levels of industrial production and the improved diets of many people across the globe, the fact that control over the food supply is concentrated in the hands of powerful—and increasingly monolithic—corporate entities has meant that governments are less able to regulate what is available for people to eat. Indeed, it should be noted that the ability of food corporations to produce enough food to feed the world has not meant an end to global food insecurity, the risk of famine and malnutrition, and overall improvements to the general health of the population.

11. In particular, Block and others have noted that in urban areas like Chicago, discount stores are concentrated in nonwhite areas and national full-service chains are concentrated in areas with lower percentages of African Americans. See D. Block and E. McLennan, (2008). "Filling In the Gaps in Food Deserts: The Distribution of Independent and Small Chain Supermarkets in the Chicago Metropolitan Area," paper presented at the Association for the Study of Food and Society annual meeting; New Orleans, La.

12. Lisa Heldke, personal correspondence, August 2009.

13. Although the article asserts the absolute significance of primary socialization by family, it's interesting that it goes on to try and alleviate the responsibility parents feel about providing home-cooked meals, suggesting that takeout food served at home can function as an equally successful way of creating family time and, thus, family itself.

Chapter 2. From Formality to Comfort

1. For example, in Douglas's lines of distance and intimacy, the mail carrier or repair person may enter the home but is not invited to sit in the living room and "relax" with food and a drink. There are cultural connotations of comfortable furniture as an aspect of the private household. For example, the comfortable chair is a recurrent theme in certain television sitcoms like *All in the Family* and *Frasier*, where the working-class man has "his own chair" and guests who sit in it are overstepping his idea of comfort and familiarity. These scenes are often used to satirize the working-class man's perception of home as private sanctuary.

2. Southern hospitality is a complicated set of ideologies. Although it was invoked by African American interviewees, sources often suggest that historically southern hospitality was a construct of wealthier whites, who were able to offer food and lodging to guests due to the labors of African American slaves and servants. In *Eating, Drinking, and Visiting in the South*, Taylor and Egerton write, "The incessant visiting characteristic of the antebellum South was an important ingredient of the cement that bound the ruling class of the region together socially, intellectually, and in time, politically. . . . Undoubtedly, the planter's hospitality was the slave's drudgery" (63). Furthermore, "It is necessary to

emphasize that in the New South as in the Old, the householder's door was not open to all. In addition to the barriers imposed by race, people of definitely lower social status were not invited to visit, and they did not come. Strangers were looked upon with suspicion. . . . Friends of friends were received but more or less on probation. In other words, the rules of hospitality in the South after the Civil War were very much as they had been for more than a century before the war" (131). For additional examples, see Cussler and de Give, *Twixt the Cup and the Lip*; and Witt, *Black Hunger*, particularly the chapter on "Servant Trouble." See Tony Whitehead for the use of southern hospitality among poor and working-class African Americans in Douglas (1984).

3. This same contrast can be seen in discussions of "comfort food" for families. While the contrast between comfort and luxury appears in popular media repeatedly after September 11, 2001, there were numerous newspaper and magazine articles about people's desire to return to "comfort foods" even when dining out. Although some of this discussion of "comfort food" is ethnically and regionally varied, it often asserts a particular model of food from the 1950s, both "home-made" and also reliant on certain commercial products, like canned soup. For a version of this argument, see Shapiro (1995).

4. Although I did not have enough data to explore this, there is a category of events entirely predicated on "extreme informality" that tends to intentionally flout formal rules of interaction and manners. Men, across some class lines, engage in informal sociability, often while the group watches sports together on television. Constructing a kind of masculinity, this sociability is modeled in beer advertisements and parodied on sitcoms as a way of characterizing gender. The requisites include take-out food, very casual clothing, and conversation about topics usually outside the boundaries of sociable activities, notably, bodily functions and sex. In my conversations with men who engage in this kind of sociability, it raised questions about the extent to which such informality really is about intimacy or about a different kind of required performance of gender, replete with its own rules about masculine behavior. For example, although probably overgeneralized, in the discussion of status production, Collins suggests that "female 'respectability' and male informality and even cynicism is one of the chronic sources of disputes in working class families" (1992, 219).

5. Visser writes, "According to Post's grand daughter-in-law and recent editor Elizabeth Post, 'When the book was first written, Emily Post thought it would be bought by the upper class but that wasn't true—they didn't need it' " (1991, 76).

6. The third point, "familiarity breeds contempt," centered on the potential sexual assaults African American women faced in public and in work, especially as many were still channeled into domestic labor, which left them alone and unprotected in private homes. Preserving black womanhood through the promotion of "respectability" was, as Victoria Wolcott points out, "a foundation of African American women's survival strategies," especially as a means of defense against sexual harassment and rape—and as a rebuttal to white stereotypes of black women's excessive sexuality. While black women of different economic and geographic backgrounds embraced respectability in different ways, it was widely promoted that community and virtue resided in black women's actions.

7. For a similar example, see Judith Carney's *Black Rice* on the role of African slaves in transporting both agricultural products (seeds and plants) and knowledge of farming techniques to the Americas, shaping the practices of major production (Harvard University Press, Cambridge, 2001).

8. Comparable examples appear in narratives by people of color whose mothers worked as paid servants. For example, Bill Cosby recounted how, traveling with his teammates to college sports events, they often ate in restaurants. His friends expressed surprise at Cosby's familiarity with foods like Beef Wellington. However, his mother had been a cook for an upper-middle-class family, so not only did she know how to make those dishes but she brought them home for her own family (in 1999 on the television show).

9. In analyzing this text, I relied on the original 1922 edition, reprinted on line, the twelfth revised edition from 1969, and a 1980 version written by one of Post's heirs. The twelfth edition was published after Post's death, but is only edited rather than substantially modified from the editions that appear in her lifetime. After 1969, her daughter-in-law (who edited the 1969 edition) revises the book significantly and re-titles it, for example, as *Emily Post's Etiquette* by Elizabeth Post. I use the 1969 version and compare it to Stewart's 1982 *Entertaining* because the dates correspond with those of the women's magazines that Warde compared in *Consumption, Food, and Taste*. He argues that these two time periods are a good representation of shifts in behavior, consumption, and taste.

10. In the film *Indiscreet*, the need for gender balance is satirized when Cary Grant is pressing Ingrid Bergman to join him at a dinner in his honor. He says, "I'm an extra man. You'd make the dinner party come out even." "How many people will there be?" she asks. "Six hundred." "Oh yes," she says, "599 guests would be very uneven."

11. In a more recent edition, modified to account for the lack of paid help, it states, "you can certainly cook for as many guests as you want, but to serve a seated dinner of more than eight efficiently and quickly it is almost essential to have an assistant . . . most of us must hire temporary help for the evening" (1980).

12. Evelyn Nakano Glenn suggests that which women of color were hired as servants varied by region: in the south, African American women "constituted the main and almost exclusive servant caste," whereas in the southwest, "Chicanas were disproportionately concentrated in domestic service," and in the far west, Asians (although mainly men) were the majority of domestic servants (1999, 67). See Bentley (1998) and Shapiro (1986) for other discussions of race, gender, and paid domestic labor in households.

13. Debates about race, ethnicity, and assimilation in relation to food habits are ongoing. Gabaccia (1998) suggests that Americans have always been "creoles" in their eating habits. The essays in Brown and Mussell (1984) provide an array of evidence for both the maintenance and shift in various ethnic and regional eating patterns. Ray (2004) finds that Bengali Americans "eat American" for one meal and Bengali for another, maintaining a kind of tension between cultural maintenance and assimilation.

14. In fact, in the 1922 edition, Post dedicates the book to her friends who are only superficially disguised by the pseudonyms she creates. This is distinctly different from Stewart, who intentionally names her dinner guests, family members, and catering clients to establish her authority as a socialite and domestic expert.

15. Bentley (2001) compares the artisanal aspect of Stewart's productions to the Arts and Crafts movement and "culinary luddism," both of which rest on ideas about tradition that are nostalgic constructions not rooted in real experience. "To achieve the simplicity of bygone days, then, often requires enormous expenditures of time, money, and resources" (12).

16. Bentley (2001) contrasts the whiteness produced by Martha Stewart food with the whiteness of *white trash cooking* and the racial-ethnic culture that permeates Barbara

Smith's food and entertaining productions. Bentley asserts, "Even so-called ethnic dishes that appear in MSL . . . are absent any real trace of ethnicity. When Martha Stewart publications do feature some ethnic fare, the entire process is glossed in a patina of whiteness" (6). People of color are "assimilated" into a white Anglo-Saxon environment.

17. At the same time, Stewart has been criticized for her recipes. Marion Burros reviewed *Entertaining* in the *New York Times* and found "many errors in recipes," concluding that Stewart "knows how to set a table, and shows how to give a party with style but can't cook" (reprinted April 2000, *New York Times)*.

Chapter 3. Dinner Parties in America

1. In terms of elite dinner parties, the *New York Times* provides ongoing cultural voyeurism into such events, many of which are, in fact, constructed entirely for display in the *Times*. For example, the annual special *Entertaining* magazine that comes in the Sunday *Times* often features dinner parties with famous actors and actresses, New York celebrities, or film directors who cook five-course Indian dinners or share their recipe for gold-dusted crème brûlée. Keeping the general public aware but outside of these events is a key factor. More recently, these meals have a rustic hew, showing a chef who cooks with local ingredients or is more "authentically" connected to the cuisine in question. Similarly Orlean (1990) finds that Saturday night is not, in fact, the usual night for dinner parties among the elite. As one person put it, "Saturday night is for amateurs." Orlean points out that Saturday night is the focus of working-class leisure, coming on the advent of the five-day work week. "As soon as Saturday night became available to ordinary Americans, ignoring it became a primary indicator and diagnostic feature of the upper class" (144). Interestingly, Orlean is permitted to interview Kempner before and after the party and observe all the preparations up to the minute that guests arrive when she is "firmly escorted out of the apartment by the back door" (156).

2. In *Stand Facing the Stove*, Ann Mendelson (1996) describes the significance of *Joy of Cooking*, not only as a cookbook for American women, but as a source of information about food, nutrition, and most significantly, social behavior. In the original editions, Rombauer commented extensively on what foods were appropriate for particular social events, be it a family's daily meal, a dinner party for twelve, or a potluck where one is expected to contribute an appropriate dish. In the 1997 *All New Joy of Cooking* ("revised for today's lifestyles," the jacket proclaims), written by Ethan Becker, Rombauer's grandson, the "Entertaining" section now reads, "It has been said that the ideal number at the dinner table is somewhere between the Three Graces and the Eight Muses; we find that the most easily managed and successful number of guests is between six and eight—enough to encourage social intercourse in numerous configurations but not so many that conversation turns to a din."

3. Although John and Marion lacked the "competent and suitable" servants required in Emily Post's definition, they may have occasionally relied on a hired waitress or their grown children to assist in their social events.

4. Bentley (1998) also argues that Rockwell's imagery reinforced both gender and racial hierarchies. As many African American women left domestic service for better war service jobs, hopeful about increase in opportunities, middle- and upper-class white women complained about "the servant problem" and viewed such changes as a crisis about "the

unraveling of social order." Because Rockwell and other illustrators portrayed black women as cooks and servers, even as their prevalence declined, the images spoke to many whites' desire "to maintain race segregation and domination" (61). In particular, "the cultural images of African American women were important to the economic order to keep African American women and others outside the economic mainstream. . . . [T]he economic motivation for [such] images . . . is significant as such images lead to societal perceptions and expectations. . . . [T]he mammy stereotype served to elevate the status of others, namely white women by representing the antithesis of idealized white women" (79).

5. However, a number of years after I interviewed her, Joanne was divorced from Ron and stated that she "didn't really do much cooking any more" for anyone other than her children. Although from the vantage point within marriage, she saw the work as her choice, changes over time suggest that she was, in some ways, responding to gendered expectations of wife and mother.

6. Heldke (2003) also points out that the marketplace then transforms the novel into the ordinary by packaging and selling it in supermarkets, mall eateries, and fast-food restaurants. As she points out, "yesterday's new exotic cuisine becomes tomorrow's supermarket special" (13). In the last fifteen years, packaged foods now include all manner of "ethnic" and gourmet items, sold in grocery stores, discount markets, and even mixed-retail outlets like T.J.Maxx.

7. Mars and Mars (1993) explore differences in sociable entertaining, using an extended participant observation of two couples in London, suggesting that entertaining styles are connected to "the working life of households and the communities they live in" (49). The suburban couple use a model of food and sociability that creates "a tight bounded and exclusive group . . . confirming a shared and ordered, highly structured and conformist lifestyle," whereas the urban couple, who work in the arts, are "into individuality and engage in a wide range of relationships," creating food and social styles that are "esoteric, fashionable, and new" (51). The differences in their approaches mirror differences between Marion and John and Joanne and Ron.

8. See Heldke (2003) for an extended discussion of the way authenticity is used in culinary adventuring. See Narayan (1997) for a critique of colonialism and food appropriation.

9. Larry also cooks for dinner parties, but he and Rita make an explicit point of sharing both the daily and the special cooking. Elsewhere I analyze the ways that Rita and Larry negotiate this arrangement, particularly because they engage in a range of sociable activities. They rely on the work of a paid nanny and housekeeper to do a majority of the invisible prep work. In effect, I suggest that the housekeeper's labors allow Larry and Rita the freedom to do gender in their marriage and social life in a more egalitarian way. As Dunne (2000) puts it, "Increasingly, we are finding a preferred solution for the achievement of equality is for both parents to prioritize their economic activities . . . and pass caretaking and domestic work onto women with less power" (19).

10. Ironically, both couples—Ron and Joanne and Amy and Evan—were divorced when I talked to them four years later.

11. Another reason is that her own food rules change—she becomes a strict vegan and can't eat any of the "heavy German food" that some of the friends cook (she describes them getting offended when all she eats is salad). Finally, an unspoken reason may be Paula's discomfort with this form of sociability. She's a musician and so is her husband.

They have lots of cultural capital, intellectual capital but very little income. There are also strains in the marriage in terms of what each one thinks is a "good" social life. He likes to have big barbecues and invite other musicians to come over and drink and hang out all day, events that are much more informal. Those are exclusively his activity. Although she started out very engaged by it, in the end, she's less invested in the class performance than most of the other people I interviewed who hold dinner parties. It turns out not to be the best strategy for her in creating friendships and regular sociability.

Chapter 4. Sweetening the Pot

1. This event was not a formal participant observation, but rather an ordinary piece of my everyday life. Gina and Sam knew about my research and we talked about it informally.

2. The concept of cultural capital is complex and hard to operationalize in observational research. In this case, I considered both formal cultural resources (like type of education and occupation) and informal dispositions and affinities. In particular, even though they lived in a New England suburb, Gina and Sam invoked a specific orientation toward urban New York culture. In fact, many of the participants in the dinner had some connection to New York City, such as having lived or attended school there, made frequent trips, or had relatives who lived in the city.

3. Currently people have been mentioning a new practice of "evites," using email invitations, which may change the nature of some of these practices.

4. This is not uniformly the case, however. Family members or close friends were sometimes encouraged to help with cooking and beverages for these parties. For example, Lavinia, a Lithuanian American woman in her eighties, often cooked for her daughters, especially when they were having parties. This was true for both her working-class daughter who lived nearby and her other daughter who was a Washington, D.C., lawyer.

5. Although, as I argue elsewhere, bread is not free of complicated symbolic associations. However, in this case, I suggest that the underlying presumption was that the bread would come from the commercial marketplace (albeit an artisanal source like a local bakery) and therefore would be standardized in its quality and less risky than asking an unknown guest to actually cook something.

6. In various editions of *The Joy of Cooking*, the authors vacillate between saving time and cooking homemade foods from scratch. Canned soup is a key indicator of the antinomy of care and convenience (Warde, 1997). Food manufacturing cookbooks suggest, "Take canned soups, season, combine, supplement or garnish them and then produce them with a great deal of pride as products of our own ingenuity" (Levenstein, 1988). See Parkin (2001) for an overview of advertisements for Campbell's from the turn of the century to World War II.

7. See Witt (1999) and Zafar (1999); both use Verta Mae Grosvenor's culinary autobiographies to grapple with the symbolic and material uses of the term "soul food," concluding that it is not "a historical entity but . . . an evolving, flexible continuum: the food may change but the identity persists. . . . [T]he 'boundaries' of culinary black America may alter (in this case foods or styles of preparation), but the group itself remains identifiable by itself and to others" (Zafar, 81). Their examples point to the way ethnic and racial groups participate in defining food as part of their cultural experience. These definitions are not static.

8. Although I did not gather enough data to say this for certain, it appeared to me that the people who engaged in this practice were like Cindy and Harry, more likely to embrace some aspects of their ethnic identity as an explanation for their culinary practices.

Chapter 5. Potlucks

1. Although people mentioned that various terms were regional, I did not find very clear boundaries around usage. In a number of online searches, "dish to pass," "covered-dish supper," and potluck turned up 189,000 Web sites. "Covered-dish supper" appeared mainly (but not exclusively) in the following areas: Florida, South Carolina, Georgia, Texas, Virginia, Western Pennsylvania, Kansas, North Carolina, Maryland, Alabama, West Virginia, and a few spots in Ohio. "Dish to pass" was often used as part of the sentence: "Please bring a dish to pass."

2. In *Whitebread Protestants* (2000), Daniel Sacks does a historical analysis of church suppers and their role in the structure of communal life in one religious organization.

3. In deciphering her own family meals, Douglas (1972) writes, "If I wish to serve anything worthy of the name of supper in one dish it must preserve the minimum structure of a meal. Now I know the formula. A proper meal is A (when A is the stressed main course) plus 2B (when B is an unstressed course). . . . A +2B is obviously not a formula that our family invented, but one that is current in our social environment. . . . To sum up, the meaning of a meal is found in a system of repeated analogies" (68). See Charles and Kerr (1988) for the significance of the "proper meal" as central to the construction of proper family in British households. See Murcott (2000) for changes and continuities in the significance of ordered meals in England. See Bentley (1998) or the ways in which the "ordered meal" has been used in the United States to reinforce gender and racial hierarchies.

4. In a personal correspondence, one woman told me about birthdays and holiday celebrations in her working-class extended family from western Pennsylvania, where, although the rule is unspoken, "no woman would dare show up without food."

5. Research librarians Barbara Haber and David Schoonover, who both specialize in food-related archives, find very little material on potlucks. Most references to potlucks appear in cookbooks (especially church and community cookbooks) and the category of "women's" magazines that focus on domestic life (*McCall's*), some cooking magazines (not gourmet or high-end cuisine ones but *Healthy Living*), and particularly regional magazines such as *Southern Living*, *Yankee*, and *Sunset*. There is also a "potluck discourse" in lesbian culture: potluck appears in *Lesbian Etiquette*, in cartoons such as *Dykes to Watch Out For*, and various other forms.

6. Certainly one strategy for people with economic and social resources is to pay a catering service. Of the professional and managerial people I spoke to, catered parties tended to occur more when the event was deemed "special," such as a graduation, bar mitzvah, or anniversary.

7. To have a situated identity is to have an organized set of impulsive responses within a defined situation, responses that are more or less shared with others and that are brought under conscious control as people utilize their own and others' perspectives to form conduct (Hewitt, 1989, 135). Situated identity can, in some cases, refer to those understandings of the self that are "public" in the sense that they are socially enacted and negotiated and that they are also bounded in time and place.

8. As Gusfield (1994) suggests, potlucks often proliferate in academic communities (although dinner parties are equally prevalent). I found many people who offered to be interviewed were part of a college or university. They all had potluck stories. Certain departments had reputations based on the type or quality of potlucks. In my own department, during a particular stage in graduate school, potlucks were a regular form of socializing. At one particular potluck, at the home of some people who often hosted, a "newer" grad student entered with store-bought chips and salsa (an act in itself that signified status in this group, where many people were "good cooks"). He handed them to the host, still in the supermarket bag. In front of other guests, she handed them back to him with a dish and said, "Didn't your mother teach you how to open a bag of chips and put it in a bowl?" From then on, a number of people referred to this incident as indicative of this man's personality, someone whose gender politics were contrary to the group norm (needs a woman to help him get food) and who didn't know how to work with others, be part of the community, and contribute in the experience.

9. Among some of the informal interviews I did with participants, there were discussions among couples about how a partner or spouse could avoid the obligation to attend parties at the Pembrokes.' That is, some people found the necessity for continued attendance restrictive and negotiated both with partners and the Pembrokes about how to maintain group membership without having to meet the same level of obligation. It was often easier for partners who were not directly members of the university community to miss events.

10. It was suggested to me that another acceptable site for scatalogical conversation was among men as a form of intimacy. Such discussions cut across class lines, but construct a form of masculinity. See, for example, the bean-eating scene in the film *Blazing Saddles*.

Chapter 6. Artfulness, Solidarity, and Intimacy

1. For an extended sociological look at the history of hospitality, see Murray (1990). He also suggests "the most comprehensive cross-cultural description of hospitality practices I know of is the series of articles on hospitality in *The Encyclopedia of Religion and Ethics*, vol. 7 (1925)." Murray, Hochschild (1983), and Olesen (1993) all discuss the effect of commercialization on hospitality.

2. Although I do not have enough narratives to assert this with certainty, among the people I spoke to there were definite hierarchies determining when a person's health issue appeared "legitimate" enough to warrant changing a menu. So, for example, people often complained about having to make special foods for vegans or vegetarians, dietary restrictions they constructed as "choices" rather than necessities, whereas food allergies or diagnosed conditions (high blood pressure or heart condition, for example) were uncontested and acceptable.

3. The advent of social media such as Facebook has also added an interesting layer to the discussion of friendship, such that "friend" has become a verb. At the same time, the social relationships developed online may encourage people to be very revealing about their everyday lives, but with a certain amount of personal control that one would not exercise if those same "friends" were invited to come to one's home and share a meal.

4. See, for example, V. Wilson, *Social Capital in the African American Community*, Western Political Science Conference, March 17, 2005, Oakland, Calif.

5. Simmel described these limits: "Sociability among members of very different social strata is often inconsistent and painful. Equality, as we have seen, results from the elimination of both the wholly personal and the wholly objective, that is, from the elimination of the very material of sociation from which sociation is freed when it takes on the form of sociablity" (Wolff, 1950, 48). However, the permeable and shifting nature of social strata make these moments the very stuff of everyday life, such that class codes are never completely fixed and often contested.

Bibliography

Abarca, M. (2001). Los Chilaquiles de mi ama: The language of everyday cooking. In Inness, S., *Pilaf, Pozole, and Pad Thai: American Women and Ethnic Food*. University of Massachusetts Press, Amherst.

Abrahams, R. (1984). Equal opportunity eating: A structural excursus on things of the mouth. In Brown, L. K., and Mussell, K., eds., *Ethnic and Regional Foodways in the U.S.: The Performance of Group Identity*. University of Tennessee Press, Knoxville.

Adkins, L. (2005). Social capital, the anatomy of a troubled concept. *Feminist Theory* 6(2):195–211.

Adler, T. (1981). Making pancakes on Sunday: The male cook in family tradition. *Western Folklore* 40:45–54.

Allan, G. (1979). *A Sociology of Friendship and Kinship*. George Allen and Unwin, London.

Allan, G. (1989). *Friendship: Developing a Sociological Perspective*. Westview Press, Boulder, Colo.

Appadurai, A. (1988). How to make a national cuisine: Cookbooks in contemporary India. *Comparative Studies in Society and History* 30:3–24.

Atkins, P., and Bowler, S. (2000). *Food in Society: Economy, Culture, Geography*. Routledge, London.

Avakian, A. V., ed. (1997). *Through the Kitchen Window: Women Explore the Intimate Meanings of Food and Cooking*. Beacon Press, Boston.

Avakian, A. V., and Haber, B., eds. (2005). *From Betty Crocker to Feminist Food Studies: Critical Perspectives on Women and Food*. University of Massachusetts Press, Amherst. .

Ayres, M. (1997). The parable of the lamb, In Avakian, A. V., ed., *Through the Kitchen Window: Women Explore the Intimate Meanings of Food and Eating*. Berg Publishing, London.

Baca Zinn, M. (1994). Feminist theorizing from racial-ethnic families. In Baca Zinn, M., and Thornton-Dill, B., eds., *Women of Color in U.S. Societies*. Temple University Press, Philadelphia.

Bahr Bugge, A., and Reidar, A. (2006). Domestic dinner: Representations and practices of a proper meal among young suburban mothers. *Journal of Consumer Culture* 6(203).

Barndt, D., ed. (1999). *Women Working the NAFTA Food Chain: Women, Food, and Globalization.* Second Story Press, Toronto.

Bates Grigsby, K., and Hudson, K. (2002). *Basic Black: Home Training for Modern Times.* Doubleday, New York.

Bauman, Z. (1991). *Modernity and Ambivalence.* Polity Publishing, Cambridge.

Beardsworth, A., and Keil, T. (1997). *Sociology on the Menu: An Invitation to the Study of Food and Society.* Routledge, New York.

Beck, U. (1992). *Risk Society: Towards a New Modernity.* Sage Publications, London.

Beecher, M. A. (2001). The mythical making Martha. *American Studies* 42(2):113–124.

Belasco, W. (1989a). *Appetite for Change.* Pantheon, New York.

Belasco, W. (1989b). Ethnic fast foods: The corporate melting pot. *Food and Foodways* 2:1–30.

Belasco, W. (1999). Why food matters. *Culture and Agriculture* 21.

Belasco, W. (2002). Food matters: Perspectives on an emerging field. In Belasco W., and Scranton, P., *Food Nations: Selling Taste in Consumer Societies.* Routledge, New York.

Belasco, W. (2008). *Food: The Key Concepts.* Berg Publishing, London.

Bell, D., and Valentine, G. (1997). *Consuming Geographies: We Are Where We Eat.* Routledge, London.

Bentley, A. (1998). *Eating for Victory: Food Rationing and the Politics of Domesticity.* University of Illinois Press, Urbana.

Bentley, A. (2001). Martha's food: Whiteness of a certain kind. *American Studies* 42(2):5–29.

Beoku-Betts, J. (1995). We got our way of cooking things: Women, food and preservation of cultural identity in African-American Sea Island communities. *Gender and Society* 9(5):535–555. Reprinted in Counihan, C. M., ed. (2002). *Food in the USA: A Reader.* Routledge, New York.

Bernstein, B. (1977). Social class, language, and socialization. In Karabel, J., and Halsey, A. H., eds., *Power and Ideology in Education.* Oxford University Press, New York.

Bezanson, K. (2006). Gender and the limits of social capital. *Canadian Review of Sociology and Anthropology* 43(4):427–444.

Biernacki, P., and Waldorf, D. (1981). Snowball sampling: Problems and techniques of chain referral sampling. *Sociological Methods and Research* 10(2):141–163.

Biltekoff, C. (2005). The terror within: Citizenship and self control in the fat epidemic. In *Hidden Hunger: Eating and Citizenship from Domestic Science to the Fat Epidemic.* PhD thesis for the American Civilization Program, Brown University.

Bliezner, R., and Adams, R. G. (1992). *Adult Friendship.* Sage Publications, London.

Blum-Kulka, S. (1994). *Dinner Talk: Cultural Patterns of Sociability and Socialization in Family Discourse.* Lawrence Earlbaum, Hillsdale, N.J.

Bordo, S. (2003). *Unbearable Weight: Feminism, Western Culture, and the Body.* University of California Press, Berkeley.

Borgmann, A. (2000). The moral complexion of consumption. *Journal of Consumer Research* 26(4).

Bouma, G. (1993). *The Research Process.* Oxford University Press, Oxford.

Bourdieu, P. (1984). *Distinction: A Social Critique of the Judgment of Taste.* Harvard University Press, Cambridge.

Bourdieu, P. (1987). What makes a social class? On the theoretical and practical existence of groups. *Berkeley Journal of Sociology* 32.

Bower, A. (2009). Recipes for history: The National Council of Negro Women's five historical cookbooks. In Bower, A., ed., *African American Foodways*. University of Illinois Press, Urbana.

Braziel, J., and LeBesco, K., eds. (2001). *Bodies out of Bounds: Fatness and Transgression*. University of California Press, Berkeley.

Brembeck, H. (2005). Home to McDonald's: Upholding the family dinner with the help of McDonald's. *Food, Culture, and Society* 8(2).

Brown, L. K., and Mussell, K., eds. (1984). *Ethnic and Regional Foodways in the U.S.: The Performance of Group Identity*. University of Tennessee Press, Knoxville.

Calhoun, C., LiPuma, E., and Postone, M., eds. (1993). *Bourdieu: Critical Perspectives*. Polity Publishing, Cambridge.

Camp, C. (1989). *American Foodways: What, When, Why, and How We Eat in America*. August House, Little Rock, Ark.

Campos, P. (2004). *The Obesity Myth: Why America's Obsession with Weight Is Hazardous to Your Health*. Gotham Books, New York.

Campos, P., Saguy, A., Ernsberger, P., Oliver, E., and Gaesser, G. (2005). The epidemiology of overweight and obesity: Public health crisis or moral panic? *International Journal of Epidemiology* 35(1):55–60.

Campos, P., Saguy, A., Ernsberger, P., Oliver, E., and Gaesser. G. (2006). Response: Lifestyle not weight should be the primary target. *International Journal of Epidemiology* 35.

Cannon, L. W., Higgenbotham, E., and Leung, M. L. (1991). Race and class bias in qualitative research on women. In Fonow, M. M., and Cook, J. A., eds., *Beyond Methodology: Feminist Scholarship as Lived Research*. Indiana University Press, Bloomington.

Carrington, C. (1995). *Constructing Lesbigay Families: The Social Organization of Domestic Labor(s) in Lesbian and Gay Families*. PhD thesis, University of Massachusetts, Amherst.

Carrington, C. (1999). *No Place like Home: Relationships and Family Life among Lesbians and Gay Men*. University of Chicago Press, Chicago.

Castells, M. (1996). *The Rise of the Network Society*. Blackwell Publishers, Cambridge, Mass.

Charles, N., and Kerr, M. (1988). *Women, Food, and Families*. Manchester University Press, Manchester.

Chesman, A. (1996). *Yankee Magazine's Church Suppers and Potluck Dinner Cookbook*. Villard, New York.

Clark, R. (1994). *Potluck: Exploring American Foods and Meals*. Vocabureader Workbook 2. Pro Lingua Associates. Brattleboro, Vt.

Clatterbargh, K. 1998. What is problematic about masculinities? *Men and Masculinities* 1(1):24–45.

Cole, H. (1999). *How to Be: A Guide to Contemporary Living for African Americans*. Simon and Schuster, New York.

Collins, P. H. (1990). *Black Feminist Thought: Knowledge, Consciousness, and the Politics of Empowerment*. Routledge, New York.

Collins, R. (1992). Women and the production of status cultures. In Lamont, M., and Fournier, M., eds., *Cultivating Differences: Symbolic Boundaries and the Making of Inequality*. University of Chicago Press, Chicago.

Coltrane, S. (1989). Household labor and the routine production of gender. *Social Problems* 36:473–490.

Coltrane, S. (1998). *Gender and Families.* Pine Forge Press, Thousand Oaks, Calif.

Colwin, L. (1993a). *A Big Storm Knocked It Over.* Harper Collins, New York.

Colwin, L. (1993b). *More Home Cooking: A Writer Returns to the Kitchen.* Harper Collins, New York.

Connell, R. W. (1995). *Masculinities.* University of California Press, Berkeley.

Coontz, S. (1992). *The Way We Never Were: American Families and the Nostalgia Trap.* Basic Books, New York.

Cooper, A. J. (1990). *A Voice from the South.* Oxford University Press, Oxford.

Counihan, C. (1988). Female identity, food, and power in contemporary Florence. *Anthropological Quarterly* 61(2).

Counihan, C. (1999). *The Anthropology of Food and Body: Gender, Meaning, and Power.* Routledge, New York.

Counihan, C. (2004). *Around the Tuscan Table: Food, Family and Gender in Twentieth Century Florence.* Routledge, New York.

Counihan, C., and van Estrik, P., eds. (1997). *Food and Culture: A Reader.* Routledge, New York.

Coveney, J. (2006). *Food, Morals, and Meaning: The Pleasure and Anxiety of Eating.* Routledge, London.

Cowan, R. (1983). *More Work for Mother.* Basic Books, New York.

Cox, K. R., ed. (1997). *Spaces of Globalization: Reasserting the Power of the Local.* The Guilford Press, New York.

Crawford, R. (1980). Healthism and the medicalization of everyday life. *International Journal of Health Services* 10(3):365–88.

Curtin, D. W., and Heldke, L. M., eds. (1992). *Cooking, Eating, Thinking: Transformative Philosophies of Food.* Indiana University Press, Bloomington.

Cussler, M., and de Give, M. (1952). *Twixt the Cup and the Lip: Psychological and Socio-Cultural Factors Affecting Food Habits.* Twayne Publishing, New York.

Daly, K. J. (2001). Deconstructing family time: From ideology to lived experience. *Journal of Marriage and Family* 63:283–294.

Daniels, A. K. (1987). Invisible work. *Social Problems* 34(5).

de Beauchaine, A. S. (1988). *The Bourgeoisie in the Dining Room: Meal, Ritual, and Cultural Process in Parisian Families of Today.* Institutet for folklivsforskning vid Nordiska museet och Stockholms universitet, Stockholm.

Deck, A. (2001). Now then—Who said biscuits? The black woman cooks as fetish in American advertising. In Inness, S., ed., *Kitchen Culture in America: Popular Representations of Food, Gender, and Race.* University of Pennsylvania Press, Philadelphia.

DeVault, M. L. (1990). Talking and listening from women's standpoint: Strategies for interviewing and analysis. *Social Problems* 37(1).

DeVault, M. L. (1991). *Feeding the Family: The Social Organization of Caring as Gendered Work.* University of Chicago Press, Chicago.

DiLeonardo, M. (1987). The female world of cards and holidays: Women, families, and the work of kinship. *Signs* 12(3).

Douglas, M. (1972). Deciphering a meal. *Daedalus* 101(1).

Douglas, M. (1982). *In the Active Voice.* Routledge, London.

Douglas, M., ed. (1984). *Food in the Social Order: Studies of Food and Festivities in Three American Communities*. Russell Sage Foundation, New York.

Douglas, M., and Nicod, M. (1974). Taking the biscuit: The structure of British meals. *New Society* 20:744–747.

Dowler, E., and Calvert, C. (1995). *Nutrition and Diet in Lone-Parent Families in London*. Family Policy Studies Centre, London.

Dunne, G. A. (2000). Opting into motherhood: Lesbians blurring the boundary and transforming the meaning of parenthood and kinship. *Gender and Society* 14(1).

Dyer, L. (1997). *Moving from Upper Classes to the Masses: Category Closeup on Lifestyle Books*. Cahners Publishing Company, New York.

Ehrenreich, B. (2001). *Nickeled and Dimed: On (Not) Getting By in America*. Metropolitan Books, New York.

Elias, N. (1978). *The Civilizing Process*. Urizen Books, Lynn, Mass.

Ellul, J. (1976). *The Technological Society*. Knopf, New York.

Etzioni, A., ed. (2004). *We Are What We Celebrate: Understanding Holidays and Rituals*. NYU Press, New York. .

Farb, P., and Armelagos, G. (1980). *Consuming Passions: The Anthropology of Eating*. Houghton Mifflin, Boston.

Fenton, A., and Owen, T., eds. (1977). Food in perspective. *Proceedings of the Third International Conference on Ethnological Food Research*. Cardiff, Wales.

Field, J., Schuller, T., and Baron, S. (2000). Social capital and human capital revisited. In Baron, S., Field, J., and Schuller, T., eds., *Social Capital, Critical Perspectives*. Oxford University Press, Oxford.

Finkelstein, J, (1989). *Dining Out: A Sociology of Modern Manners*. Polity Press, Oxford.

Fournier, S., Winig, L., Herman, K., and Wojnicki, A. (2001). *Martha Stewart Living Omnimedia (A), HBS Case 9-501-080*. Harvard Business School Publishing, Cambridge. .

Fowlkes, M. (1980). *Behind Every Successful Man: Wives of Medicine and Academe*. Columbia University Press, New York.

Franklin, J., and Thomson, R. (2005). (Re)claiming the social, A conversation between feminist, late modern and social capital theories. *Feminist Theory* 6(2).

Friedberg, S. (2007). Supermarkets and imperial knowledge. *Cultural Geographies* 14(321).

Gabaccia, D. (1998). *We Are What We Eat: Ethnicity and the Making of Americans*. Harvard University Press, Cambridge.

Gans, H. (1971). The uses of poverty: The poor pay all. *Social Policy* 2.

Gans, H. (1990). Deconstructing the underclass: The term's danger as a planning concept. *Journal of the American Planning Association* 56(3).

Gard, M., and Wright, J. (2005). *The Obesity Epidemic: Science, Morality, and Ideology*. Routledge, New York.

Germann Molz, J. (2007). Eating difference: The cosmopolitan mobilities of culinary tourism. *Space and Culture* 10:77.

Gerson, J., and Peiss, K. (1985). Boundaries, negotiation, consciousness: Reconceptualizing gender relations. *Social Problems* 32(4).

Glenn, E. N. (1985). *Issei, Nisei, Warbride: Three Generations of Japanese American Women in Domestic Service*. Temple University Press, Philadelphia.

Glenn, E. N. (1999). The social construction and institutionalization of gender and race: An integrative framework. In Ferree, M., Lorber, J., and Hess, B., eds., *Revisioning Gender*. Sage Publications, New York.

Goldman, A. (1996). *Take My Word: Autobiographical Innovations of Ethnic American Working Women*. University of California Press, Berkeley.

Goode, J., Theophano, J., and Curtis, K. (1984). A framework for the analysis of continuity and change in shared sociocultural rules for food use: The Italian American pattern. In Brown, L. K., and Mussell, K., eds., *Ethnic and Regional Foodways in the U.S.: The Performance of Group Identity*. University of Tennessee Press, Knoxville.

Goody, J. (1982). *Cooking, Cuisine, and Class: A Study in Comparative Sociology*. Cambridge University Press, Cambridge.

Goody, J. (1997). Industrial food: Towards the development of a world cuisine. In Counihan, C., and van Estrik, P., eds., *Food and Culture: A Reader*. Routledge, New York.

Gorman-Murray, A. 2006. Queering home or domesticating deviance. *International Journal of Culture Studies* 9(2):227–247.

Goudsblom, J., and Mennell, S., eds. (1998). *The Norbert Elias Reader*. Blackwell Publishers, Malden, Mass.

Green, E. S. (1920). *National Capital Code of Etiquette*. A. Jenkins Co., Washington, D.C.

Grover, K. (1987). *Dining in America, 1850–1900*. University of Massachusetts Press, Amherst.

Guerron-Montero, C. (2004). Afro-Antillean cuisine and global tourism. *Food, Culture and Society* 7(2).

Gupta, S. (1999). The effects of transitions in marital status transitions on men's performance of housework. *Journal of Marriage and the Family* 61:700–711.

Gusfield, J. (1994). The social meaning of meals: Hierarchy and equality in the American potluck. In Platt, G. M., and Gordon, C., eds., *Self, Collective Behavior and Society: Essays Honoring the Contributions of Ralph H. Turner*. JAI Press, Greenwich, Conn.

Guthman, J. (2012) *Weighing In: Obesity, Food Justice, and the Limits of Capitalism*. University of California Press, Berkeley.

Gutierrez, R., and Fabre, G., eds. (1995). *Feasts and Celebrations in North American Ethnic Communities*. University of New Mexico Press, Albuquerque.

Haber, B. (2005). Follow the food. In Avakian, A. V., ed., *Through the Kitchen Window: Women Explore the Intimate Meanings of Food and Eating*. Berg Publishing, London.

Hall, E. J. (1993). Waitering/waitressing: Engendering the work of table servers. *Gender and Society* 7(3):329–346.

Harnack, L., Story, M., Martinson, B., Neumark-Sztainer, D., and Stang, J. (1998). Guess who's cooking? The role of men in meal planning, shopping, and preparations in U.S. families. *Journal of the American Dietetic Association* 98:995–1000.

Harris, M., and Ross, E. B., eds. (1987). *Food and Evolution: Toward a Theory of Human Food Habits*. Temple University Press, Philadelphia.

Hawkins Brown, C. (1940). *The Correct Think To Do—To Say—To Wear*. G. K. Hall and Co. (1995 reprint), New York.

Heath, Shirley Brice. (1983). *Ways with Words*. Cambridge University Press, Cambridge.

Heldke, L. (1992). Food making as a thoughtful practice. In Curtin, D., and Heldke, L., eds., *Cooking, Eating, Thinking. Transformative Philosophies of Food*. Indiana University Press, Bloomington.

Heldke, L. (2003). *Exotic Appetites: Ruminations of a Food Adventurer*. Routledge, New York.

Heldke, L. (2012). The unexamined meal is not worth eating, or why and how philosophers (might/could/do) study food. *Food, Culture, and Society* 9(2).

Herd, P., and Harrington Meyer, M. 2002. Care work: Invisible civic engagement. *Gender and Society* 16(5):66–68.

Hess, B. B. (1990). Beyond dichotomy: Drawing distinctions and embracing differences. *Sociological Forum* 5(1).

Hewitt, J. P. (1989). *Dilemmas of the American Self*. Temple University Press, Philadelphia.

Higgenbotham, E., and Weber, L. (1992). Moving up with kin and community: Upward social mobility for black and white women. *Gender and Society* 6(3):416–440.

Hochschild, A. (1983). *The Managed Heart: Commercialization of Human Feeling*. University of California Press, Berkeley.

Hochschild, A. (1989). *The Second Shift: Working Parents and the Revolution at Home*. Viking Press, New York.

Hollows, J. (2002). The bachelor dinner: Masculinity, class and cooking in *Playboy*, 1953–1961. *Continuum: Journal of Media and Cultural Studies* 16(2).

Hollows, J. (2005). Feeling like a domestic goddess: Postfeminism and cooking. *European Journal of Cultural Studies* 6(2):179–202.

hooks, b. (1992). *Black Looks: Race and Representation*. South End Press, Boston.

hooks, b. (1998). Eating the other: Desire and resistance. In Scapp, R., and Seitz, B., eds., *Eating Culture*. SUNY Press, Albany.

Hopley, C. (1994). Four women meet monthly for food and friendship. *Amherst Bulletin*, Amherst, Mass.

Hunt, A. (1997). The "moral panic" and moral language in the media. *British Journal of Sociology* (online) 48(4).

Hyland, M. G. (2001). Martha Stewart's living landscapes. *American Studies* 42(2):101–112.

lmeling, R., and Saguy, A. C. (2005). Fat Panic! The "Obesity Epidemic" as Moral Panic. Paper presented at the annual meeting of the American Sociological Association, Marriott Hotel, Loews Philadelphia Hotel, Philadelphia.

Jerrome, D. (1984). Good company: The sociological implications of friendship. *Sociological Review* 32(4).

Johnson, L. (2006a). Browsing the modern kitchen—A feast of gender, place and culture (Part 1). *Gender, Place and Culture: A Journal of Feminist Geography* 13(2).

Johnson, L. (2006b). Hybrid and global kitchens—First and third world intersections (Part 2). *Gender, Place and Culture: A Journal of Feminist Geography* 13(6).

Julier, A. (2004). Entangled in our meals: Guilt and pleasure in contemporary food discourses. *Food, Culture, and Society* 7(1).

Julier, A. (2005). Hiding race, class, and gender in discourses of commercial food. In Avakian, A., and Haber, B., eds., *From Betty Crocker to Feminist Food Studies: Critical Perspectives on Women and Food*. University of Massachusetts Press, Amherst.

Julier, A. (2007). Food preparation and work. Entry for the *Oxford Encyclopedia of Women in World History*. Oxford, New York.

Julier, A. (2008). The political economy of obesity: The fat pay all. In Counihan, C., and van Estrik, P., eds., *Food and Culture: A Reader*, 2nd edition. Routledge, New York.

Julier, A. (2009). Keynote: Deciphering Another Meal: Douglas, DeVault, and the Gendered Rhetoric of Domestic Food Labor Conference. Association for the Study of Food and Society/Agriculture.

Julier, A., and Lindenfeld, L. (2005). Mapping men onto the menu: Food and masculinities. *Food and Foodways: Explorations in the History of Human Nourishment*. Double Issue on *Men and Masculinities* 13(1, 2).

Kalcik, S. (1984). Ethnic foodways in America: Symbol and the performance of identity. In Brown, L. K., and Mussell, K., eds., *Ethnic and Regional Foodways in the U.S.: The Performance of Group Identity*. University of Tennessee Press, Knoxville.

Kasson, J. (1990). *Rudeness and Civility: Manners in Nineteenth-Century Urban America*. Hill and Wang, New York.

Kemmer, D. (2000). Tradition and change in domestic roles and food preparation. *Sociology* 34(323).

King, D. K. (1988). Multiple jeopardy, multiple consciousness: The context of a black feminist ideology. *Signs* 14(1).

Kopytoff, I. 1986. The cultural biography of things: Commoditization as process. In Appadurai, A., ed., *The Social Life of Things: Commodities in Cultural Perspective*. Cambridge University Press, Cambridge.

Kovalainen, A. (2004). Rethinking the revival of social capital and trust in social theory: Possibilities for feminist analysis. In Marshall, B., and Witz, B., eds., *Engendering the Social: Feminist Encounters with Social Theory*. Open University Press, Berkshire, U.K.

Laslett, B. (1993). Feminism, families, and family sociology. *Sociological Forum* 8(2).

Lauden, R. (1996). A plea for culinary modernism: Why we should love new, fast, processed foods. *Gastronomica* 1(1).

Leavitt, S. (2001). It was always a good thing: Historical precedents for Martha Stewart. *American Studies* 42(2):125–131.

Lemert, C., and Branaman, A., eds. (1997). *The Goffman Reader*. Blackwell Publishers, Malden, Mass.

Levenstein, H. (1988). *Revolution at the Table: The Transformation of the American Diet*. Oxford University Press, Oxford.

Levenstein, H. (1993). *Paradox of Plenty: A Social History of Eating in Modern America*. Oxford University Press, Oxford.

Levine, D. N., ed. (1971). *Georg Simmel: On Individuality and Social Forms*. University of Chicago Press, Chicago.

Lien, M., and Nerlich, B., eds. (2005). *The Politics of Food*. Oxford University Press, Oxford.

Long, L. (1998). Culinary tourism: A folkloristic perspective on eating and otherness. *Southern Folklore* 55(3):181–204.

Long, L. (2000). Holiday meals: Rituals of family tradition. In Meiselman, H., ed., *Dimensions of the Meal: The Science, Culture, Business, and Art of Eating*. Aspen Publishers, New York.

Long, L. (2003). *Culinary Tourism*. University Press of Kentucky, Lexington.

Lupton, D. (1993). Risk as moral danger: The social and political functions of risk discourse in public health. *International Journal of Health Services* 23(3).

Marling, K. (2001). The revenge of Mrs. Santa Claus or Martha Stewart does Christmas. *American Studies* 42(2):133–138.

Mars, G., and Mars, V. (1993). Two contrasting dining styles: Suburban conformity and urban individualism. *Food, Culture, and History: The London Food Seminar* 1:49.

Massey, D., and Denton, N. (1993). *American Apartheid: Segregation and the Making of the Underclass*. Harvard University Press, Cambridge.

Maurer, D., and Sobal, J. (1999). *Weighty Issues: Fatness and Thinness as Social Problems*. Aldine de Gruyter, New York.

McFeely, M. (2002). *Can She Bake a Cherry Pie? American Women and the Kitchen in the Twentieth Century*. University of Massachusetts Press, Amherst.

McIntosh, W. (1996). *Sociologies of Food and Nutrition*. Plenum Press, New York.

McIntosh, W., and Zey, M. (1989). Women as gatekeepers of food consumption: A sociological critique. *Food and Foodways* 4:317–332.

Mechling, J. (2001). Introduction: Martha Stewart and taste cultures. *American Studies* 42(2):67–69.

Meiselman, H., ed. (2000). *Dimensions of the Meal: The Science, Culture, Business, and Art of Eating*. Aspen Publishers, New York.

Mendelson, A. (1996). *Stand Facing the Stove: The Story of the Women Who Gave America The Joy of Cooking*. Henry Holt Publishers, New York.

Mennell, S., Murcott, A., and van Otterloo, A. H., eds. (1993). *The Sociology of Food: Eating, Diet, and Culture*. Sage Publications, London.

Mintz, S. (1986). *Sweetness and Power: The Place of Sugar in Modern History*. Penguin Books, New York.

Miztal, B. (2005). The new importance of the relationship between formality and informality. *Feminist Theory* 6:173.

Moisio, R., Arnould, E., and Price, L. (2004). Between mothers and markets: Constructing identity through homemade food. *Journal of Consumer Research* 4(3).

Moore, L. (1995). Beautiful grade. *New Yorker*. December 25, 1995.

Murcott, A. (1982). On the social significance of the "cooked dinner" in South Wales. *Social Science Information* 21(4/5):677–695.

Murcott, A. (1997). Family meals—A thing of the past? In Caplan, P., ed., *Food, Health and Identity*. Routledge, London.

Murcott, A. (2000). Is it still a pleasure to cook for him? Social changes in the household and the family. *Journal of Consumer Studies and Home Economics* 24(2).

Murray, H. (1990). *Do Not Neglect Hospitality: The Catholic Worker and the Homeless*. Temple University Press, Philadelphia.

Nakayama, T., and Kuzek, R. (1999). Whiteness as a strategic rhetoric. In Nakayama, T., and Kuzek, R., eds., *The Communication of Social Identity*. Sage Publications, New York.

Narayan, U. (1997). *Dislocating Cultures. Identities, Traditions, and Third World Feminism*. Routledge, New York.

Nardi, P., and Sherrod, D. (1994). Friendship in the lives of gay men and lesbians. *Journal of Social and Personal Relationships* 11:185–199.

Nestle, M. (2002). *Food Politics: How the Food Industry Influences Nutrition and Health*. University of California Press, Berkeley.

Neuhaus, J. (2003). *Manly Meals and Mom's Home Cooking: Cookbooks and Gender in Modern America*. Johns Hopkins University Press, Baltimore.

Neustadt, K. (1992). *Clambake: A History and Celebration of an American Tradition*. University of Massachusetts Press, Amherst.

Newman, K. (1988). *Falling from Grace: The Experience of Downward Mobility in the American Middle Class*. Free Press, New York.

Newman, K. (1993). *Declining Fortunes: The Withering of the American Dream*. Basic Books, New York.

Oakley, A. (1981). Interviewing women: A contradiction in terms. In Roberts, H., ed., *Doing Feminist Research*. Routledge & Kegan Paul, London.

Olesen, V. (1993). Selves and a changing social form: Notes on three types of hospitality. *Symbolic Interaction* 17(2).

Omi, M., and Winant, H. (1994). *Racial Formation in the United States: 1960–1990*, 2nd edition. Routledge, New York.

Orlean, S. (1990). *Saturday Night*. Random House, New York.

Orlean, S. (1993). Homewrecker. *New Yorker*. August 23, 1993.

Ostrander, S. (1984). *Women of the Upper Class*. Temple University Press, Philadelphia.

Pader, E. J. (1993). Spatiality and social change: Domestic space-use in Mexico and the United States. *American Ethnologist* 20(1):114–137.

Pader, E. J. (1994). Sociospacial relations of change: Rural Mexican women in urban California. In Altman, I., and Churchman, A., eds., *Women and the Environment*. Plenum Press, New York.

Parasecoli, F. (2008). *Bite Me: Food in Popular Culture*. Berg Publishing, London.

Parkin, K. (2001). Campbell's soup and the long shelf life of traditional gender roles. In Inness, S., ed., *Kitchen Culture in America: Popular Representations of Food, Gender, and Race*. University of Pennsylvania Press, Philadelphia.

Paules, G. F. (1991). *Dishing It Out: Power and Resistance among Waitresses in a New Jersey Restaurant*. Temple University Press, Philadelphia.

Pillsbury, R. (1998). *No Foreign Food: The American Diet in Time and Place*. Westview Press, Boulder, Colo.

Pleck, E. (2000). *Celebrating the Family: Ethnicity, Consumer Culture, and Family Rituals*. Harvard University Press, Cambridge.

Poe, T. (1999a). *Food, Culture, and Entrepreneurship among African Americans, Italians, and Swedes in Chicago*. PhD diss., American Studies, Harvard University.

Poe, T. (1999b). The origins of soul food in black urban identity: Chicago, 1915–1947. *American Studies International* 37(1).

Pollan, M. (2006). *The Omnivore's Dilemma: A Natural History of Four Meals*. Penguin Books, New York.

Poppendieck, J. (1998). *Sweet Charity: Emergency Food and the End of Entitlement*. Viking, New York.

Post, E. *The Emily Post Institute*. www.emilypost.com. Accessed September 2012.

Post, E. (1922). *Etiquette in Society, in Business, in Politics, and at Home*. www.bartley.com/95. Accessed September 2012.

Post, E. (1969). *Etiquette*. Funk and Wagnalls, New York.

Post, P. (1997). *Emily Post's Etiquette*, 16th edition. Harper Collins, New York.

Power, E. M. (1999). An introduction to Pierre Bourdieu's key theoretical concepts. *Journal for the Study of Food and Society* 3(1):48–52.

Probyn, E. (2000). *Carnal Appetites: FoodSexIdentity*. Routledge, London.

Putnam, R. (2000). *Bowling Alone*. Simon and Schuster, New York.

Putnam, R. D. (1995). Bowling alone: America's declining social capital. *Journal of Democracy* 6(1):65–78.

Pyke, K. (1996). Class-based masculinities: The interdependence of gender, class, and interpersonal power. *Gender and Society* 10(5).

Raspa, R. (1984). Exotic foods among Italian Americans in Mormon Utah: Food as nostalgic enactment of identity. In Brown, L. K., and Mussell, K., eds., *Ethnic and Regional Foodways in the U.S.: The Performance of Group Identity*. University of Tennessee, Knoxville.

Rawlins, W. (2009). *The Compass of Friendship: Narratives, Identities, and Dialogues*. Sage Publications, Newbury Park, Calif.

Rawlins, W. K. (1992). *Friendship Matters: Communication, Dialectics and the Life Course*. Aldine de Gruyter, New York.

Ray, K. (2004). *The Migrant's Table: Meals and Memories in Bengali-American Households*. Temple University Press, Philadelphia.

Reay, D. (2004). Gendering Bourdieu's concepts of capitals? Emotional capital, women, and social class. In Adkins, L., and Skeggs, B., eds., *Feminism after Bourdieu*. Blackwell Publishers, Oxford.

Riesman, D., Potter, R., and Watson, J. (1960). The vanishing host. *Human Organization* 19:17–21.

Riessman, C. K. (1987). When gender is not enough: Women interviewing women. *Gender and Society* 1(2).

Riessman, C. K. (1993). *Narrative Analysis*. Qualitative research methods series #30. Sage Publications, Newbury Park, Calif.

Ritzer, G. (2000). *The McDonaldization of Society*. Pine Forge Press, Thousand Oaks, Calif.

Rombauer, I., and Becker, M. R. (1975). *The Joy of Cooking*. Bobbs-Merrill, Indianapolis.

Rosenthal, C. (1985). Kinkeeping in the family division of labor. *Journal of Marriage and the Family* 47(4).

Rozin, E. (1982). The structure of cuisine. In Barker, L., ed., *The Psychobiology of Human Food Selection*. AVI Publishing, New York.

Sacks, D. (2000). *Whitebread Protestants: Food and Religion in American Culture*. St. Martin's Press, New York.

Saguy, A. (2006). Are Americans too fat? Conversation with Stanton Glantz. *Contexts* 5(2).

Saguy, A., and Riley, K. (2005). Weighing both sides: Morality, mortality, and framing contests over obesity. *Journal of Health Politics, Policy, and Law* 5.

Sahlins, M. (1990). Food as symbolic code. In Alexander, J., and S. Seidman, S, eds., *Culture and Society*. Cambridge University Press, Cambridge.

Santino, J. (1996). *New Old-fashioned Ways: Holidays and Popular Culture*. University of Tennessee Press, Knoxville.

Scanlon, C. (2004). What's wrong with social capital? *Arena Magazine* 64:12–28.

Scott, J. (1993). A biting analysis of society: The deeper meaning of dining. *Los Angeles Times*, A1–A11.

Sen, A. (1981). *Poverty and Famines: An Essay on Entitlement and Deprivation*. Clarendon Press, Oxford.

Shapiro, L. (1986). *Perfection Salad: Women and Cooking at the Turn of the Century*. Farrar, Straus and Giroux, New York.

Shapiro, L. (1995). The home-cooked meal is enjoying a comeback. *Newsweek* 126(13):64.

Shapiro, L. (2005). *Something from the Oven: Reinventing Dinner in 1950s America*. Penguin Books, New York.

Sharman, A., Theophano, J., Curtis, K., and Messer, E., eds. (1991). *Diet and Domestic Life in Society*. Temple University Press, Philadelphia.

Sharp, R. (1986). *Friendship and Literature: Spirit and Form*. Duke University Press, Durham.

Shields-Argeles, C. (2004). Imagining the self and other: Food and identity in France and the United States. *Food, Culture, and Society* 7(2).

Shortridge, B., and Shortridge, J., eds. (1998). *A Taste of American Place: A Reader on Regional and Ethnic Foods*. Rowman and Littlefield Publishers, Oxford.

Shulman, M., and Anderson, C. (1990). The dark side of social capital. *Rural Sociology* 64(3):351–372.

Sisnroy, W. (1999). What's for Lunch? Ritual, Identity and Ethnicity at the Office Potluck. Unpublished thesis, Vermont College of Norwich University.

Smith, B. (1995). *Entertaining and Cooking for Friends*. Artisan Publishing, New York.

Smith, B. (1999). *Rituals and Celebrations*. Random House, New York.

Smith, C. D. (2000). Discipline—"It's a good thing": Rhetorical constitution and Martha Stewart Living Omnimedia. *Women's Studies in Communication* 23(3):337–366.

Smith, D. (1993). The standard North American family: SNAF as an ideological code. *Journal of Family Issues* 14:1.

Smith, D. E. (1987). *The Everyday World as Problematic: A Feminist Sociology*. Northeastern University Press, Boston.

Smith, D. E. (1992). Sociology from a woman's standpoint: A reaffirmation. *Sociological Theory* 10(1).

Sobal, J. (1995). The medicalization and demedicalization of obesity. In Maurer, D., and Sobal, J., eds., *Eating Agendas: Food and Nutrition as Social Problems*. Aldine de Gruyter, New York.

Sobal, J. (2000). Sociability and meals: Facilitation, commensality, and interaction. In Meiselman, H., ed., *Dimensions of the Meal: The Science, Culture, Business, and Art of Eating*. Aspen Publishers, New York.

Sobal, J., and Nelson, M. K. (2003). Commensal eating patterns: A community study. *Appetite* 41:181–190.

Sobal, J., Bove, C., and Rauschenberg, B. (1999). Weight and weddings: Constructing beautiful brides. In Sobal, J., and Maurer, D., eds., *Interpreting Weight: Social Management of Fatness and Thinness*. Aldine de Gruyter, New York.

Sobal, J., Bove, C., and Rauschenbach, B. (2002). Commensal careers at entry into marriage: Establishing commensal units and managing commensal circles. *Sociological Review* 50(3).

Spain, D. (1993). Gendered spaces and women's status. *Sociological Theory* 11(2).

Stacey, J. (1900). Can there be a feminist ethnography? *Women's Studies International Forum* 11(1):21–27.

Stacey, J., and Thorne, B. (1985). The missing feminist revolution in sociology. *Social Problems* 32(4):301–316.

Stack, C. (1974). *All Our Kin: Strategies for Survival in a Black Community*. Harper and Row, New York.

Stewart, M. (1982). *Entertaining*. Crown Publishers, New York.

Stewart, M. (1994a). *Martha Stewart's Menus for Entertaining*. Clarkson Potter, New York.

Stewart, M. (1994b). *Special Occasions: The Best of Martha Stewart Living*. Oxmoor Publishing, New York.

Stewart, M. (1997). *Great Parties: The Best of Martha Stewart Living Recipes, Menus, and Ideas for Perfect Gatherings*. Clarkson Potter, New York.

Strasser, S. (1982). *Never Done: The History of American Housework*. Pantheon, New York.

Strathern, M. (1987). An awkward relationship: The case of feminism and anthropology. *Signs* 12(2).

Sutton, D. (2001). *Remembrances of Repasts: An Anthropology of Food and Memory*. Berg Publishing, Oxford.

Swartz, D. (1997). *Culture and Power: The Sociology of Pierre Bourdieu*. University of Chicago Press, Chicago.

Symons, M. (1994). Simmel's gastronomic sociology: An overlooked essay. *Food and Foodways* 5(4):333–351.

Taylor, J. G., and Egerton, J. (1982). *Eating, Drinking, and Visiting in the South: An Informal History*. Louisiana State University Press, Baton Rouge.

Taylor, R. J., Chatters, L. M., Tucker, M. B., and Lewis, E. (1992). Developments in research on black families: A decade review. In Skolnick, A. S., and Skolnick, J. H., eds., *Family in Transition: Rethinking Marriage, Sexuality, Child Rearing and Family Organization*. Harper Collins, New York.

Thompson, C., Locander, W., and Pollio, H. (1990). The lived meaning of free choice: An existential-phenomenological description of everyday consumer experiences of contemporary married women. *Journal of Consumer Research* 17(3).

Tierney, W. G. (1997). *Academic Outlaws: Queer Theory and Cultural Studies in the Academy*. Sage Publications, Thousand Oaks, Calif.

Trubek, A. (2000). *Haute Cuisine: How the French Invented the Culinary Profession*. University of Pennsylvania Press, Philadelphia.

Tuchman, G., and Levine, H. G. (1993). New York Jews and Chinese food: The social construction of an ethnic pattern. *Journal of Contemporary Ethnography* 22(3):382–407.

Turner, K. (2006). Buying, not cooking: Ready-to-eat food in American urban working class neighborhoods, 1880–1930. *Food, Culture, and Society* 9(1).

Valentine, G. (1999). Eating in: Home, consumption, and identity. *Sociological Review* 47(3).

Vinitzky-Seroussi, V. (1998). *After Pomp and Circumstance: High School Reunion as Autobiographical Occasion*. University of Chicago Press, Chicago.

Visser, M. (1992). *The Rituals of Dinner: The Origins, Evolution, Eccentricities and Meaning of Table Manners*. Penguin Books, New York.

Visser, M. (2003). Etiquette and eating habits. In Katz, S., *Encyclopedia of Food and Culture*. Scribners, New York.

Wacquant, L. (2001). Taking Bourdieu into the field. *Berkeley Journal of Sociology* 46.

Wade-Gayles, G. (1997). Laying on hands through cooking: Black women's majesty and mystery in their own kitchens. In Avakian, A., ed., *Through the Kitchen Window: Women Explore the Intimate Meanings of Food and Cooking*. Beacon Press, Boston.

Wadja, S. T. (2001). KMartha. *American Studies* 42(2):71–88.

Walker, K. (1996). Men, women, and friendship: What they say, what they do. *Gender and Society* 8(2):246–265.

Wann, M. (1999). *Fat!So?: Because You Don't Have to Apologize for Your Size*. Ten Speed Press, Berkeley.

Warde, A. (1997). *Consumption, Food and Taste*. Sage Publications, London.

Warde, A., and Martens, L. (2001). *Eating Out: Social Differentiation, Consumption, and Pleasure*. Cambridge University Press, Cambridge.

West, C., and Fenstermaker, S. (1995). Doing difference. *Gender and Society* 9(1).

West, C., and Zimmerman, D. H. (1987). Doing gender. *Gender and Society* 1(2).

Weston, K. (1990). *Families We Choose: Lesbians, Gays, Kinship*. Columbia University Press, New York.

Whitehead, T. L. (1984). Sociocultural dynamics and food habits in a southern community. In Douglas, M., ed., *Food and the Social Order*. Russell Sage Foundation, New York.

Wilkes, C. (1990). Bourdieu's class. In Harker, R., Mahar, C., and Wilkes, C., eds., *An Introduction to the Work of Pierre Bourdieu: The Practice of Theory*. St. Martin's Press, New York.

Wilkinson, D., Zinn, M. B., and Chow, E. N.-L. (1992). Guest editors' introduction. *Gender and Society* 6(3):341–345.

Williams, B. (1984). Why migrant women feed their husbands tamales: Foodways as a basis for a revisionist view of Tejano family life. In Brown, L., and Mussell, K., eds., *Ethnic and Regional Foodways in the United States: The Performance of Group Identity*. University of Tennessee Press, Knoxville.

Williams, P. J. (1991). On being the object of property. *The Alchemy of Race and Rights: Diary of a Law Professor*. Harvard University Press, Cambridge.

Williams, S. (1987). *Savory Suppers and Fashionable Feasts: Dining in Victorian America*. Pantheon Books, New York.

Williams-Forson, P. (2006). *Building Houses out of Chicken Legs: Black Women, Food, and Power*. University of North Carolina Press, Chapel Hill.

Willmott, P. (1987). *Friendship Networks and Social Support*. Report 666, Policy Studies Institute.

Witt, D. (1999). *Black Hunger: Food and the Politics of U.S. Identity*. Oxford University Press, Oxford.

Wolff, K., ed. (1950). *The Sociology of Georg Simmel*. The Free Press, New York.

Wood, R. (1995). *The Sociology of the Meal*. Edinburgh University Press, Edinburgh.

Wright, R., and Houston, S. (2007). "It's just that people mix better here": Mixed household narratives of belonging and displacement in Seattle, Washington. In Hanley, L., and Ruble, B., *Immigration and Integration in Urban Communities*. Johns Hopkins University Press, Baltimore.

Wright, R., Ellis, M., and Parks, V. (2004). Work together, live apart? Geographies of racial and ethnic segregation at home and work. *Annals of the Association of American Geographers* 94(3).

Zafar, R. (1996). Cooking up a past: Two black culinary narratives. *GRAAT: Ethnic Voices* II(14).

Zafar, R. (1999). The signifying dish: Autobiography and history in two black women's cookbooks. *Feminist Studies* 25(2).

Index

ALICE P. JULIER is an associate professor and the director of the graduate program in food studies in the School of Sustainability and the Environment at Chatham University.

The University of Illinois Press
is a founding member of the
Association of American University Presses.

_____

Composed in 10.5/13 Adobe Minion Pro
by Lisa Connery
at the University of Illinois Press
Manufactured by Sheridan Books, Inc.

University of Illinois Press
1325 South Oak Street
Champaign, IL 61820-6903
www.press.uillinois.edu